Large-Scale Agile Frameworks

Sascha Block

Large-Scale Agile Frameworks

Agile Frameworks, Agile Infrastructure and Pragmatic Solutions for Digital Transformation

 Springer

Sascha Block
Hamburg, Germany

ISBN 978-3-662-67781-0   ISBN 978-3-662-67782-7   (eBook)
https://doi.org/10.1007/978-3-662-67782-7

Translation from the German language edition: "Large-Scale Agile Frameworks" by Sascha Block, © Springer-Verlag GmbH Deutschland, ein Teil von Springer Nature 2023. Published by Springer Berlin Heidelberg. All Rights Reserved.

This Springer imprint is published by the registered company Springer-Verlag GmbH, DE, part of Springer Nature.
The registered company address is: Heidelberger Platz 3, 14197 Berlin, Germany

Preface

My decision to write this book matured in connection with my master's thesis at the University of Hamburg, which deals with the suitability of Large-Scale Agile Frameworks as an organizational model for software manufacturers. The decision to complete a master's program at an "advanced age" was significantly influenced by the fact that I missed agile organizational forms in many aspects of my professional practice. It was never the individual teams or colleagues who opposed such methodology - quite the contrary!

It was regularly observed that best practices and mature agile organizational models were missing or simply unknown. In any case, I was determined to deal precisely with this complex of topics of Large-Scale Agile Frameworks. To this day, I perceive how difficult it is for companies to anchor agile working methods holistically in their organization.

I developed this book to help establish agility as a permanent part of our modern working culture in companies and organizations of all kinds. Regardless of the level of maturity you or your colleagues and employees are currently at, this book is intended to serve as a guide to anchor an agile mindset and agile working methods in your professional everyday life. Whether you are a manager or a team member who wants to learn more about agile methodology, this work should serve as a compass and navigate you along the currently highly topical issues such as cloud technologies, DevOps, and IT security. Another goal is to raise awareness of IT security and to demonstrate practical strategies and solutions for implementation. It is my concern to help you expand your knowledge beyond the basics of agility. This specialist book was created based on years of experience in countless IT projects and against the background of various corporate environments. There are many books that introduce agility and the associated basics. My plan was to write a book that goes beyond that. This book is intended to effectively support you and your organization in getting started with agility and establishing a new organizational form so that you, together with your colleagues and teams - and above all with fun - can achieve a successful digital transformation!

The period in which this book was created and grew was shaped by the Corona pandemic; not only the immense importance but also the urgency of agile methodology was intensified once again. As an IT architect in the context of telematics infrastructure, the results of my daily work are heavily dependent on many individuals and teams, with external organizations, legal frameworks, and new subject areas - in and beyond software architectures - playing a significant role.

In this context, I was able to help shape and experience the introduction of numerous collaboration tools during this formative time and see their positive effects; I also learned how important individual and community feedback is and how well-suited an agile mindset is for mastering challenges in a team.

Because I know from my work as an IT architect how important visual representations are for developing a common understanding - especially across individual teams - and how effective graphical artifacts are for successfully designing accepted solutions, I have expanded this book with numerous illustrations. As the saying goes, a picture is worth a thousand words ...

This book is the result of countless iterations, influenced by ever-new ideas, be it during my daily work as an IT architect and in dialogue with colleagues or with friends and other IT specialists at numerous online events and meetups.

Structure of the Book

The book structures the problem in the context of agile software development and focuses on Large-Scale Agile Frameworks, which meet the special requirements of companies that are confronted with a multitude of agile teams in various, often parallel, digitization projects.

Part I – Digital Transformation with Large-Scale Agile Frameworks
Practical methodology based on real project experience

Chapter 2 describes the problems that project participants and stakeholders face in digital transformation. The **agile prioritization** is regularly a challenge for all involved.

Through clearly defined **goals of digital transformation** and the change to agile working methods, the importance of agile processes and Large-Scale Agile Frameworks is illustrated.

Agile concepts and basic terms are explained and examined in the context of multi-project management and portfolio management.

Software license products and **custom software** must be distinguished from a **software platform**, the **software product family**, and a **software product line** because different framework conditions must be taken into account on the requirements side. The **product life cycle of software** as well as **software releases, release management, software architecture**, and **knowledge management** as well as DevOps have a significant influence on agile software development.

Agile concepts and the **agile project model** are presented in the context of **Scaled-Agile** and **Large-Scale Agile**, Agile Teams, their roles, tasks, and processes.

Chapter 3 introduces the concept of Large-Scale Agile Frameworks and presents the most relevant and proven models in practice, showing their differences and limitations.

Chapter 4 provides practical support for introducing a Large-Scale Agile Framework in an organization. With the **method of *Action Design Research***, you have a modern approach to practice-oriented problem solving in organizations.

With a **fact-based summary of the most relevant influencing factors of the cloud trend and virtualization**, not only are highly current technology topics taken into account, but also their effects on the requirements of agile organizational forms are considered.

Software architecture and IT security play a central role in all digitization activities. Not only are the paradigms of the approaches **IT-Security-by-Design** and the **Zero-Trust Strategy** presented, but also effective secret management and the extended protection requirements of virtual container environments. This results in a holistic view.

In this context, the aspects of **public-key infrastructures, microservice architectures, REST APIs,** and **RESTful design**, the **architecture pattern of service meshes**, and related quality characteristics must not be neglected.

Based on the **OWASP guidelines**, IT security can be demonstrably improved through iterative, accompanying penetration testing. Penetration tests, on the other hand, document examined properties at a specific point in time under defined conditions, along with agreed test criteria, and thus attest to IT security in relation to a defined test scope. Combined, both measures complement each other as effective means to harden software, i.e., to increase IT security.

With the methodology of **threat modeling**, an effective mechanism is explained to identify threats early and systematically eliminate these security risks.

You will comprehensibly learn why early, agile deployment and automated tests are suitable means to develop robust and **IT security-hardened software solutions**.

In this context, the relatively young discipline of **DevSecOps** is introduced, and with the working tools of **code reviews** and **pair programming**, practical methods for software development are presented.

The often-neglected requirement for **logging and monitoring** has its focus on IT security and data protection aspects to be considered in this section.

To cope with these challenges, the necessary **agile teams, roles, tasks, and processes** are outlined, which an agile organizational model requires. By introducing the respective specializations, a comprehensible and easily understandable classification of the individual disciplines is provided. At the same time, this section can effectively support organizations in sharpening or supplementing their own teams and role profiles.

In the context of **design thinking** and **prototyping**, the required basic knowledge for prototypical approaches, rapid prototyping, and the prototype phase model is presented.

Chap. 5: Agile prioritization model for software manufacturers reflects companies in the role of a software manufacturer using three well-known companies, thus illustrating the scope and importance of software development for organizations. In **Sect. 5.2**, the **agile teams and roles typical for organizations in the role of a software manufacturer** are presented, and in **Sect. 5.3**, the corresponding **processes and activities** are presented.

Based on the requirements and results of the previous chapters, the *developed agile model for cross-cutting prioritization within different company constellations* is presented and explained why this model is suitable for harmonizing requirement prioritization and agile software development for a wide variety of software projects.

To effectively address hurdles, "**Chap. 6** presents the **agile teams, roles, processes, and activities** that are typical for organizations in the role of a software manufacturer.

– Challenges in establishing a large-scale agile framework in the company" presents appropriate measures so that you can also master the regular challenges in your organization that stand in the way of effective application of agile methodology.

With the establishment of **Friendly User Tests**, you will learn why development stages within an organization cannot be skipped, but must be taken with **agile maturity levels**. In addition, you will read about how **innovative development and test environments with an abstracted hardware level** provide you with reliable tests as well as solid test results. The **importance of transparent decision-making processes and agile requirements management** is also illustrated.

Section 6.2 clarifies **how and why good digital leadership works**. From vision to strategy, the concept of a **product/service roadmap** is introduced. Moreover, the roles of the **Chief Information Officer (CIO)** and the new leadership role of the **Chief Digital Officer (CDO)** are explained in detail.

Likewise, the essential points of **change management** are explained, which are particularly relevant during the introduction of new organizational structures. These include, in particular, the procedures essential for software development, such as **change request and release management**, the establishment of agile capabilities through an Agile Academy, and the establishment of agile values.

The explanations on **emergency management** conclude the first part with a forward-looking view on agile and appropriate reactions in emergency situations.

Part II – Agile Infrastructure
Chap. 7 – Agile Tools: Toolbox for Product Owners & Agile Teams
The second part of the book is dedicated to agile tools and serves as a toolbox for Product Owners & Agile Teams.

In addition to the **Agile Manifesto**, **agile goals**, the agile concepts of **Personas, User Stories, Epics, Tasks** and **Sub-Tasks**, and the **Backlog** are explained.

Collaboration Tools are the agile tools with which stakeholders and members of the countless agile teams cooperate and exchange information. You will learn the importance and functionality of **Git repositories** as well as **OpenAPI** as a **tool for API design**.

In order for **agile architectures to form the foundation of software-based digitalization**, you will learn which important influencing factors apply to an agile infrastructure.

With Sect. 7.5, you will receive a **guide to creating a pragmatic software architecture documentation** and learn how to create **meaningful visual artifacts for your software architecture** and which **standards, criteria, and norms** are useful.

The following questions are also answered: Who are the **recipients and** what are the **subject areas of software architecture documentation**? How do you formulate meaningful questions for essential software architecture decisions? The relevance of **technical debt** is also illustrated. The **Arc42 template** finally provides you with a **directly usable tool for software architecture documentation**. And the standard of **ISO/IEC 25010** defines the **quality of software**.

In Sect. 7.6 **DevOps methods** and **DevOps tools** are introduced with the transition to **BizDevOps**.

Section 7.7 presents **content** and the **goals of a content strategy** and explains what requirements should be placed on valuable content and how to **measure the effectiveness of content**. We also devote ourselves to the **presentation and visualization of content** and introduce the special **content formats of infographics and dialogue images**.

In Sect. 7.8 possibilities for **implementing monitoring and controlling** based on **Key Performance Indicators (KPI)** are explained and which strategies and tools can be used to implement such reporting.

Section 7.9 introduces **methods and tools for agile prioritization** that provide real relief for product owners and agile teams in the software development environment to prioritize requirements and make existing dependencies between requirements visible. Both **timeboxing** and **feature-driven development** are among the most popular and proven methods. With the introduction of **Liquid Democracy**, you will learn an agile voting procedure and find out how to live transparency within an organization together.

The conclusion is Chap. 8, which is dedicated to data quality and thus the lifeblood of digitization. From the basics and prerequisites for excellent data quality, it goes on to data cleansing techniques and effective control mechanisms for optimizing data quality.

Acknowledgment
My personal thanks go especially to the mental support of my wife Martina and the patience of our daughter Coco. My special thanks go to my mother, who passed away after a long illness during the creation of this book, and who always wholeheartedly supported and encouraged me in my goals. This book should accompany Aileen and Jean Paul on their journey and show that every great goal can be achieved – even in small steps.

Your questions & your personal feedback are welcome!
Feedback from our readers is always welcome!

Because an agile mindset, transparency, and open dialogue are very important to me personally, I ask you as the reader to please direct any feedback to me as the author of this work.

If you have any questions about any aspect of this book, please send me an email at info@large-scale-agile-frameworks.com

Errata: Although I have taken every possible care to ensure the accuracy of my content, errors can occur. If you have found an error in this book, we would be grateful if you could report it to us.

Of course, we also welcome your general feedback: Send us an email and mention the title of the book in the subject of your message.

You can also find up-to-date information on the website www.large-scale-agile-frame-works.com

Share your thoughts in the form of a book review!
If you have read Large-Scale Agile Frameworks – Agile Frameworks, Agile Infrastructure, and Pragmatic Solutions for Digital Transformation, we would love to hear your opinion!

Your review is important to us and the tech community and helps us ensure that we deliver excellent quality content.

Hamburg   Sascha Block
Germany

Contents

Abbreviations

ADR	Action Design Research
API	Application Programming Interface
ART	Agile Release Train
AWS	Amazon Web Services
B2B	Business to Business
B2C	Business to Customer
BizDevOps	Business, Development & Operations
BL	Area Management
BSI	Federal Office for Information Security
CI	Configuration Item
CR	Change Request
CWA	Closed World Assumption
DDD	Domain Driven Design
DEV	Development
DevOps	Development & Operations
DoS	Denial of Service
DSVGO	General Data Protection Regulation
EAM	Enterprise Architecture Management
FAQ	Frequently Asked Questions
HTTPS	Hypertext Transfer Protocol Secure
IaaS	Infrastructure as a Service
IAM	Identity Access Management
IDLE	Infrastructure Services
IoT	Internet of Things
IT	Information Technology
KPI	Key Performance Indicators
LDAP	Lightweight Directory Access Protocol
MPM	Multi-Project Management
MVC	Model View Controller

MVP	Minimum Viable Product
NIST	National Institute of Standards and Technology
OLAP	Online Analytical Processing
OLTP	Online Transaction Processing
OPS	Operations (IT Operations)
OWA	Open World Assumption
PaaS	Platform-as-a-Service
PI	Program Increments
PJM	Project Manager
PM	Product Management
PO	Product Owner
RTE	Release Train Engineer
SA	Software Architect
SaaS	Software-as-a-Service
SAFe	Scaled Agile Framework
TLS	Transport Layer Security
TOM	Technical Organizational Measures
UML	Unified Modeling Language
UX	User Experience
VCS	Versioning Control System
Ver	Sales
VMM	Virtual Machine Monitor
XP	Extreme Programming
XML	Extensible Markup Language

List of Figures

List of Tables

Part I

Digital Transformation with Large-Scale Agile Frameworks

Introduction

1

This book presents practical solutions for cross-cutting prioritization of requirements and documentation using the example of an organization in the role or with essential characteristics of a software manufacturer. In doing so, the interaction of current technology topics such as the cloud trend or the organizational requirements with regard to microservices is reflected. Under the requirement of customer-centric and service-oriented products and services, organizations are increasingly confronted with the need to align their IT strategy closely with the needs of their customers. In addition, tightened requirements in the direction of IT security and in the context of digital transformation using cloud technologies and containerization require a radical realignment of previous IT strategies.

Companies struggle in the environment of unpredictable markets with increasing competitive pressure, rapidly changing customer requirements, regulatory changes, and rapid technological progress to achieve the best possible business success. Under such conditions, long-term strategic plans are limited and require continuous control and agile adjustment mechanisms to best support manufacturers of B2C or B2B products or service providers in any industry in such a difficult market environment.

Not only a gentle, but also largely flexible handling of the available, limited resources significantly relaxes the competitive situation. If software is defined through customer-relevant digital services and is agilely oriented towards the real needs of customers, then IT becomes an enabler in the company and contributes maximally to business success.

Software development is not only considered a complex problem area itself, but the value of software is also sometimes difficult to verify. In doing so, software must cover the strategic and economic interests of a company as extensively, simply, and cost-effectively as possible. The complexity of software increases with the heterogeneous interests of different customer groups. Thus, individualized software solutions that are optimally aligned with specialized customer interests and their agile handling become indispensable.

S. Block, *Large-Scale Agile Frameworks*, https://doi.org/10.1007/978-3-662-67782-7_1

The economic efficiency of optimized procedures seems to contradict the individu-alization of software. The more individual a market-oriented offer is designed, the more complex and elaborate the requirements become, and the more relevant the necessity of cross-cutting prioritization becomes. In this way, desired scale effects can be real-ized through structured digital services, economic aspects regarding the corresponding resource determination for the implementation of software, the need for manageable maintainability, the highest demands on IT security, and the shortest possible time-to-market. How important agile and science-based action is, is shown in the phases of the recent Corona crisis and in the context of national and European security efforts for criti-cal infrastructures all the more.

This book analyzes and explains the special requirements of a differentiated offer of software services and to what extent agile principles are suitable for effectively solving this problem, using practice-proven agile methodology. In addition to considering the product life cycle and a basic classification of software, the processes, activities, and roles required for this are particularly highlighted. Based on these requirements, suita-ble agile frameworks are selected, presented, and examined for possible weaknesses and strengths.

In doing so, this book presents the close relationship and optimization potential along software product lines. A software product line is a group of software products that rep-resent variants of a base product and share a common software architecture.

This consideration is in the context of so-called Large-Scale Agile Development. Large-Scale Agile Development becomes relevant when it comes to extending an agile approach to the structures of larger organizations. In this way, projects with large teams and a wide variety of different projects can be extended according to the principles of agile development—beyond the boundaries of individual agile teams—to the entire organization.

Motivation and Goals

The book aims to support organizations in an effective digital transformation. To this end, suitable process models, methods, and agile tools are described and explained so that companies can sustainably change their organizational structure towards a compre-hensive, agile prioritization. With such agile organizational structures, also known as Large-Scale Agile Frameworks, an adaptable implementation of, for example, cloud-based microservices and the prioritization of business units organized in agile teams is optimally supported.

Within the framework of recommendations oriented towards examples and use cases, a practice- and science-oriented analysis is carried out with regard to the overarching requirement prioritization between product-specific development teams and cross-func-tional teams with overarching support functions as well as product-independent expert teams with specialized tasks.

Novel is the reflection of highly topical technical issues and the consideration of the requirement for the best possible IT security in relation to the described technologies and with regard to the impact on agile organizational models and prioritization models.

As a result, a suitable agile organization and prioritization model is presented that effectively supports organizations that are at the beginning or already in the middle of the agile transformation process to improve the service-wide organization and prioritization.

With a focus on the efficient design of agile software services, the optimization, dimensions of the technical framework, professional documentation, and inter-process communication are at the center of such a model.

Who is this book for?
I have developed this book to help establish agility as a permanent part of our modern working culture in companies and organizations of all kinds. Regardless of the level of maturity you, your colleagues, and employees are currently at, this book is intended to serve as a guide to anchor agile mindset and agile working methods in your professional everyday life. Regardless of whether you want to learn more about agile methodology as a manager or team member, this work is intended to serve as a compass and navigates along the currently highly topical issues such as cloud technologies, DevOps, and IT security. Another goal is to sharpen awareness of IT security and to demonstrate practicable strategies and solutions for implementation. It is my concern to help you expand your knowledge beyond the basics of agility. It was created based on years of experience in countless projects and against the background of various corporate environments. There are many books that introduce agility and the associated basics. My plan was to write a book that goes beyond that. This book is intended to effectively support you and your organization in getting started with agility and establishing a new organizational form so that you, together with your colleagues and teams—and above all with fun—can achieve a successful digital transformation!

Process Models, Frameworks, and Standards
Which process models, frameworks, and standards are ideally suited to successfully complete agile software projects or transfer them to the next process phase?

A process model describes how a team solves a task within a project and how the team cooperates effectively. It is important that the approach is repeatable and successful so that comparable projects can be tackled in a similar form—in terms of cost, quality, and time—in an optimized manner.

A process model defines three essential elements [1]:

- **Roles**
- **Artifacts/Products**
- **Activities and Workflows**

If requirements are fully known at the beginning of a project, waterfall models are considered a proven process model, provided that there is also no need to change these requirements during the further course of the project [1, page 759].

A second important prerequisite for the application of the waterfall model, which is not given in the project context, is that an experienced project team with established technology takes over the development. In addition, change costs during the course of the project are a relevant decision criterion.

The diagram 1.1 "Change costs during the course of the project" schematically illustrates the amount of change costs during the course of the project, depending on how late these adaptation requirements are recognized [2, pages 71/72].

To partially compensate for the mentioned disadvantages, projects can be implemented iteratively, with the aim of recognizing adaptation requirements earlier and benefiting from the partial results sooner. Even projects following the waterfall model can be carried out in stages instead of in a single large waterfall. Each stage corresponds to a small waterfall. Requirements can change from stage to stage, and lessons learned can be implemented. Customer feedback is also provided after the first stage, not just at the end of the project. Each stage can be treated as a separate fixed-price project.

With increasingly shorter intervals for changes in requirements, an iterative, prototypical approach is now suitable in most cases.

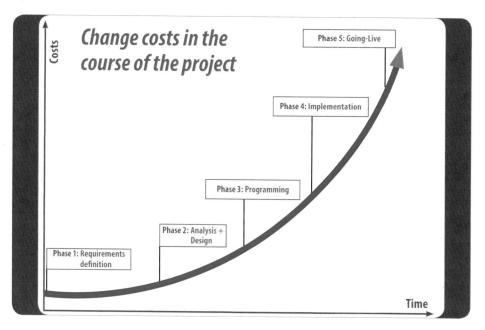

Fig. 1.1 Change costs during the course of the project. (Source: Sascha Block—Own illustration)

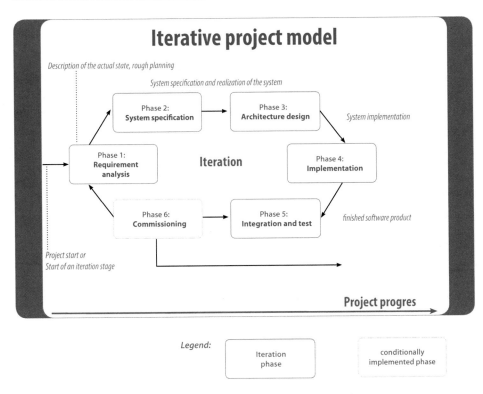

Fig. 1.2 Iterative project model. (Source: Sascha Block—Own illustration)

In iterative process models, a project is organized in several small iterations, see Fig. 1.2 "Iterative project model". According to the iterative model, all phases are completed with each iteration.

Learning is possible within the team from iteration to iteration. Customer feedback is also quickly taken into account, as functioning software is available after the first iteration. This reduces the project risk for all project partners, as the project can be terminated after each iteration [1, page 760]. In more recent iterative process models, this approach is explicitly included as a build-measure-learn cycle or principle.

In addition, a distinction is made between evolutionary and incremental development in iterative approaches. In **incremental** development, the software grows from iteration to iteration. The range of functions is also continuously expanded, while requirements remain largely unchanged.

In **evolutionary iteration** of software solutions, on the other hand, specifications and requirements in the software can change from one iteration to the next. Thus, with evolutionary iteration—hence the name of this iteration model—a complete restructuring of software systems is possible if the architecture of the software cannot meet changed requirements.

For starting situations with unclear project specifications, agile process models such as Scrum are suitable. As a process management framework, Scrum has a very close relationship to the product artifacts created in a project and provides a procedure for managing and planning requirements. The specific approach in the ongoing development process is determined by the project team [3, pages 3 and 4].

In contrast to plan-driven process models, the team itself is responsible for the outcome and thus learns independently in the specific approach how it can work most productively. The iterations, referred to as sprints, usually last a maximum of 30 days. For each sprint, requirements are selected that are implemented directly. This also allows for the flexible and independent adaptation of requirements within the project team from sprint to sprint. Requirements are not necessarily defined in writing, but often in personal conversations with stakeholders. Agile methods use product increments or prototypes, which are delivered to project customers at short, regular intervals for evaluation. Valuable feedback is thus always immediately and directly available to the project team.

This book follows the motivation to present additional mechanisms for synchronizing and prioritizing requirements between agile teams, the conducive methods, processes, and tools, as well as agile concepts of large-scale agile frameworks.

Agile Processes and Knowledge Management
How can agile processes for software development be made simple, understandable, transparent, and pragmatically documented?

Requirements for the Product Owner
What requirements should a Product Owner meet and which methodology proves successful for recurring tasks and agile documentation?

References

1. Ernst, H., Schmidt, J., & Beneken, G. (2016). *Grundkurs Informatik: Grundlagen und Konzepte für die erfolgreiche IT-Praxis. – Eine umfassende praxisorientierte Einführung* (6th ed., p. 757). Springer/Vieweg. hier Kapitel 17.4 „Vorgehensmodelle".
2. Schoeneberg, K.-P. (Eds.). (2014). *Komplexitätsmanagement in Unternehmen: Herausforderungen im Umgang mit Dynamik, Unsicherheit und Komplexität meistern* (1st ed.). Springer/Gabler.
3. Schwaber, K., & Sutherland, J. (2017). „The Scrum Guide" – Edition November 2017. http://www.scrumguides.org. Accessed 3 Nov 2022.

Digital Transformation & Agile Prioritization

2

The digital transformation is the driving force behind agile prioritization. The central theme in the overarching prioritization in the context of IT projects is the organization and cooperation between agile teams: How are coordination processes in the agile environment—especially overarching requirements in complex IT systems and software projects—ideally regulated? In addition, the question arises as to how—in software development in a technical domain with several technically separate products—the technical aspects of the domain and the technical documentation of the software products complement each other and how such documentation can be created and updated agilely.

With regard to the primary goal—the development of an agile organization and prioritization model for IT projects—this chapter reflects the current state of research and all aspects relevant to the development of such a model.

2.1 Agile Models for Organizing Digital Transformation

The Large-Scale Agile Frameworks presented in this book are the agile models for digital transformation in large organizations. Digital transformation places diverse demands on organizations and requires a rethinking of organizational structures. Highly specialized teams are in demand, and new tools are desired as working tools for effective communication between teams. Agile collaboration brings new rules of behavior into play and demands an agile mindset from all participants. The following section helps to understand the challenges posed by digital transformation and the new opportunities that arise through agile organizational models.

2.1.1   Digital Transformation—a Challenge With Many Opportunities

Digital transformation is the strategic realignment of companies to meet today's requirements of an increasingly digitally oriented business environment [1, page 1].

What is the Digital Challenge?
In particular, the digitization of existing processes within the company and the mapping of digital sales and marketing strategies towards modern online commerce shape the concept of digital transformation. Every company is therefore equally challenged to perfectly align existing structures, processes, and IT infrastructure so that the maximum value contribution is guaranteed even under increasing competitive conditions.

Why digital transformation?
Information systems for the integration of production and services play a central role. With the increasing importance of digital media, companies are more dependent than ever on customer-centric structures and problem-oriented solutions.

Shortest reaction times and perfectly interlocked IT systems
Complex service, eCommerce, and business scenarios require the shortest reaction times for digital service offerings and online commerce in both B2C and B2B. As customers increasingly expect shorter response times, the internal corporate requirements for IT, logistics, marketing, sales, and support to perfectly interlock all used systems automatically increase in the course of digital transformation.

Why digitization projects fail
Digitization is driving companies in every industry. However, many IT projects still fail. A study by the University of St. Gallen estimates the damage caused by failed IT projects in the European Union at €142 billion annually. "Digitization means change. Processes are being redesigned, employees are being assigned new tasks. But companies find it difficult to design the change," explains Dr.-Ing. Regina Zeitner from the Competence Center Process Management Real Estate in search of the causes and possible solutions [2, page 24].

"Only half of the companies have a digital agenda"—90% of companies in Germany, Austria, and Switzerland assume that competition will be fundamentally different in 2025 than it is today due to digitization and global events. But only half of the companies in this country have a digital agenda. For comparison: In Switzerland, it is 60%. At the same time, companies face a number of obstacles when it comes to concrete implementation.

No later than the Corona pandemic, the importance and urgency of a consistent digital transformation has been demonstrated in all respects for all areas and organizational forms. Drastically changing supply chains demand agile action just as much as the need to respond to IT security concerns without delay. In addition to a digital agenda, many companies still lack an IT strategy and, even more so, an agilely lived practice for implementing IT security and associated emergency concepts.

Why digital change is indispensable
A significant peculiarity of digital transformation is that the starting point of the digital revolution is for the first time not initiated by the companies themselves, but by consumers [3, Chap. 6, page 159].

As digital technologies have now reached a high level of dissemination with the rapid expansion of internet technologies and digital services, broadband availability, or smart devices, digital technology is dissolving many previously existing and traditionally analog customer relationships, forcing companies to address and serve consumers, partners, and suppliers via digital platforms.

The new threat: Digital Disruption
The principle of digital disruption can be traced back to the American economist Clayton M. Christensen. Clayton describes a digital innovation that completely displaces an existing technology, an existing product, offer, or a proven business model ideally [4, pages 17/18].

New markets emerge – even for established companies – often unexpectedly and initially appear uninteresting. As early as 1942, the Austrian economist Joseph Schumpeter coined the term "creative destruction" (analogously "creative destruction") to describe the importance of disruptive technologies that, over time, show ever-increasing growth and completely displace existing markets, products, and services [5]. According to this, an innovative entrepreneur becomes a monopolist through his innovation only as long as new imitators appear or his innovation fades due to other developments. For digital transformation, this means a constant interplay between the willingness to merely imitate other market participants or, instead, to outperform and displace competitors directly through one's own innovation.

Digital Disruption in Retail – Why almost every retailer needs to revise their business model
Driven by the emergence of new digital trading platforms, retailers – predominantly in the B2C sector and increasingly in the B2B sector – are forced to radically revise their business models in order to create new, global trading forms in the course of digital transformation [6, page 30 in the article "Reinvention of trade through digital disruption"].

When customers can have interchangeable goods from a multitude of arbitrary providers delivered directly and flexibly to any address of their choice via countless distribution

channels and at the fastest possible speed with just a click, and prices are easily comparable, both suppliers and manufacturers come under enormous competitive pressure.

A large number of retailers – without actively used digital sales strategies – are
already threatened in their existence by highly customer-centric services like Amazon
Prime.

The risk of not participating in the digital transformation is thus unacceptable, as the
standstill and consequently the economic decline of a company would be the inevitable
consequence.

2.1.2   What Factors Influence Digital Transformation?

To digitize a company, certain basic prerequisites must be created in the organization, at
the professional level, and in the alignment and implementation of the IT strategy.

Customer Experience

Customers want to be able to freely choose the communication channel through which
they contact a company. If digital marketing seamlessly interlocks traditional offline
channels with modern online channels and achieves a comprehensive customer-centric
approach, the digital customer approach is successful all around. This also includes systems at the center of customer dialogue in the form of a responsive company website and
the online shop, as well as all connected contact channels including social media.

The basic rule for success in customer experience management is:

> *"Only those who deliver more than promised will generate enthusiasm!"* [1, page 173]

Operational Excellence

In practice, a coordinated approach with all involved departments in close cooperation
with all integrated executives in the company has proven successful for implementing
changes. Digital transformation requires additional expertise:

Excellent understanding of business processes

To successfully lead the transformation to a digital company, an excellent understanding
of business processes is required. Based on a careful as-is analysis, the target architecture is determined and it is checked to what extent existing systems can be integrated or
replaced.

Transfer of analog to redesigned digital processes

The redesign of operational processes goes hand in hand with the changed business models brought about by digital transformation. This includes, for example, the immateriality
of the performance result in the form of operational processes, such as maintenance, up

to business processes, such as operating plants [1, page 128]. For each process step in the company, it must be specifically examined to what extent analog processes can be digitized.

Optimization of the organizational structure
With digital transformation, the focus shifts from internal processes to external processes that are controlled by customers, suppliers, and partners and are aligned with them. This goes hand in hand with the optimization of the organizational structure as well as adaptive processes and IT strategies.

Sensors and embedded digital systems
In order to specifically support logistics with digital services or align digital services with customers (e.g., by providing tracking information and sensor data with relevant additional information for users and customers), the implementation and use of appropriate sensors are required, which generate digital data and pass it on to connected digital systems.

The technology in the form of GPS-based positioning systems or RFID chips for digital coding of serial numbers in the GTIN process is inexpensive in terms of hardware; the focus should rather be on the associated usage scenarios and the resulting process orientation and IT-supported connection and data utilization [7, page 19 ff.].

Optimization of the Supply Chain
In addition, the supply chain can be supported, for example, by specifically accelerating delivery chains and planning processes, such as by connecting new technologies like SAP's In-Memory solution HANA to speed up reporting, provided the ERP solution in the company is based on SAP solutions [7, page 22].

Legal and organizational foundations
To specifically exploit rationalization effects and all the advantages of digitization, responsible handling of digital data is inevitably required. With fine-grained consent management, a tiered model is proposed that only allows access to stored data when there is demonstrable necessity. In this context, legal framework conditions are the focus. Furthermore, decentralized and anonymized data storage must be taken into account so that the creation of a personal profile is only partially possible and not accessible to everyone [8, page 45].

2.1.3   Goals of Digital Transformation

The goals of digital transformation projects are equally based on the opportunities that arise from consistent digitization. The following goals are cross-industry and independent of the size of a particular company.

Internal efficiency improvement

Efficiency is an important long-term criterion in the value creation model of every company. Internal efficiency improvement also includes looking at production and manufacturing costs as well as the careful use of all resources used in the value creation process. All activities that do not contribute to value creation, i.e., do not produce value for customers or the company, are wasteful and should be eliminated. It is also necessary to examine to what extent scale effects can be used to achieve efficiency improvements with certain target sizes. In most cases, digital offerings no longer incur additional costs once the digital strategy has been successfully established. Marginal costs thus tend to approach zero, even as user numbers and revenues in the company increase [9, page 211].

Productivity improvement

Whether cloud computing enables productivity improvement has not yet been proven. In general, productivity depends heavily on the specific processes within a company, so that process optimizations can only be identified and implemented based on in-depth analyses. Digitization offers companies an opportunity in this regard, as processes can be re-examined, evaluated, and redesigned in an optimized form through digital transformation. As previously explained in the Operational Excellence section, the highest degree of attention must be paid to process analysis; appropriate resources must be planned (e.g., lead time, financial resources, employees, and efforts through external support based on objective process consulting).

Quality improvement

Quality improvement in the context of digitization primarily aims at the previously described process optimization and, in particular, at data quality within companies.

For *data quality*, the highest requirements apply with regard to:

- **Completeness**
- **Consistency**
- **Timeliness**
- **Accuracy**
- **Reliability**

Data quality poses challenges to digital transformation projects in two respects. First, it is necessary to establish homogeneity between the existing different IT systems and identify redundancies. Second, digitization projects involving the integration of partners and suppliers on the data side require newly acquired data to be monitored before import to ensure the best possible data quality continuously [10, page 276]. The improvement of quality for software applies to at least the same extent to usability and IT security. Since IT security is of significant importance with the cloud trend and containerization, a separate section is dedicated to this topic.

Establishing Agility
Agility in relation to modern development concepts – such as the establishment of a novel leadership style – are crucial success factors for digital transformation projects and are explained in detail in Agile Organization and further in the concept of Large-Scale Agile Frameworks.

Revenue Increase
Revenue increases can be achieved through lower prices as a result of internal efficiency improvements (see point Internal Efficiency Improvement) as well as through new products and services. In the strategic (re)orientation towards specific market segments and securing market shares or targeted expansion through the conquest of new market shares through internationalization, revenues can be specifically increased with digitalization strategies.

New Products + Digital Services
Those who understand the challenges of digital transformation as a real opportunity for change to better products and customer-centric services will be rewarded with success on the project side as well as with expected revenue increases.

Own Sales Structures and Innovative Services
Foresighted manufacturers build their own digital distribution channels and thus enter into direct competition with their dealers. On the dealer side, new offers and services are required as well as complementary sales and marketing strategies. The value of goods can only be justified to the customer on the basis of tangible and convincing arguments. Only in this way can customer loyalty be won and maintained.

Secure and Expand Market Shares
As mentioned in the point Revenue Increase, digitalization strategies specifically aim to secure and expand market shares.

Address Customers Worldwide Online
While companies have so far bundled their sales strategy on a few sales channels and distributed their products and services mainly nationally or in the surrounding European economic area, digital platforms already have customers worldwide in focus from the start phase.

Expand Market Shares and Win New Customers Without Additional Costs
While the digital platform attracts customer contact in a very short time and binds customers to the company in the long term with the right digital strategy, digital companies benefit from addressing customers in new market segments without significant marketing costs, in order to safely gain revenue shares in new markets.

Increasing Customer Loyalty

Customer loyalty can be demonstrably increased through multi-channel marketing and personalized customer approach. In this context, the quality requirements listed under point Quality Improvement regarding data quality play a decisive role.

Maximum Customer Orientation and Convenience Increases Profit

Focus specifically on usability and customer-oriented solutions! Based on already established customer relationships and a high degree of comfort zone (keyword: Convenience) on the customer side, Amazon can sometimes actively test high-price strategies. For the technology company Amazon, it is a matter of course to adjust its offer prices for each individual product online several times a day if necessary. Such a need arises simply because the evaluation based on big data analyses with an evaluation of customer behavior shows that higher prices can be enforced.

2.1.4 Digital Transformation and Large-Scale Agile Frameworks

Companies that do not use purely standard software products, but rather establish their processes and services on individualized software solutions, face the following challenges when developing software – as part of complex IT systems:

While companies desire highly individualized software based on their individual requirements, software manufacturers are interested in largely standardized software products. From the dilemma between individualization and efficient standardization, corresponding prioritization requirements arise.

Organization of cross-functional prioritization for a software system

As soon as a software consists of various subsystems, whose development is independently driven by several development teams, the question of organizing cross-functional prioritization arises. Is this in contradiction to the agile mindset?

In almost every company, independent software products have developed over the course of the business years from various individual projects, which functionally complement each other. Initial basic requirements regularly deviate in parts or, in the worst case, completely from today's requirements, especially with regard to software architecture:

Redundancies have arisen; accumulated requirements from the current design concept can only be implemented with considerable effort on all individual components of the software or an IT infrastructure. Also, with a growing number of interdependent subsystems, components, and modules, testing efforts increase significantly and currently account for about one-third of project costs – thus, the creation of new or the adaptation of existing software. In addition, technical questions arise, such as: "Which systems are leading?" and "How should corresponding process specifications be designed?" This organizational task is an important mandatory discipline in the design of every IT architecture. Effective processes and role models are required for this. The focus is on prioritizing requirements. Dependencies, roles, and required processes and options for team and project coordination are considered. A suitable, agile model for cross-functional prioritization and organization is desired.

Domains and tension fields of agile transformation

Carr's provocatively formulated thesis "IT does not matter" [11] "triggered a controversial and long overdue discussion about the role of IT" [12]. Typically, the IT domain is not only leading in technical matters and solely focused on the development, provision, and operation of IT systems. The importance of IT and software development increasingly shapes strategic and creative, economically successful business processes. The role of IT has changed significantly: from being perceived as a mere cost center, to IT as a service provider, to IT as an enabler and even a driving force in companies. With the trend towards digitalization, software is understood as a strategic competitive instrument that creates differentiated and entirely new business models [13, page 98]. Traditionally, a higher-level, organizational domain within the company is responsible for corporate strategy, management of processes and activities, and resource planning.

The focus is primarily on problem areas that affect the IT environment and organizational business processes [14, page 40]. With agile transformation, companies in these tension fields increasingly face challenges that can hardly be solved with traditional methods. Complemented by the technical domain, the benefit-oriented reference that software projects should fulfill is established. This extends the technical role of IT to include strategic and marketing-related aspects.

Changed tasks require new roles, activities, and processes within the company. The diagram 2.1 Domains and Roles in a Company illustrates the different perspectives of various roles and domains in the agile context of a company.

2.1.5   The Importance of Agile Processes and Large-Scale Agile Frameworks

Agile methodology promises significant advantages for software development, e.g., in the form of shorter release cycles, a positive influence of regular feedback, and thus overall higher-quality software. Therefore, agility practices are now widely established as a standard for manageable project teams and moderately complex software development projects.

Increasingly, companies are now interested in extending agile methods to larger organizational units and the collaboration, coordination, and communication between such teams. The growing number of agile frameworks can be seen as evidence of this. Starting with the method set "Crystal Family" by Alistair Cockburn in 1992, there are now at least 20 frameworks specifically designed for larger organizations [15, page 125].

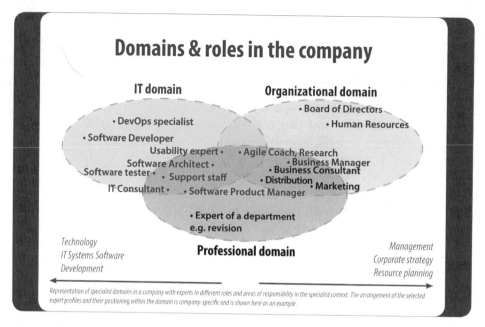

Fig. 2.1 Domains and roles in a company. (Source: Own representation – Sascha Block)

The economic success of young and agilely organized companies like Spotify, which created their own organizational model for the purpose of agility scaling against this background – the Spotify Engineering Model – should have aroused interest in verifiable reasons and causes. Especially the introduction of agile approaches in large projects is either associated with considerable difficulties for many companies or fails completely.

What criteria should be used to select such a framework, and how can an agile organizational model be transformed to larger business units?

Balance between Agility and Prioritization
The most difficult task is to recognize when the need for overarching prioritization arises, which stakeholders should be involved in decision-making processes, and which procedural model can efficiently solve these challenges.

In addition to the actual development efforts, a large portion of time is spent on planning and coordination processes. Legal frameworks, changing user requirements, error corrections, and customer requests continuously flow into software development in the form of changes, software releases, and new solutions. Agile methods promise the most effective solution approach for this.

Specifics of Isolated Software Projects within an IT Strategy
In practice, isolated software projects are created over the years, which are powerful individual solutions within the company and which – each taken separately and in the

form of separately licensable individual products – perform specific functions in very specific task areas.

Individual Products, Product Packages, and Software Suites from Various Components

From a company perspective, a uniform behavior in professional functions and system monitoring as well as a uniform usability with a central configuration is regularly desired. From an internal developer's point of view, the question arises as to how existing redundancies in software architecture and functionality can best be avoided. Against this background, the "agility in software development" is examined to what extent optimization potentials can be realized and how these can be achieved most easily through coordination and coordination processes and transparent knowledge management. It should be determined which fundamental decisions have to be made and which agile procedural models are particularly suitable for such mutually complementary software components.

2.2   How Proven Are Agile Approaches?

The fact that agile approaches are proven is theoretically substantiated. For the first time, Serrador and Pinto dedicate themselves to a quantitative study of 1386 projects in over 60 countries, examining the relationship between agile methodology and project success. They used regression analysis to investigate criteria for goal achievement, budget, time, and project evaluation by stakeholders. As a result, project success increased demonstrably with the increasing application of agile methods. According to their observations, projects that apply agile methods to a high degree have a similarly high effort for project planning as traditional approaches [16, page 1047]; Dybå and Dingsøyr, on the other hand, believe that agile projects apparently require higher planning efforts [17].

What seems to be less researched, however, is the direct practical relevance and the aspects of existing dependencies within software products combined with the solution approaches of agile methodology. Letho and Rautiainen, for example, consider the challenges of transformation towards agile software product development in a comparable case study, but do not take into account the dependencies between software products within a software portfolio [18].

Wnuk et al. criticize that approaches to release planning that support continuous dynamic replanning currently seem to be underrepresented in the literature [19, page 49u.].

Against the background of fragmented system landscapes and the organization of decentralized distributed teams, the scientific examination of the topic *Scaled Agile* is gaining increasing importance. With the aspect of multi-product development, the relevant artifacts and roles as well as relevant tools, methods, and agile approaches move into the focus of consideration. A validation through practice-oriented evaluations of existing *Scaled Agile Frameworks* (SAFe) also seems to be lacking so far.

In a study conducted in 2016, Dikert et al. question the still very limited practical experience with Scaled Agile Frameworks: According to their results, only six research papers deal with the topic at this point in time; the researchers are all the more surprised by the fact that SAFe, based on a survey, already has an astonishingly high acceptance and dissemination rate [20, page 106]. Against this background, the authors propose practice-oriented case studies on agile transformations, studies on the use of scaling practices and Scaled Agile Frameworks, as well as on company-wide use of Agile and surveys on Agile on a large scale.

The current state of research on agile software development in larger organizational structures largely refers to the explanation of agile methods and the subsequent consideration of agile frameworks; this approach is followed by the present book.

2.3 Agile Concepts and Basic Terms

Compared to classical process and approach models, which are organized according to the waterfall model, completely different requirements are placed on the organization of corporate units and processes in agile processes. Consequently, the management and handling of activities and roles in the company do not necessarily become easier. Changes towards agile models should always be supported as extensively as possible by the employees and thus pose new challenges and difficulties for management with regard to the associated change processes.

Currently, there are no concrete guidelines in the literature regarding the implementation of an agile prioritization and organization model that contributes to making software releases—traditionally referred to as software product lines—economically efficient and customizable at the same time. This book examines this topic and presents models and methodology that best meet the aforementioned requirements for efficiency and customizability.

Concepts relevant to agile collaboration
Different concepts influence software development and agile collaboration in teams and beyond organizational boundaries.

The Table 2.1 "Classified Concepts with Relevance for Agile Collaboration" illustrates the relevant concepts that are significant in the context of Large Agile Frameworks and agile software development.

This reflects all relevant agile methods as well as the overarching control of a multitude of projects. The important topics for cross-cutting prioritization in software development are examined in detail.

These include the equivalent terms *"Portfolio Management"* and *"Multi-Project Management"*, which are used synonymously in the literature and, by definition, form the framework for the strategic and organizational management of software projects.

Table 2.1 Classified Concepts with Relevance for Agile Collaboration

Conceptswith Relevance for Agile Software Development	Multi-Project Management/Portfolio Management
	Software Concepts: • **Software License Products and Custom Software** • **Software Platform, Product Family, and Product Line** • **Product Lifecycle of Software** • **Software Releases and Release Concept**
	Domain Driven Development
	Software Architecture and Knowledge Management
	Requirement Management/Prioritization
	DevOps and DevOps Model
	Agility and Agile Project Model
	Scaled Agile/Agile Frameworks

Suitability and Quality of Agile Processes and Activities

These concepts will be presented in the following chapters and reflected in the context and with regard to their relevance in direct relation to the Large-Scale Agile Frameworks.

2.3.1   Multi-Project Management

Multi-Project Management (MPM) is an annual and intra-annual portfolio process for the organization, control, and development of multiple projects [21, page 20]. Multi-project management is situated in a field of tension between various interests and domains within the company. Figure 2.2 "Multi-Project Management" illustrates the complex interplay of various activities and responsibilities.

MPM is anchored in a strictly hierarchical organizational structure to achieve company-relevant goals through projects. In this respect, MPM appears to be well-suited for the overarching prioritization of the software portfolio at a software manufacturer. Rohner confirms that success in projects depends on the control and leadership activities in the parent and project organizations, the given framework conditions, and the handling of these [22, page 21]. Framework conditions that cannot be controlled or led by the project include market dynamics, organizational structure, corporate dynamics, the IT landscape, and general operational capability—for example, in terms of available resources [22, pages 22, 24].

In MPM, a *project portfolio* bundles projects and programs—possibly also other project portfolios—in a delimited area of responsibility for the purpose of overarching planning and control [23, page 28]. A project portfolio can be structured according to different criteria; e.g., by products, markets, project types, or risk and economic aspects. The initiation of projects is an important task in MPM; it can be done through a program, the project portfolio, or by a department or management. Figure 2.3 "Synchronization

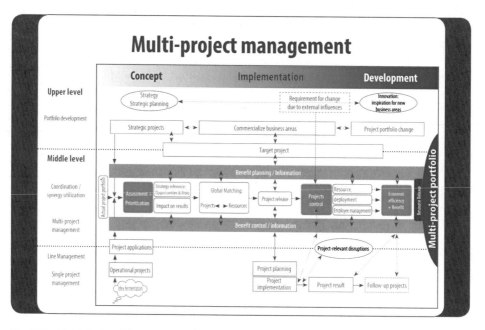

Fig. 2.2 Multi-Project Management. (Source: Own representation based on Steinle et al.)

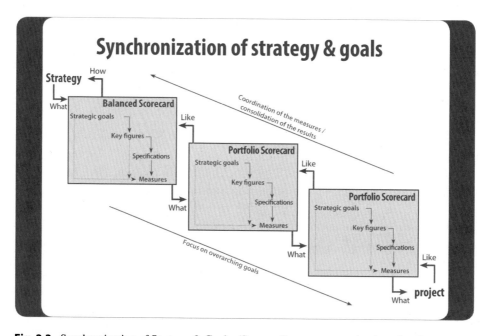

Fig. 2.3 Synchronization of Strategy & Goals. (Source: Own representation based on Lang et al.)

of Strategy & Goals" shows, based on Lang et al., how measures are coordinated and results are condensed with a focus on overarching goals.

Following a three-stage logic, project portfolios bundle initiated programs. *Programs* in turn combine projects according to professional, strategic, or organizational aspects. In a *project*, the actual implementation of strategic guidelines takes place. Projects can serve purely for the optimization of internal support processes or be directly aimed at the development and provision of products and services. In this context, top management is challenged to create concrete synergies between project and strategy work and to make decisions. To achieve this, a coordination of methods is required. Classically, goals are broken down *Top-Down* – from strategy to project portfolio and finally to programs and projects—and results are then condensed accordingly *Bottom-Up* [23, pages 38/39].

2.3.2 Portfolio Management

Regularly, various software products complement each other and form an overarching software system within a company when interacting with each other. A distinct feature that is examined in software companies in the role of software manufacturers as well as in companies that develop their software components independently and complement each other is discussed in the following section.

The *portfolio-* or *multi-product management* refers to the organization of a customer-oriented offer in the form of a *product portfolio* and controls the product distribution strategy. In the context of software development, these are individual licensable and combinable software products that complement each other and are thus functionally related to each other.

Strategic Control of the Software Product Portfolio
Product management assumes overarching prioritization responsibility for several software products, which are typically arranged within product families with subordinate product lines.

Thus, the portfolio management of software products carries out the pre-evaluation of product ideas regarding prioritization, budget, and feasibility, including a recommendation in the form of a project ranking to the company management [21, page 20]. In this context, multi-product management is responsible for compliance with the project management guideline and intervention with the relevant committees.

Not only in a classic process organization do the above-listed subprocesses of multi-product management take place at fixed intervals; this is also necessary within an agile model.

Thus, the product strategy of product management (PM) serves both controlling and providing the individual agile product teams with important guidelines for delimiting the software products they are responsible for from other products within the portfolio. From an "In-Scope/Out-Scope orientation," through the direct reference to practicable architectural concepts and software development strategies, the influence of PM extends to prioritizing functionalities to be implemented. Additionally, PM can assume a feedback function for evaluating team-internal processes. Furthermore, PM ensures reliable framework conditions for the agile teams concerning the project dimensions of time, costs, and resources and provides the teams with planning security and the information necessary for their product planning. Important tools of PM are a transparent product vision, the product roadmap, and the release plan with the individual release dates for main releases and release patches.

Cross-functional Control and Controlling

For effective portfolio management in a software company, it is particularly important to ensure that a cross-functional team—consisting of representatives of product management, specialists for software architecture, and specialists for the functional requirements of the respective solutions, based on cost-oriented controlling specifications, ensures the required quality of project ideas and project proposals. The goal of this team is to ensure products within a product family that correspond to the corporate strategy, evaluate the feasibility of innovations and product changes, ensure quality assurance, harmonize the solutions, and, if necessary, promote appropriate alternatives. To do this, the resulting efforts, dependencies, and side effects of the respective solution approaches must be evaluated; these can then be related to each other and ultimately contribute to making recommendations and documenting them accordingly. If necessary, the core team can involve appropriate experts from the product-specific specialist teams.

2.3.3   Software License Products and Custom Software

Software is an intangible product and, as such, has no physical properties. The value of software is often difficult to perceive; also, the benefits and what distinguishes a specific software product are to a large extent subjective [24, page 5].

Evaluation Criteria for Software

Software must—with regard to customer-oriented sales arguments—convince. In this context, software products are primarily defined by:

- Functional and performance features
- Price
- Quality
- Scope of service

Classes and Types of Software Products

In contrast to clearly definable and distinguishable software products, *"Embedded Software"* is a software component that cannot be marketed as a standalone software product, but only in combination with a real—non-software-based product—[24, page 6]. A concrete example of this is the integrated engine control within physical assemblies in the vehicle interior.

Another important category is *OEM software products;*—the abbreviation OEM stands for Original Equipment Manufacturer—here, a software manufacturer distributes software to a company that sells it as an integrated part of its own products, usually without visibly marking it [24, page 7].

License Products

Software license products can also be *standardized solutions* that are not further customizable and are therefore typically aimed at a large market segment as a software product. Representative examples of such mass license products are Microsoft Word or Adobe Photoshop.

Custom Software

In contrast, *customizable software license products* are at least to a small—if not to a large—extent customizable for specific customer needs. Thus, the standardized software product forms a product superclass, with the customer-specific customization of this product consequently forming the class instances. This reference point is given appropriate weight in prioritization, because—even without further detailed consideration—it becomes immediately clear that the complexity increases continuously with each individual customization variant: After all, each individual software variant must be kept updatable and maintainable.

Software development has the character of a very heterogeneous, service-oriented service. The benefit of a service is largely created on both sides; i.e., on the part of the service provider as well as on the part of the customer [25, slide 36]. This also applies to a large extent to the development of custom software: The customer of the software manufacturer becomes, due to the intensive interaction in the design process, the "co-creator of the benefit". Therefore, it is advisable to intensify cooperation with the customer; after all, only the customer himself generates the actual benefit through the application in his context. The software manufacturer only provides the necessary resources for this. In diametrical contrast to this is the self-interest of the software manufacturer to pursue its own software strategy, which may be contrary to customer interests.

In addition, service-oriented individual solutions have a low degree of standardization, are difficult or impossible to compare with each other, make market transparency difficult, are difficult to measure in terms of their quality level, and are highly diverse in their perceived benefit by customers [25, slide 24]. The marketing of software is further complicated by the fact that the resources, know-how, and technical specifications used in the software production process remain largely hidden from the customer. In the prioritization process, this is of great importance because the sales department has a special, compensating role to play in highlighting the advantages of this hidden information in interaction with the customer. In addition, it is important to keep the risk for the customer as low as possible due to uncertainties in the development process; after all, the customer of custom software only receives the usable result at the very end of the software development process. This directly reveals the need for agile approaches, as agile feedback and frequent iterations can effectively reduce this risk in both directions.

Internal and External Perspectives on Software License Products
Both the internal perspective—from the software manufacturer's point of view—and the external view of end users and licensees are crucial. Software license products are often not perceived as independent services, but rather as a part of a multifaceted software landscape or as an integral part of a licensee's service—and not understood as an independent service object.

The Strategic Importance of Software Components
What role do software components play as integral parts of complex software systems? License products such as online shop systems are often an integral part of a core process or a service component in a company that has procured a software product or several mutually complementary software components for this purpose. These individual software products or software components, on the other hand, are not perceived by end users—for example, in the role of customers of an online shop for medical products—although the service performance of online ordering would be inconceivable without these integrated software license products. This aspect is crucial in terms of prioritization, as it has a significant influence on the strategic orientation of the overarching product strategy. The definition of industry-specific performance features serves to differentiate from competitive products and influences the decision-making of customers and their long-term commitment to the software manufacturer.

PayPal as an Example of a Perfectly Arranged Software Product
PayPal is an outstanding example of a perfectly arranged software product because the provider of this digital payment component has managed to turn its actual software product into a distinctive digital service in a perfect way. Technically speaking, PayPal is a payment service like many other online payment services, but it sets itself apart from all competitors in the market with a meticulously designed customer loyalty strategy—primarily focused on the convenience and additional features of the money transfer service—and has established itself as a currently indispensable payment component in eCommerce and beyond. Just think about how often you have ordered goods simply because PayPal was offered as a payment method.

PayPal's success is based on its close customer loyalty strategy in the form of an easy-to-integrate software component for online shop systems, and the monetization model through the seller-supported fee model is well known to everyone.

Transform Your Software into Distinctive Digital Services!
In the same way, successful companies transform their previous product and service strategies into distinctive digital services with an independent character. This, in turn, has a direct impact on the way software should be designed to offer customers optimally functioning processes. It is no longer sufficient for all involved software components to work together smoothly; attention is now focused on the customer experience in the form of a perfectly optimized user experience.

2.3.4 Software Platform, Software Product Family, and Software Product Line

A *software platform* is a collection of similar elements—usually in the form of a basic underlying technology—and as such is not yet an independent software product.

Software Platforms as Control Instruments for Innovations
A suitable example for almost every company is the Java runtime environment, which has been available as freeware until now; a standardized software platform that is required to run developed Java programs. With Oracle's strategy change as the provider of Java, this free freeware model has now turned into a license-based fee model. The impact on existing software projects and, above all, software products from software manufacturers is—as you can easily imagine—enormous!

This is relevant for prioritization because architectural decisions constantly fall into the context of software platforms and such decisions are closely related to the strategic product orientation and the innovation capability of software products. Accordingly, it should be ensured that an organized process identifies, analyzes, and evaluates technologies.

Marketing instrument software product family
The *software product family* is a group of software products that are marked as related for strategic marketing reasons. In this case, the software architecture plays a subordinate role; rather, this circumstance results in the requirement that no disadvantages regarding the software architecture arise from a specific product constellation in the future [24, page 11].

Optimization potential along software product lines
A *software product line* is a group of software products that represent variants of a base product and have a common software architecture. According to the definition by Clements and Northrop, software product lines are based on a set of identical base

components that are incorporated into each individual product of this line according to prescribed architectural specifications [26, page 23]. Thus, software product lines play an essential role in a prioritization concept for a software manufacturer: The domain-based architecture approach within a software product line enables scaling effects to develop for a large number of similar systems—in favor of lower costs, shorter time, and higher quality—[27, page 70/71]. Therefore, according to Clements and Northrop, software product lines offer medium and long-term measurable scaling and synergy effects and demonstrable economic benefits within a product portfolio as well as strategic advantages through a differentiable orientation.

With the proper organization of processes and activities, there should be—at the same time through simplified maintenance of the basic architecture—room for shared product support and reduced development activities in scope. In an idealized change process—a basic component for one of the line products—this modification should automatically be incorporated into the other components without significant additional effort if desired.

Pohl/Metzer optimistically suggest that this could even result in up to 10% higher productivity and quality, a reduction in costs of up to 60%, a decrease in development effort of up to 87%, and a shortening of time-to-market of up to 98%; they also see the possibility of serving new markets not in cycles of years, but within a few months [27, page 185]. This requires an architecture concept geared towards this, combined with organized version control management and appropriate DevOps practices. Dehmouch fundamentally confirms the concept of software product lines and also sees advantages in reusability, which can be achieved by considering commonalities and variability within the product line; this can result in lower costs, shorter time-to-market, and higher quality requirements [28].

The main task of product management—in the context of software engineering oriented towards software product lines—is the alignment of a product portfolio through the definition of distinguishable product features that characterize the essence of each individual line product. In defining such characteristics, there is a risk that the scope of a software product line becomes too large and domain artifacts become too general, and ultimately the effort to realize them becomes too high. On the other hand, if the scope is defined too narrowly, the required features as well as functional and quality requirements of many customers may not be covered; consequently, only very few applications can be derived from the product line. In both cases, the product line may not be economically viable [27, page 189]. Therefore, a reliable forecast of cost estimates, achievable product advantages, and technical expertise should be equally taken into account.

2.3.5 Product Life Cycle of Software

The *product life cycle* is a model according to which products have a limited lifespan in the market due to societal and/or technological changes [29, page 116 ff.]. It describes the process from market introduction to the withdrawal of a product from the market. During this time span, software products—depending on their current life cycle phase—contribute to economic success to varying degrees. It is possible that software products do not go through the entire life cycle, as they may be displaced or abandoned during their market deployment.

Development of sales, profitability, and liquidity over the product life cycle
Software is unique in that the largest capital expenditure occurs during the main development phase; after that—apart from major improvements—mainly small variable costs and high marginal profits are incurred [24, page 23]. The overarching product management monitors the individual software products and their phases with an active product policy. The following phases are distinguished:

1. Introduction phase
2. Growth phase
3. Maturity phase
4. Saturation phase

The *introduction phase* provides a new software product with market access; it is characterized by sales efforts and increased marketing expenses, and first customers are acquired [29, page 118]. This is to be distinguished from follow-up products in the form of new software releases: Such new release versions can—especially with larger version jumps—have a highly innovative product character in the form of so-called major releases, i.e., version 2.0 follows version 1.0. However, the product to be introduced to the market may already have a significant market presence, making the introduction phase easier. Initially low and gradually increasing sales are offset by high expenditures in software development and corresponding sales costs. Distribution costs for software are not only negligibly low but also promise regular follow-up sales for software companies through implementation and training. However, internal costs, e.g., for training sales and support teams, should not be neglected. Efforts related to software documentation updates are also often overlooked. With the start of sales, software manufacturers face the internal demand to demonstrate profits and significant annual sales growth.

These characteristic phases of a product life cycle are shown in Fig. 2.4 "Development of sales, profitability, and liquidity over the product life cycle." The graphical representation clearly illustrates the interplay of the relevant factors such as the development of sales, profitability, and liquidity in relation to the individual phases within the product life cycle.

In the *growth phase*, the demand and thus the revenue for a software product steadily increases. This leads to the profitability reaching its peak in the growth phase. Software manufacturers with innovative software products benefit from their competitive advantage and can skim so-called *pioneer profits* from the market [29, page 119]. An advantage is that the demand in this phase is predominantly characterized by licensees

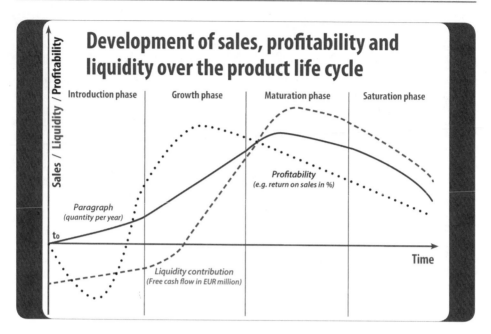

Fig. 2.4 Development of sales, profitability, and liquidity over the product life cycle. (Source: Sascha Block)

classified as *innovators*, who are generally less price-sensitive. For software manufacturers, the otherwise typical rule for product manufacturers that investments only burden the fixed assets to the extent of the depreciation on profits is only partially applicable, as additional expenses typically arise for bug fixes and release updates. Such expenses should correctly burden the portfolio controlling—at least in part—the budget of this release version. The competitive situation during the growth phase is predominantly moderate. Competition in growing market segments of software products is even less intense.

The *maturity phase* is characterized by a slowed increase in sales volume, caused by the emerging saturation limit of initial demand and the emergence of alternative products due to technological progress [29, page 119]. Accordingly, revenue growth and investment expenses for the further development of this software release decrease, so that the cash flow reaches its maximum. Depending on market intensity, market segment, and the degree of individualization of the software, profitability decreases if increasing competition puts pressure on market prices and other conditions.

In the *saturation phase*, both the cash flow and profitability for a software product decline [29, page 119]. Once software is introduced to a licensee, they only invest in it when there is a particular need—usually triggered by regulatory requirements, market-related changes, or especially due to the necessity of technological progress. It remains open how relevant innovations can be reliably identified, analyzed, and evaluated, and when they should be included in the development strategy.

2.3.6   Software Releases and Release Management

A *software release* is a version with a defined scope of functions and maturity level of a software application or app that can also be specified for a particular user group.

Types of Different Releases
An *initial software release* generally represents the first generation of a new or improved software application. In the context of software development for software products, the term *release candidate* is alternatively used.

Before a release, the distribution of the application in the form of *alpha and* then *beta releases*—also called alpha and beta versions—precedes as testable pre-versions.

The Major Release defines the main version of a software version and includes significant innovations of a software product. Such innovations can be completely new functional areas or special technologies that are supported for the first time. Not infrequently, such functional extensions are accompanied by changes to the system or software architecture.

In addition, the main version with the Major Release also replaces additions and extensions that have been published since the last release approval. A *minor release*, on the other hand, contains "smaller" application additions and software extensions to existing functions.

An Emergency Release is relevant in terms of IT security and refers to short-term available software versions that fix serious problems. It is therefore an "emergency release" that usually contains only significant bug fixes and no additional features. Alternative terms for Emergency Releases are Bugfixes, Emergency Fix, or Hotfixes. Before the publication of an Emergency Release, specifically defined test cases for quality assurance should be defined and passed.

A Stable Release usually indicates a release status that is approved for productive use and meets the appropriate stability criteria.

Release Management
In agile software development, a release is a deployable software package that represents the culmination of several iterations.

In the incremental development of software, features are incorporated into the respective release versions, and a release-ready release usually has to pass defined tests successfully within the scope of quality assurance. With this agile approach, releases can be created before the end of an iteration, and software functions are made available as early as possible in the form of adapted or supplemented functions published with the release.

Accordingly, an agile model must include an effective mechanism for controlling software releases. Such a release concept must be aligned with how different software products and software services relate to each other.

A Software Release Cycle is the result of individual development and maturation phases of computer software. The release cycles range from the initial software development to the final release of a software application. Software Releases include updated versions, patches, and updates of the released version with the aim of improving software quality or fixing software errors still present in previous release versions.

The deployment of software releases is now mapped in most organizations using Git-based repositories as part of release management. Here, software releases are planned and implemented. In the course of release management, a release plan is traditionally used. Based on release plans, software developers plan the scope, content, and timing of deployments in releases. Depending on the software products and individual company strategy, corresponding release cycles vary greatly from one another. The short-term implementation and deployment of bug fixes, software quality control, agreed criteria for release publication, maintenance of change logs, and the provision of release keys for the release of functions can also be the responsibility of release management.

How this is achieved is explained in the concept of Release Trains in a separate section. Test management is the mechanism that must ensure that each published software release is error-free and establishes effective usability tests before your customers report serious software errors to you at worst.

Thus, all stakeholders immediately get a sense of the value of individual functions and have the opportunity to provide feedback early in the process. Each system version as a software release is an addition of further functions, containing optimizations that are, for example, aimed at stability and a positive user experience.

Indispensable, of course, is also the aspect of IT security. Each software release must be subjected to appropriate hardening tests, so that test management and IT security merge seamlessly.

2.3.7   Software Architecture and Knowledge Management

Software describes both static and dynamic aspects, thus providing a blueprint and process plan for software. The following aspects are particularly relevant for software architecture:

Software Architecture Definition
Software architecture ...

- ...**shapes** structures at different levels (software layers),
- ...**enables functioning** solutions for software-based use cases,
- ... **defines** design decisions,
- ...**forms the transition** from analysis to implementation,
- ...**consists of** various views,
- ...**leads to** easier comprehensibility,

- …**is the** framework for flexible **and** agile systems,
- …**is** abstraction,
- …**creates** quality.

Thus, software architecture encompasses significant decisions about:

- the organization of a software system: structuring a system, decomposition into parts, responsibilities and interaction of these parts, as well as interfaces between the parts;
- the selection of structural elements and their interfaces, through which the overall system is composed, along with the behavior defined with respect to the interaction of the aforementioned elements;
- the composition of these elements into increasingly larger subsystems;
- the architectural style with regard to these elements and interfaces to ensure optimal interaction of individual components and optimal performance of the overall system.

Because many aspects are difficult or costly to change later, decisions on software architecture and their justifications must be recorded by the stakeholders involved at the time of the decision!

This leads to the fact that software architecture always requires a close connection to knowledge management. How modern knowledge management can be effectively designed with modern collaboration tools is discussed in the second part of this book. Collaboration tools are software-based tools that have a positive impact on agile collaboration across team and organizational boundaries.

2.3.8   Requirement Management/Prioritization

A functioning software architecture is based on coordinated requirements and constraints among all stakeholders. Both the decision-making process with the clarification of requirements and their prioritization, as well as the activity of analyzing and evaluating requirements in relation to each other, must be continuously documented.

Large Agile Frameworks also provide the appropriate methodology for managing requirements and their prioritization during implementation, which can be effectively implemented in practice using collaboration tools.

The distribution of requirements to actors from different teams, including the communication that takes place, is preferably supported by software-based tools in agile teams. Atlassian, with its software solutions Confluence and Jira, currently dominates the market, but alternatives do exist. For example, GitHub now offers a repository-based approach as a serious alternative, which—when consistently applied—brings about a significant and revolutionary change: not only the source code, but the entire requirement management is made public through a repository. At the same time, it becomes possible

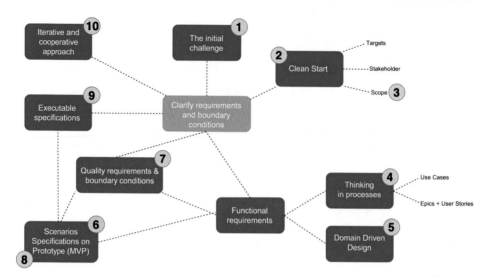

Fig. 2.5 Arc42-Workflow based on Hruschka/Starke

to design the prioritization process as an active participation process with the software community—the actual users of software solutions.

Direct Relation to Software Architecture

Requirements and constraints are directly related to the tasks of software architects. The Fig. 2.5 "Arc42-Workflow based on Hruschka/Starke" shows the central activity of IT and software architects, namely clarifying requirements and constraints in relation to the connected activities. Starting with—iteratively—specifying an initial challenge and documenting it in writing in the software architecture documentation, solid starting conditions are created, whereby the focus is defined by delimiting In-Scope and Out-Of-Scope. Agile mindset also means thinking in processes that are specified as Epics, User Stories, and Use Cases.

With the understanding of a Domain-Driven Design, IT and software architects shape the active participation of all relevant stakeholders and actors, so that they regularly rely on the expertise of domain experts in the role of other software developers and subject matter experts. Based on the prototypes created through User Stories and Use Cases, determined quality requirements, and defined constraints, the work becomes more precise in the form of usable software artifacts and digital services.

Prototyping is an iterative quality process with continuous optimization, which—due to constantly changing conditions—is carried out continuously. This becomes particularly clear when you think about how quickly browser versions, new smartphone models, and many other factors continuously affect software development. With each realization and optimization of runnable prototypes, these executable specifications are immediately

usable. At the latest when applying this prototypical approach, interactive and cooperative behavior and true agility, beyond individual teams, is realized!

2.3.9   DevOps and DevOps Model

Consequently, an exact definition for DevOps is particularly difficult because the
DevOps concept is aligned with the **DevOps cycle** and at the same time includes several
relevant parts and aspects. In addition, DevOps is a highly topical subject area, so there
is no standardized definition yet.

The main attributes and thus leading characteristics of the DevOps method include:

1. **Resources and capabilities**
2. **DevOps culture**
3. **DevOps technologies**

DevOps Definition
Jabbari, Nauman bin Ali, and Petersen have characterized DevOps in their scientific
study and identified central DevOps components of DevOps definitions [30]:

> "DevOps is a development methodology that aims to bridge the gap between development
> (Dev) and operations, with a focus on communication and collaboration, continuous integra-
> tion, quality assurance, and deployment with automated deployment using a set of develop-
> ment practices."

DevOps Model
The "DevOps Model" shown in Fig. 2.6 becomes easy to understand with a look at the
DevOps lifecycle. Instead of a classic division into separate business areas Development
and Operations, the model realizes an agile corporate culture and agile software development.

In terms of creating and managing software, the DevOps model introduces a range of
new methodologies to significantly improve collaboration between different stakeholders
and to get software up and running faster.

Especially with regard to the current cloud trend and containerization, the DevOps
model has already proven itself in practice. Effective DevOps strategies also aim to
achieve platform independence, i.e., keeping software operational in fast release cycles
regardless of a specific operating environment. This platform independence and fast
release cycles are indispensable in the migration of software towards the cloud, reinforced by IT security requirements.

By using a set of development practices, specialized DevOps tools, and best practices, communication and collaboration between the traditionally separated organizational units Development and Operations are promoted. In addition, DevOps drives the

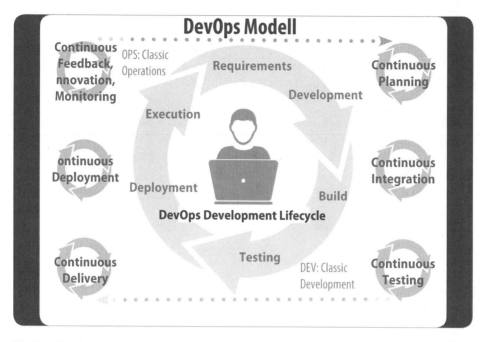

Fig. 2.6 DevOps Model. (Source: Sascha Block)

continuous integration of ongoing software solutions and positively influences their quality assurance. With the provision of automated **deployment mechanisms**, the commit-to-live time can be significantly reduced.

In agile software development, DevOps now plays an essential role and is taken into account in every agile framework accordingly.

2.3.10 Agility and Agile Project Model

Conboy has formulated a very tangible definition of agility in relation to software development; he describes agility as a continuous readiness to create changes quickly or inherently, to proactively or reactively embrace them, and to learn from them, thus contributing to perceived customer value (economy, quality, and simplicity) through collective components and relationships to its environment [31].

The failure of many IT projects fuels the need for agile project models that are capable of responding appropriately and flexibly in any situation to successfully manage projects. Agility is therefore an important topic for project management because software projects are highly complex and agile approaches seem better suited to effectively control decisions based on the right priorities within complex system environments.

Agile approaches help manage complex systems and organizational structures

Agile approaches are largely based on the system-theoretical principles for controlling complex systems [32, page 9 f.]: Complex systems behave unpredictably in many aspects, but are based on causal chains and are therefore not chaotic. Due to extremely complex causal chains, cause and effect are difficult to predict; moreover, each cause is simultaneously an effect and each effect is in turn a cause. Gains in knowledge can predominantly be obtained retrospectively. The behavior of complex systems is extremely difficult to predict—runtime behavior is a suitable example for this.

Agility and the central importance of iterative feedback

If the behavior of complex systems is so difficult to predict, traditional concepts based predominantly on anticipatory planning are hardly suitable. Instead, retrospective analyses at short intervals and on different levels are needed for control and prioritization. A distinction must be made between direct feedback, such as that provided by unit tests in test-driven development, and longer-running, calibrating feedback loops, such as those provided by result reviews or retrospectives at the end of each iteration. Both forms of agile feedback complement each other and are indispensable for managing complex projects. Agile action only becomes possible and can actively shape optimization-oriented changes through agile feedback loops and the inclusion of feedback for correction [also 1, page 3]. Heikkilä et al. confirm the positive effect of iterative and incremental releases, which enable frequent feedback from users and customers and thus improved prioritization of requirements as their evaluations change over time [33, page 138].

Agility in terms of innovations, strategy, and conflicting interests

Software manufacturers act as innovation drivers and are even more challenged in this agile role than other companies; they must demonstrate leadership in digital solutions both internally and towards their customers. Startups are under at least as much innovation pressure; however, it is short-sighted to assume that other companies can rest on their past successes or approach software projects with reduced interest in innovation. Certainly, traditional companies are never required to always rely on the latest technologies. While the use of new technologies is indeed associated with increased risk, as has been extensively demonstrated elsewhere, every company is continuously challenged to critically examine existing processes and optimize them accordingly. Often, the optimization or even expansion of digital service scenarios—and this is by no means limited to a web, app, or cloud strategy—is only possible in most cases through new software technologies.

To what extent does agile project management differ and provide reliable solutions for cross-functional prioritization within a company? In the sense of a competitive (product) vision, software manufacturers must be highly strategic and, at the same time, agile—i.e., flexible—even with regard to contradictory interests. This requires a new leadership style that can no longer be managed with purely classically organized processes.

Agile strategic corporate management means that companies can react more quickly to new developments and changing framework conditions, and in this way, strategic goals can be continuously adapted. This significantly shortens the cycles in which new control impulses become necessary. Implementation phases of several years are a thing of the past in agile software development [34, page 14].

Self-organization of agile teams
The self-organization of agile teams is an essential characteristic of agile approaches and helps in an appropriate way to better cope with complexity. The focus is on self-organized teams that independently organize their internal processes—i.e., those that take place within their team—and continuously develop further based on knowledge. The importance of this horizontal organizational form is not entirely new but was already described in 1967 by Thomson with regard to the special advantages of mutual ad-hoc adjustments, by solving problems as soon as they arise [35, pages 40/41].

Because insights cause changes, all structures often have only a temporary character. To a certain extent—for example, limited by regulatory requirements for legally compliant software—self-organization is a property of every group.

Agility includes accompanying analysis and the ability to react quickly
Continuous observation and evaluation of the relevant environment are typical for agile strategic management. Agile processes are intended to enable companies to react quickly and flexibly to changing requirements [36, page 11]. Agile approaches aim to support companies in the best possible way even in turbulent times and volatile markets by aligning processes across departments flexibly and competitively [37, page 120]. In particular, in software development, it is important to recognize early on newly prioritized goals and changes with analytically oriented processes in order to be able to react correctly and quickly through an adapted strategy.

Focusing on the customer leads to increased competitiveness
With agile processes, the customer and their needs are the focus. Agility is dynamic and thus an ongoing process within the company without a predetermined end [38, page 27]. Agile approaches, therefore, require permanent attention to involve employees organizationally and in favor of optimal performance readiness concerning their individual abilities. Likewise, the focus of agile approaches is particularly on the constantly changing requirements of markets and customers, which requires ongoing optimization of products and services of companies to align them precisely with the currently relevant customer needs.

Accompanying controlling and regular feedback processes improve software
For this purpose, agile models use accompanying controlling, regular feedback processes, and evaluation to improve the strategy and software products. Agility also

requires fast capabilities for implementation and deployment of software. A well-organized and smoothly functioning software architecture and DevOps skills within the company are important characteristics to assess the digital maturity [39, page 126].

In the current IT landscape, a bimodal mode prevails: Some organizations still have a large proportion of technically outdated legacy systems in use in certain areas—under the premise of stability and reliability—(Mode 1). In contrast, other parts of organizations are urgently required to place innovations agilely, reactively, and quickly due to competitive pressure and market expectations, thus having an urgent need for rapidly adaptable frontends. Increasingly, organizations—driven by disruptive factors of change pressure as primary drivers—are forced to switch from Mode 1 to Mode 2. In this process, Mode 1 ultimately does not become irrelevant but must adapt its processes to this changeability. DevOps practices effectively support this change. For this purpose, DevOps requires fundamentally different tools and an architecture with adapted processes and smaller teams. More frequent changes in software lead to rapid development of small features, and the goal is to deliver small-scale software releases to customers according to a Minimum Viable Product (MVP) approach. It is important to note that the IT operations departments (Ops)—due to capacity constraints—are the bottleneck of flexibility in an agile software environment. In such a DevOps environment, a close connection between the different teams such as development, testing, quality assurance, operations, and the production environment is required.

Cooperations to Increase Competitiveness
Friedli points out the great potential of cooperations between companies in a dynamic environment—characterized by shortening product life cycles and volatile market needs—to secure competitiveness [40, pages 381/382]. For example, cooperations with licensees can also be designed in such a way that the time required for commissioning supplied software components is significantly reduced. The DevOps approach with shortened release cycles and accelerated commissioning is thus transferred from the software manufacturer to its customers.

A current example of such a cooperation, which can become a serious threat in the banking environment, is the agreement between PayPal and Google with the integration of the digital payment function Google Pay into Android smartphones. With this, around 20 million PayPal customers can now make mobile payments at German store checkouts [41]. The increasing competitive pressure on the solutions of the Sparkassen and Volksbanken is also intensifying since the market launch of Apple Pay [42]. The importance of contactless payment became clear at the latest with the Corona crisis. The newcomer N26 is already present in every banking market—even before the traditional banks themselves—and is completely digitally positioned in all customer-centered services.

Agile Corporate Culture, Values, and Philosophy

With the transition to agile processes, there is also a change in direction of the existing corporate culture. With agile principles, the people who shape and live a process come to the forefront of events. As a result, employees are also involved in the further development of processes to optimize work effectiveness and thus have a significant impact on the success of projects. Resources available in projects are always limited. The realization that people should be treated differently from the resources used is the first step towards successful projects [43, page 15]. Chin and Benne—as representatives of classical motivation theory in the sense of an empirical-rational strategy—fundamentally see employees as rational and acting in favor of their personal advantage, and only open to their own corporate goals and intrinsic needs [44, pages 24 ff.]. In contrast, an agile company requires a changed, modern value model. In the study "Value Worlds Working 4.0", 1200 people (1000 working people, two control groups of 100 people each) were surveyed based on the microcensus about their ideas on the topic of "work in Germany". According to this empirical investigation by the Federal Ministry of Labor and Social Affairs, seven different value models compete equally alongside one another and thus represent completely different, individual needs of employees [45, pages 14/15]. A rational change strategy in a company is therefore based on showing employees how they can achieve their personal goals by aligning them with given framework conditions and corporate goals. Financial security, positive career development, social recognition, and self-realization have generally been considered primary factors of intrinsic employee motivation. With the development of increasingly complex products and services, motivational factors and requirements on the corporate side also change. Specifically, due to digital transformation, organizational structures and processes in companies across industries are undergoing a special change. Digital transformation is often associated with a strategic realignment; at least always with an agile alignment of corporate processes in an increasingly digitally oriented corporate field [1, pages 1 ff.]. In particular, the Agile Manifesto has shaped clear basic ideas in this context, which are crucial for the successful transition to agile methodology:

Basic Values of Agile Processes: The Agile Manifesto

The Agile Manifesto was created out of the desire for lightweight and iterative methods for software development. The compact result of the Manifesto for Agile Software Development is reflected in the basic values and the twelve principles.

With the goal of developing better software, the values of the Agile Manifesto have emerged as an integral part and guiding principles of action.

These values of agile processes are shown in Fig. 2.7. According to the philosophy *"We discover better ways of developing software by doing it and helping others do it."* A prioritization of regularly recurring processes in software development has emerged [46].

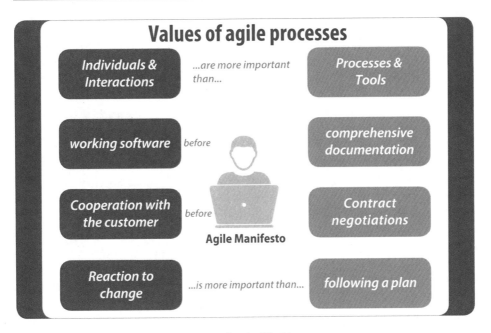

Fig. 2.7   Values of agile processes. (Source: Sascha Block)

In practice, the following core values should prove themselves:

- Individuals and interactions are valued over processes and tools.
- Working software is valued over comprehensive documentation.
- Collaboration with customers is valued over contractual agreements.
- Responding to change is more effective than following a strict plan.

That means, even though the values on the right side are meaningful and important, the value of the core values on the left side outweighs them. While the core values of the Agile Manifesto represent guidelines that quickly clarify the basic attitude of agile practice, the 12 principles of the Agile Manifesto concretize these basic ideas into specific action recommendations [46]: The Agile Manifesto thus aims to ensure that all employees in the company follow a common value system and internalize the agile philosophy from within. Consequently, a higher-level control system must also correspond to this ideal value system and the claim of short iteration and release cycles—in combination with an open feedback culture.

2.3.11 Scaled Agile/Large-Scale Agile Development

The term Scaled Agile or synonymously Large-Scale Agile Development is used when it comes to extending agile approaches to the structures of larger organizations in order to cover projects with large teams and a multitude of different projects, and thus to extend the principles of agile development—beyond the boundaries of agile teams—to the entire organization. In a large agile development environment, where more than two teams are working towards a common goal, coordination between the teams becomes particularly relevant [47].

Dingsøyr and Moe have compiled definitions that characterize such a Large-Scale Agile Development environment [48, page 3]:

- More than 50 developers OR ½ million lines of code OR more than three time zones.
- Over 50 people OR more than 5 teams develop the same product together using agile methods.
- Agile principles are applied to more than one team, one project/product.
- Agility is applied at the organizational level.
- The Agile methodology includes a context that affects more teams than a single person can organize.
- When the coordination of teams is only possible through new agile project forms— such as through a "Scrum-of-Scrums forum".
- Several venues (arenas) are needed for coordination—such as a multitude of "Scrum of Scrums".
- Large teams require a solution to integrate each individual into the agile framework.
- Large projects in which many stakeholders are decision-relevant.
- Customer-centered orientation/Flexible changes.
- As soon as it is no longer possible to know every individual who is working on the same project/on the same product.
- Agile organizations are characterized by rapid learning ability and effective value creation.
- Many teams work together to deliver software artifacts.
- Driven by a multitude of different requirements and challenges.
- Emergent, complex, and adaptable approach that is culture-based and requires a new way of thinking.

Large-Scale Agile Development is aimed at covering software architecture, inter-team coordination, portfolio management, and scaling in terms of software solutions and organizational structure.

A *Scaled Agile Framework* is designed to provide an effective agile organizational model for a complex environment. In particular, it avoids focusing the responsibilities of coordination and information exchange on a single role, but instead promotes exchange between as many team members as possible [47].

Analogous to Gustavsson, existing Scaled Agile Frameworks should not be considered as strictly binding prescriptions from a practical perspective, but rather serve as inspiration or as a toolbox for one's own model [47]. In this context, it makes sense that neither Scrum, SAFe, nor Large-Scale Scrum (LeSS) require the role of a project manager, but this role should be largely avoided; nevertheless, many agile organizations still consider such a role to be relevant [47, page 3].

References

1. Kreutzer, R. T., Neugebauer, T., & Pattloch, A. (2017). *Digital Business Leadership – Digitale Transformation – Geschäftsmodell-Innovation – agile Organisation – Change-Management* (1st ed.). Springer/Gabler.
2. Wiederhold, L., Zeitner, R., & Peyinghaus, M. (2016). *Warum IT-Projekte scheitern.* In: Immobilienzeitung, p. 24. ISSN 1433-7878. http://www.htw-berlin.de/forschung/online-forschungskatalog/publikationen/publikation/?eid=9014. Accessed 31 Mar 2020.
3. Kollmann, T., & Schmidt, H. (2016). *Deutschland 4.0 – Wie die Digitale Transformation gelingt* (1st ed.). Springer/Gabler.
4. Christensen, C. M., & Matzler, K. (2013. Korrigierter Nachdruck in deutscher Übersetzung des amerikanischen Orginalwerks). *The innovator's dilemma: Warum etablierte Unternehmen den Wettbewerb um bahnbrechende Innovationen verlieren* (1st ed.). Vahlen.
5. Schumpeter, J. A. (1947). *Capitalism, socialism and democracy* (2nd ed.). Allen & Unwin.
6. Heinemann, G., Gehrckens, M. H., & Wolters, U. J. (2016). *Digitale Transformation oder digitale Disruption im Handel – Vom Point-of-Sale zum Point-of-Decision im Digital Commerce* (1st ed.). Springer/Gabler.
7. Bousonville, T. (2017). *Logistik 4.0 – Die digitale Transformation der Wertschöpfungskette* (1st ed.). Springer/Gabler.
8. Berberich, O. (2016). *Trusted Web 4.0 – Konzepte einer digitalen Gesellschaft. Konzepte der Dezentralisierung und Anonymisierung* (1st ed.). Springer/Vieweg.
9. Weinreich, U. (2016). *Lean Digitization – Digitale Transformation durch agiles Management* (1st ed.). Springer/Gabler.
10. Breyer-Mayländer, T. (2016). *Management 4.0-Den digitalen Wandel erfolgreich meistern: Das Kursbuch für Führungskräfte.* Carl Hanser Verlag GmbH Co KG.
11. Carr, N. G. (2003). *IT doesn't matter.* Harvard Business School Publishing Corporation. *Educause Review, 38,* 24–38.
12. Smith, H., & Fingar, P. (2003). *IT doesn't matter – Business processes do: A critical analysis of Nicholas Carr's IT article in the Harvard business review.* Meghan-Kiffer Press.
13. Ebert, C., & Paasivaara, M. (2017). Scaling agile. *IEEE Software, 34*(6), 98–103.
14. Sein, M. K., et al. (2011). Action design research. *MIS Quarterly,* 40.
15. Uludağ, Ö., et al. (2017). Investigating the role of architects in scaling agile frameworks. In *Enterprise distributed object computing conference (EDOC), 2017 IEEE 21st international.* IEEE.
16. Serrador, P., & Pinto, J. K. (2015). Does Agile work? – A quantitative analysis of agile project success. *International Journal of Project Management, 33*(5), 1040–1051.
17. Dybå, T., & Dingsøyr, T. (2008). Empirical studies of agile software development: A systematic review. *Information and Software Technology, 50*(9–10), 833–859.
18. Lehto, I., & Rautiainen, K. (2009). Software development governance challenges of a middle-sized company in agile transition. In *Software development governance, 2009. SDG'09. ICSE workshop on* (pp. 36–39). IEEE.
19. Wnuk, K., et al. (2016). Supporting scope tracking and visualization for very large-scale requirements engineering-utilizing FSC+, decision patterns, and atomic decision visualizations. *IEEE Transactions on Software Engineering, 42*(1), 47–74.

20. Dikert, K., Paasivaara, M., & Lassenius, C. (2016). Challenges and success factors for large-scale agile transformations: A systematic literature review. *Journal of Systems and Software, 119*, 87–108.

21. Steinle, C., Eßeling, V., & Eichenberg, T. (Eds.). (2010). *Handbuch Multiprojektmanagement und -controlling: Projekte erfolgreich strukturieren und steuern* (2nd ed.). Erich Schmidt Verlag GmbH & Co KG.

22. Rohner, P. (9 November 2015). *Warum scheitern große Projekte?* AWF IWI-HSG.

23. Lang, M., Kammerer, S., & Amberg, M. (2012). *Projektportfoliomanagement in der IT – Priorisierung, Investition, Steuerung* (1st ed.). Symposion.

24. Kittlaus, H.-B., & Clough, P. N. (2008). *Software product management and pricing: Key success factors for software organizations.* Springer Science & Business Media.

25. Böhmann, T. (2017). Vorlesungsunterlagen/Foliensätze. *Modul Service Lifecycle Management.* Stand 09/2017, Universität Hamburg.

26. Clements, P., & Northrop, L. (2012). *Software product lines: practices and patterns* (8th ed.). Addison-Wesley.

27. Metzger, A., & Pohl, K. (2014). Software product line engineering and variability management: Achievements and challenges. In *Proceedings of the on future of software engineering* (pp. 70–84). ACM.

28. Dehmouch, I. (2014). Towards an agile feature composition for a large scale software product lines. In *Research Challenges in Information Science (RCIS), 2014 IEEE eighth international conference on* (pp. 1–6). IEEE.

29. Baum, H.-G., et al. (2013). *Strategisches Controlling* (5th ed.). Schäffer-Poeschel.

30. Jabbari, R., et al. (2016). What is DevOps? A systematic mapping study on definitions and practices. In *Proceedings of the scientific workshop proceedings of XP2016* (pp. 1–11).

31. Conboy, K. (2009). Agility from first principles: Reconstructing the concept of agility. *Information Systems Research, 20*(3), 329–354.

32. Vigenschow, U. (2015). *APM-Agiles Projektmanagement – Anspruchsvolle Softwareprojekte erfolgreich steuern* (1st ed.). Dpunkt.

33. Heikkilä, V. T., et al. (2015). Operational release planning in large-scale Scrum with multiple stakeholders-A longitudinal case study at F-Secure Corporation. *Information and Software Technology, 57*, 116–140.

34. Thiel, G., & Meinke, I. (2018). Agile Statistikbehörde – eine Herausforderung für den strategischen Verbund. In *WISTA – Wirtschaft und Statistik.* Herausgeber Statistisches Bundesamt, Ausgabe 3.

35. Thompson, J. D. (1967). *Organizations in action: Social science bases of administrative theory.* McGraw-Hill.

36. Eckstein, J. (2012). *Agile Softwareentwicklung in großen Projekten – Teams, Prozesse und Technologien für den Wandel im Unternehmen* (2. Aufl.). dpunkt.

37. Overby, E., Bharadwaj, A., & Sambamurthy, V. (2006). Enterprise agility and the enabling role of information technology. *European Journal of Information Systems, 15*(2), 120–131.

38. Gunasekaran, A. (2001). *Agile manufacturing: The 21st century competitive strategy* (1st ed.). Elsevier.

39. Uludağ, Ö., et al. (2017). Investigating the role of architects in scaling agile frameworks. In *Enterprise distributed object computing conference (EDOC), 2017 IEEE 21st international* (pp. 125 ff.). IEEE.

40. Friedli, T. (2006). *Technologiemanagement: Modelle zur Sicherung der Wettbewerbsfähigkeit* (1st ed.). Springer.

41. *Paypal schließt einen Pakt mit Google.* (10. Oktober 2018). *Süddeutsche Zeitung.* https://www. sueddeutsche.de/wirtschaft/mobiles-bezahlen-paypalschliesst-einen-pakt-mit-google-1.4164040. Accessed 10 Oct 2021.

42. *Apple Pay: Teilnehmende Banken in Europa und dem Nahen Osten.* https://support.apple.com/ de-de/HT206637. Accessed 10 Oct 2021.

43. Prescher, H. (2015). *Projektmanagement, aber richtig – Der Weg aus der Kapazitätsfalle. Ein Leitfaden für Organisation, Kommunikation und Führung in Projekten* (1st ed.). tredition.

44. Chin, R., & Benne, K. D. (1969). *General strategies for effecting changes in human systems.* Human Relations Center, Boston University.

45. *Wie wir arbeiten (wollen).* (2016). Werkheft 02 in der Reihe Arbeit weiter denken, Initiative Arbeiten 4.0, Herausgeber: Bundesministerium für Arbeit und Soziales, Stand August 2016. https://www.arbeitenviernull.de/fileadmin/Downloads/BMAS_Werkheft-2.pdf. Accessed 15 Oct 2021.

46. *Manifesto for Agile Software Development.* http://agilemanifesto.org/. Accessed 7 Aug 2021.

47. Gustavsson, T. (2017). Assigned roles for Inter-team coordination in Large-Scale Agile Development: A literature review. In *Proceedings of the XP2017 scientific workshops* (p. 15). ACM.

48. Dingsøyr, T., & Moe, N. B. (2014). Towards principles of large-scale agile development (May 2014). In: *Agile methods: Large-scale development, refactoring, testing, and estimation,* XP 2014 international workshops, revised selected papers, Rome.

Large-Scale Agile Frameworks

3

If the criteria summarized in the Scaled Agile/Large-Scale Agile Development section apply to your organization, a Large-Scale Agile Framework offers you effective methods for competitive software development. Regardless of the size of an organization, agile frameworks provide effective strategies for implementing digital transformation and suitable methodology for working collaboratively agile across countless teams and individuals.

Large-Scale Agile Frameworks provide usable best practices for collaboration in agile teams
Each Large Agile Framework provides an adequate solution for modern software development and for taking into account constantly changing, diverse requirements of various stakeholders and often divergent tasks. The goal is always to solve software-based problems effectively and economically within complex IT projects using agile methodology and the available resources.

The approach varies from model to model in how the different agile teams organize themselves. Each of the Large Agile Frameworks is based on close collaboration between the different agile teams and their goals.

3.1   Evaluation criteria for Large-Scale Agile Frameworks

The requirements for a Large-Scale Agile Framework typically differ according to the size and type of an organization as well as the defined corporate goals. However, less measurable factors such as the mindset of an organization also influence the suitability of a specific Large-Scale Agile Framework.

© The Author(s), under exclusive license to Springer-Verlag GmbH, DE, part of Springer Nature 2023
S. Block, *Large-Scale Agile Frameworks*, https://doi.org/10.1007/978-3-662-67782-7_3

Agile maturity and adaptability of a Large-Scale Agile Framework
Rather bureaucratic organizational forms, such as public authorities or administrative and research institutions, have a very different level of maturity with regard to agile methodology. Agile methodology is relatively new, and new ways of working may seem unfamiliar and perhaps too changeable or unproven to some.

It is important to effectively counter such reservations, especially when processes have been handled strictly formally and strictly separated by responsibilities and departments for decades. For these and other good reasons, it is not only important that we understand new agile methods precisely, but also that a Large-Scale Agile Framework is adaptable and changeable for our organization and its needs.

Design Thinking for your optimal organizational form
Principles and phases of Design Thinking can also be incorporated into the introduction phase of a Large-Scale Agile Framework, as it has become indispensable to place a special focus on the needs of your employees and the users of (software) solutions themselves. Only in this way can a valuable prototype and finally a real application be created for the user—usually the paying customers of a company or your employees who use the software for your corporate goals. Ultimately, research-backed findings should always be incorporated into software development.

Design Thinking takes time, but rewards you richly with added value
Since Design Thinking already requires an intensive observation phase and a longer project duration overall, you should be aware at the beginning of the project that it is advisable to carry out a comprehensive process analysis with regard to all areas of the target group. Only in this way can the advantages of the creative elements from Design Thinking be brought to bear as much as possible.

Relevance of prototyping and IT security
Overall, the different selected elements and methods of the approach in IT projects are oriented towards various requirements on the part of stakeholders and the task at hand, which require an iterative approach, an opportunity for evaluation of results and user requirements, as well as the use of prototypes.

IT security plays a central key role for both software and hardware-based IoT solutions (Internet of Things) that your organization uses. The responsibility for IT security grows with the role and importance of your organization for third parties. This includes taking into account legal framework requirements and the resulting data protection. If your organization acts in the role of a software manufacturer, the responsibility attributed to you increases immensely. The rule here is: As soon as you and your organization use digital services and offer these digital services to third parties—such as your customers—you are already acting very quickly in the role of a software manufacturer.

The responsibility for this has already been clarified with the legal validity of the GDPR in relation to the website services used by your organization.

With an app or any other software-based service, the role of a software manufacturer applicable to your organization comes more into focus.

However, even if you do not clearly identify your organization in the role of a software manufacturer, prototyping and IT security should undoubtedly play a central role in an organizational model.

Therefore, these and other requirements for your organization should play a decisive role both in assessing the suitability of a particular large-scale agile framework and in introducing the large-scale agile model you prefer.

For this reason, a proven model is required that brings easily implementable and practical approaches and methods into play in order to adapt and introduce a large-scale agile framework for your organization.

The direct inclusion of agile methodology, such as orientation towards design thinking and prototyping, and alignment with a predominantly incremental-iterative process are the primary benchmarks. The inclusion of further aspects such as IT security and data quality are additional dimensions that such a model should take into account for your organization and make easily implementable.

3.2   Selected Scaled Agile Frameworks

Horlach et al. have examined existing scaled agile frameworks and classified them into three different categories and evaluated them based on IT governance criteria [1].

In this context, each framework assigns a different importance to the decision domains, so that these decisions are either predominantly prioritized as top-down or bottom-up, or as a compromise, both approaches are combined accordingly.

Out of scope in the considered context are scaled agile frameworks that primarily focus on agile transformation within the company. In contrast, according to Horlach et al., organization-oriented frameworks are considered, which focus on agility with regard to the emergence of products in companies, as well as the blueprint of an agile organization. Here, Horlach et al. differentiate two subcategories—namely frameworks that—like *SAFe*—focus on the company or—like the *Spotify Engineering Model*—are based on the basic idea of close cooperation between teams. In order to decide which approach is better suited in the examined context, a representative of both categories is examined in more detail. According to the evaluation by Horlach et al., SAFe offers the broadest coverage in terms of the dimensions of IT principles, IT architecture, IT infrastructure, strategies, and requirements for business applications. In addition, SAFe generally receives widespread attention in professional circles—as well as in [2]—and is reflected in scientific literature.

The Spotify Engineering Model was rated as interesting and considered because of its particularly consistent inter-team focus and numerous adaptations by other companies.

3.3   Domain-Oriented Model/Domain-Driven Design

[History and Background]

The *Domain-Oriented Model* is also an agile approach to software development. The fundamental conceptual ideas of this methodology come from Eric Evans, who first published a book in the form of a reference guide in 2003 and coined the term *Domain-Driven Design* (DDD) [3]. Evans initially defined the following terms, which are relevant for understanding the model [3, page VI]: A *domain* is a sphere of knowledge, influence, or activity. The subject area to which a user applies a program is the domain of the software. A *model* is an abstraction system that describes selected aspects of a domain and can be used to solve problems related to that domain. The *ubiquitous language* is a language structured around the domain model and used by all team members within a limited context to connect all team activities with the software. The *context* in turn denotes the environment in which a word or statement occurs, determining its meaning. Statements about a model can only be understood within this context. *Bounded context* defines and describes the boundaries—typically for a subsystem or the work of a specific team—within which a particular model is applicable. According to Evans, Domain-Driven Design is an approach to developing complex software that focuses [3, page 1]: 1) on the core of a domain; 2) enables the discovery of models in creative collaboration between domain and software users; and 3) uses the ubiquitous language within an explicitly defined *bounded context*.

[Prioritization Model, Core Values, Philosophy, and Principles]

Consequently, DDD is based on the realization that the modeling process of software is primarily influenced by the domain-specific functionality to be implemented, as dictated by the application domains. As a framework, DDD does not define any technical-specific rules but provides purely methodological recommendations for the processes of software development. DDD assumes agile approaches in the form of iterative software development and close collaboration between software developers and domain experts—the so-called *domain experts*.

Regarding the modeling of different architectural layers, Evans recommends a clear isolation of business logic in the design of software applications to separate any dependencies related to infrastructure, user interface, or application logic that do not correspond to the business logic. To achieve this, complex programs should be organized in layers, with explicit attention to ensuring that individual layers are cohesive—closely connected—to each other and that dependencies of a layer exist only in the direction of the underlying layer [3, page 10].

Analogous to architectural patterns that follow the same strategy, DDD recommends establishing only a loose coupling between an architectural layer and the layers above it.

Thus, the entire code of a domain model is isolated at one level and completely detached from the user interface, the application, and the infrastructure. Such an architectural principle offers, in addition to the maximum possible level of abstraction from the user interface, the following advantages:

It supports specialized division of labor in the creation of software products, the functionality of the layers is clearly specified and prescribes to other layers in a strict manner how they interact with each other. Finally, such a layer structure supports a software system with a high degree of portability; it thus offers maximum agility concerning its fundamental platform architecture, which can be changed at any time on a component-by-component basis.

Thus, DDD is more generally positioned, but closely related to the architectural model of the *Model-View-Controller concept* (MVC). The MVC concept allows for an agile, highly adaptable software architecture model through the strict separation of program logic, data source, and visualization [4, page 847]. Figure 3.1 "Model-View-Controller concept" illustrates this widely used architectural concept, not least due to the influence of modern cloud infrastructures.

Goll's objection that the MVC concept is often associated with a deterioration in performance is relevant [4, page 856].

In his model, Evans describes a large-scale structure for strategic design and limits himself to recommending the creation of a pattern of rules or roles and relationships that cover the entire system and thus enable an overall understanding of the whole system—even without detailed knowledge [3, page 47].

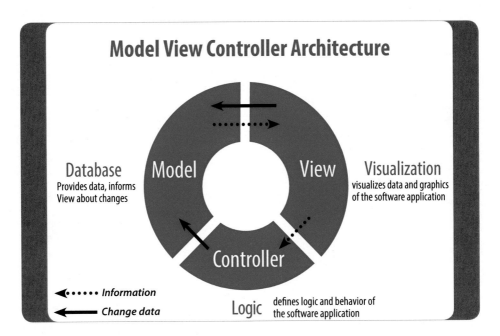

Fig. 3.1   Model-View-Controller concept. (Source: Sascha Block)

To manage complexity in software systems, Evans recommends describing individual objects in terms of their structure and behavior based on the basic model and also making clear restrictions. By dividing such rules into concrete system specifications and general rules and knowledge, a modular system architecture is enabled, allowing a user or super-user to flexibly adapt the system behavior as needed [3, page 51].

3.4   Spotify Engineering Model

History and Background

The streaming service known as Spotify and the platform behind it is the model for the framework of an agile organizational model. Founded in 2006 as a Swedish start-up, Spotify AB is now active in 237 countries and, with a community of 406 million users *(as of February 2022)* and payouts of over 9 billion EUR to rights holders *(as of December 31, 2021)* – according to its own statements—is one of the most significant drivers of revenue in the music business [5].

The *Spotify Engineering Model* combines lean start-up methods into a novel approach for agile scaling, primarily addressing corporate culture while also suggesting adjustments for agile processes and an agile corporate structure.

The representation of the *Spotify Engineering Model* in Fig. 3.2 "Organizational Model Spotify Engineering Model" is based on the conference paper [6] by Agile/Lean

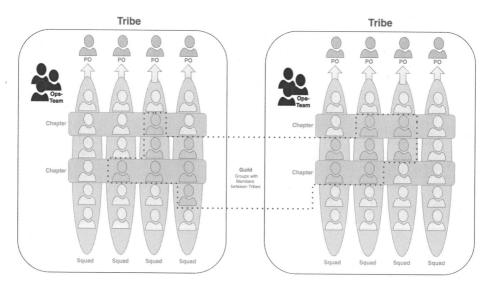

Fig. 3.2 Organizational Model Spotify Engineering Model subject areas. (Source: Sascha Block based on Kniberg/Ivarsson: Scaling Agile @ Spotify with Tribes, Squads, Chapters & Guilds—10/2012.—Source: Sascha Block)

Coach Henrik Kniberg [7] and "organizational Coach" Anders Ivarsson [8] working for Spotify, and presents the organizational model, its agile organizational structures, roles, and framework-specific methods. According to Ivarsson, he deliberately chooses the title of organizational coach because he places particular emphasis on building a strong, effective, and entertaining organization.

Prioritization Model, Core Values, Philosophy, and Principles
Striking is the fundamental philosophy of the autonomy striving communicated in the framework of the agile teams involved in the model.

In doing so, the agile teams pursue both autonomous independent project goals and collaborative goals to achieve overarching company objectives together and efficiently. *Squads* are independent agile teams. A squad is the basic unit for software development at Spotify.

Teams
Squads resemble Scrum teams and are designed to be as flexible as miniature start-ups. Each squad has all the necessary skills and tools to cover design, development, testing, and release to the production level. Squads are independently organized agile teams and autonomously decide on the way and methods they work. Some use Scrum Sprints, others Kanban, or a mix of both approaches. Each squad pursues a long-term mission; for example, developing an Android client, scaling backend systems, or providing payment methods. Squads are specifically encouraged to practice Lean start-up principles—such as creating a Minimum Viable Product or validated learning. Because a squad is entrusted with the same specific tasks and specific components of a product for a long time, experts can develop on specialized topics. In addition, each squad can independently and directly contact its stakeholders. It is essential to continuously ensure that there are no critical dependencies on other agile teams.

A tribe is a group of several squads working in a similar subject area—such as backend, infrastructure, or the music player. Tribes act as incubators for the squad mini-start-ups, providing them with the necessary degrees of freedom. Given that it is hardly possible for individuals to maintain social contact with more than 100 people, a tribe comprises a maximum of 100 members. Moreover, experience shows that the bureaucratic effort and the need for freedom-restricting rules and additional management levels increase disproportionately for larger groups. Tribes regularly hold events where current work results—especially demos of functioning software, new tools and methods, and noteworthy hack day results—are presented and discussed. These events are public and thus accessible to people outside the tribe network.

Every organizational form has at least one disadvantage. The most relevant disadvantage of complete autonomy is the loss of economies of scale. The tester in Squad A could be struggling with a problem that the tester in Squad B has already successfully solved. If all testers could organize themselves across squads and tribes, then these experts could meaningfully share their knowledge and create helpful tools for everyone. The solution to this problem lies in the organizational form of the *Chapter*: A chapter is a small unit of specialized employees who have similar skills and generally work in a related field of competence within the same tribe. Chapters hold regular meetings on their subject areas—for example, on testing procedures, web development, or backend technologies.

In addition, the *Guild* is an organic and broadly based association of interest group members who share an interest in specific topics and want to share their knowledge— such as appropriate tools, code, and best practices. While chapters are always arranged within a tribe, guilds are cross-location associations.

For cross-team DevOps support, there is a separate operations team whose task is to provide support to the squads in publishing their code independently. By providing infrastructure, scripts, and deployment routines, as well as internal knowledge transfer, this team paves the way to production, so to speak.

All squad members can influence their work at any time; they actively participate in planning and help determine which tasks should be worked on.

Regular surveys (e.g., quarterly) can ensure that processes are continuously optimized and that the need for organizational support can be effectively determined.

The representation visualized with Fig. 3.3, "Status Surveys of the Spotify Engineering Model," is intended to identify subject areas with current problems (red). Circles reflect the current status, and arrows indicate the trend for the next phase. A green status signifies a smooth process; a yellow status indicates a need for optimization. Based on Table 3.1 "Aspects of Agility Valid in the Spotify Model," a pattern for difficulties in the release process can be identified through the feedback from three squads (3, 4, 5). This implies an urgent need for action in the uncovered subject area.

Dependencies are hardly avoidable among a large number of squads and do not necessarily have to be negatively connotated. Nevertheless, it is essential to recognize such

Topics	Squad 1	Squad 2	Squad 3	Squad 4	Squad 5
Product Owner	○ ⬈	● ⬊	● ⇨	○ ⇨	○ ⇨
Agile Coach	● ⬈	● ⬈	● ⇨	● ⬈	● ⬊
Service development	○ ⬈	○ ⬈	○ ⇨	● ⬈	●
Easy to release	○ ⬈	● ⬈	● ⬊	● ⇨	○ ⬊
Processes that fit the team	○ ⇨	● ⬈	● ⬈	● ⬈	○
One mission	○ ⬈	● ⬊	○ ⬊	○ ⬊	● ⇨
Support within the organization	● ⇨	●	○	○ ⇨	○

Fig. 3.3 Status surveys of the Spotify Engineering Model for defined topics. (Source: Sascha Block, based on Kniberg/Ivarsson: Scaling Agile @ Spotify with Tribes, Squads, Chapters & Guilds—10/2012)

Table 3.1 Aspects of Agility Valid in the Spotify Model

Agility aspects	Explanation
Easy to release:	Simplicity in terms of release capability. A squad team is always able to deploy to an existing release version without any obstacles.
Process that fits to the team:	The team has sovereignty over their agile process and can continuously optimize it.
Mission:	Every squad member is aware of the mission and contributes to its fulfillment. All stories in the squad backlog effectively contribute to achieving the goal.
Organisational support:	The squad team knows who to turn to for problem-solving when issues arise, both for technical and team-related matters.

[Table footer—please overwrite]

dependencies; each squad will then be outlined in a report, and dependencies to other teams will be determined.

For this purpose, a simple Excel table can be used as a practical tool and overview, listing the squads in the first column, showing an existing dependency to one or more squads in a second column, and classifying the type of dependency and visualizing it with a traffic light status in a third column. A fourth comment column provides space for explanations, and a fifth column adds information about a simple Yes (green)/No (red) indication of whether the listed squad belongs to the same tribe.

Problematic dependencies can usually only be eliminated through reprioritization, reorganization, architectural changes, or with the help of technical solutions.

Roles and Responsibilities
Product Owner (PO) coordinate and manage the backlog, prioritize tasks, and organize coordination between the squads: Each agile squad team has an assigned Product Owner who is responsible for prioritizing work and supporting the team in achieving its goals without being involved in the implementation process. In doing so, Product Owners take into account both the business strategy and relevant KPIs as well as technical aspects. The Product Owners of different squads cooperate to continuously update an overarching roadmap that transparently tracks the direction in which Spotify as a whole is developing. To this end, each Product Owner maintains a product backlog for their squad. The role of the PO is closest to that of an entrepreneur and product champion. An entrepreneur is focused on realizing the best possible product. The *Chapter Lead* is the organizer of a chapter and thus a line manager responsible for all chapter members and has traditional responsibilities such as personnel development. Since the Chapter Lead is a regular member of a squad and involved in its daily work, they are familiar with the real conditions in the teams and thus have a realistic reference (Fig. 3.4).

Fig. 3.4 Organization of
subject areas according to the
Spotify Engineering Model.
(Source: Sascha Block,
based on Kniberg/Ivarsson:
Scaling Agile @ Spotify with
Tribes, Squads, Chapters &
Guilds—10/2012)

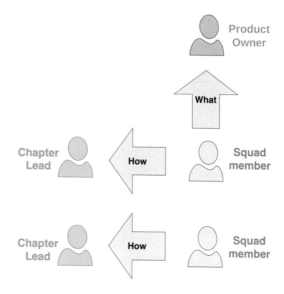

In doing so, the Chapter Lead ensures the most effective methods for knowledge dissemination and the most impactful tool usage for sharing code in the horizontal company dimension.

In matrix terminology, the vertical dimension ensures the "what" through the role of the PO and the horizontal dimension ensures the "how" through the role of the Chapter Lead.

Thus, each squad member receives certainty regarding the questions "What is to be realized in terms of code next?" and "How do we build the code artifact?" The Chapter Lead holds the competence leadership in relation to a specific technical expertise, such as deployment or web technologies.

The *Tribe Lead* is the organizer of a tribe and ensures the appropriate environment for their tribe in their role. Typically, all squads belonging to a tribe are located close to each other in the same building due to their thematic connection. The *Guild Coordinator* organizes the events of a guild association and ensures that everyone interested in a planned guild event can participate. An *Agile Coach* supports the teams in their development by helping to identify and eliminate obstacles. Typically, agile coaches support continuous process improvement through retrospectives, sprint meetings, and individual or group coaching sessions.

The squad teams act as efficient feature teams and, as such, usually need to update multiple systems to make new features production-ready. The challenge of such a liberal architectural model is to keep the overall system lean and performant, as no one focuses on the integrity of the system as a whole. To ensure controlled evolution of the individual components of the overall system, system owners take care of defined subsystems. For system-critical software parts, a DevOps team consisting of a software developer and an operations expert is defined. The *System Owner* (SO) is the central contact person for all technical or architecture-related aspects. They guide the developers within the system they supervise, thus ensuring quality, documentation, stability, scalability, and an unimpaired release process. It is not necessary for the SO to make all decisions independently, code themselves, or be solely responsible for the release process. Rather, the SO is typically a squad member or chapter lead who, in addition to their everyday tasks, takes on the supervision of a system part. To meet this responsibility, the SO—whenever necessary—sets a "System Owner Day" to meet these requirements and to perform "housekeeping" of their system. A *Chief Architect* coordinates the software architecture at the highest level. In doing so, the independent subsystems are architecturally combined into a high-performance overall solution. Their tasks include reviewing new system parts and maintaining and documenting the architectural vision. They always remain at the level of recommendations and technical input; the final design decisions remain with the respective squad teams. To effectively synchronize the agile teams with each other, a *Scrum of Scrum Meeting* regulates existing dependencies between the teams. At Spotify, however, such regular meetings are largely dispensable because the lived agile organizational form with its control mechanisms effectively controls existing dependencies. If project-related collaboration of several squads is required over a longer period, the squads synchronize daily to identify and clarify dependencies. A single board with "sticky notes" used by all squads has proven effective for this purpose.

According to Schettino et al., the prioritization model of the Spotify Engineering Model is geared towards the further development of the Spotify platform, which is considered a complex ecosystem with a wide variety of stakeholders [9] and aims for the shortest possible release cycles of features and changes to the online platform to incorporate feedback into software development as quickly as possible. The framework is specifically designed for the enormous employee growth in the company, which has grown from originally 300 employees to 3,000 employees in six years [10]. With a modern value system, this agile framework also establishes a tolerant error culture: errors are understood as part of the learning process according to the lean start-up approach and are intended to enable genuine innovations. Alqudah and Razali indirectly confirm that the entire organizational model ultimately presupposes the role of a platform operator in order to enable the continuous optimization of a very specific platform economy through consistent DevOps control under permanent user feedback [11, page 831].

3.5 Scaled Agile Framework (SAFe)

History and Background

The Scaled Agile Framework (SAFe) is an agile concept for methodical organization in software development. As a framework, SAFe provides methodical knowledge in the form of a documented procedural model and proven process patterns from practice and was founded in 2011 by book author Dean Leffingwell, who, according to his own statements, is an entrepreneur of various start-ups and a software and system developer [12, page XII] and already recognized the need for documented best practices in 2007 with an initial concept [12, page XIV]. The Scaled Agile Inc. officially provides the knowledge free of charge and generally accessible via the freely accessible online platform www.scaledagileframework.com. In addition, Scaled Agile Inc. offers certifications, training, and courses [13].

Prioritization Model, Core Values, Philosophy, and Principles
In addition to portfolio management, SAFe is particularly specialized in organizing the alignment, collaboration, and delivery process of software across a large number of agile teams in a structured manner. Release Engineering is the process that aims to achieve high software quality for end users through individual changes made by developers [14, page 1]. The Agile Release Train (ART) is a central component in the model and represents a mechanism that is the responsibility of a permanently defined group—consisting of members of agile software development teams—to ensure continuous release delivery [12, page 2, 6, and 12].

The concept of the Agile Release Train becomes understandable through the metaphor of a subway train with a regular schedule. At regular intervals, the Agile Release Train offers the various development teams the opportunity to integrate their current features into the latest release; the programmer calls this deployment.

If the team misses the deadline, it must wait for the next opportunity, in the form of the next release date for deployment (Fig. 3.5).

The ART concept with the Release Train Engineer represents a model specifically designed for DevOps practices and the needs of agile teams to synchronize various development strands—in the form of modular individual components—into a complete release. Such an approach requires jointly defined tools and is only possible in combination with modern development tools, such as GIT-based versioning tools. Organizationally, the ART team uses a series of iterations of fixed length. The time window for the iteration steps is set for defined program increments (PI) within the PI timebox—as a program step width. The Agile Release Train aligns the teams involved in an agile project with a common business strategy and technology mission and takes on the following tasks [12, page 2/3]:

- Aligning management, teams, and stakeholders on a shared mission based on a single, fundamental vision, roadmap, and program backlog.
- Delivering features in the form of ready-to-use user functions.
- Synchronizing the iterations of all involved teams using the same duration for start and end dates.
- In doing so, each ART should deliver valuable and tested system-level increments in a two-week cycle.

Fig. 3.5 Agile Release Train—Photography and Image Editing: Sascha Block

- Program increments (PIs) represent longer-term, fixed-schedule increments for planning, execution, analysis, and adaptation.
- Solutions can be released as needed; during or at the end of a PI, focused exclusively on the needs of the business (customer). Regular or continuous integration of completed features from all teams is the ultimate measure of progress.
- The ART concept is based on face-to-face personal communication to enable smooth collaboration, alignment, and the fastest possible implementation.
- ARTs build and maintain the Continuous Delivery Pipeline, which is required for software development and release of manageable releases and thus for smaller optimizations to the customer's value contribution.
- Provide a shared and consistent approach to improving the user experience through the application of Lean UX principles and practices.
- DevOps—which combines mindset, corporate culture, and a set of technical practices for communication, integration, automation, and close collaboration among all those involved in software development—supports the Agile Release Train in effectively planning, developing, testing, deploying, releasing, and maintaining various solution scenarios.

According to the ART concept, each development team always has two options:

Plan A A desired functionality is integrated at the defined time. In this case, the team deploys its code at the earliest possible date.

Plan B In the event that the functionality is not yet fully completed or sufficiently tested, the agile team must not prevent a timely release date. In this constellation, the software team must still ensure that there are no side effects due to the delay. The team ensures that there are no dependencies on development modules of other agile teams, nor is the infrastructure or software architecture affected. If necessary API changes are implemented to avoid breaking existing functionality.

SAFe is based on nine fundamental Lean and Agile principles, which guide the roles and practices in SAFe and summarize the underlying logic [12, Part 3, page 133 ff.]:

1. Take an economic perspective.
2. Apply systems thinking.
3. Assume variability, preserve options.
4. Build incrementally, with fast integrated learning cycles.
5. Base milestones on objective evaluation of the running system.
6. Visualize and limit work-in-progress, reduce batch sizes, and manage queue lengths.
7. Use rhythm (timing), synchronize with cross-domain planning.
8. Unlock the intrinsic motivation of knowledge workers.
9. Decentralize decision-making.

The portfolio concept of SAFe is largely based on the logic presented in the sections on multi-project management, multi-product development, and portfolio management, using the same terminology, extended by the concept of agility and the influence of iterative feedback [12, Part 8, page 575 ff.]. According to the introduced ART logic, a total of 5–10 SAFe teams form an "Agile Release Train," so that typically 50 to 125 people— including software development teams and other stakeholders—work together on a product program. This ensures the synchronization of iteration dependencies, and every two weeks, the delivered artifacts are integrated into the live environment. SAFe does not address the specifics of software product lines.

A point of criticism is that the authors remain very general in many relevant areas, such as in the "Value Streams" section, and often only superficially address topics: How "Value Streams" [12, page 587 ff.] are concretely defined or what rules "Lean Budgets" [12, page 599 ff.] follow remains unanswered.

3.6   Comparison of the Three Selected Large-Scale Agile Frameworks

The *domain-oriented model* is a collection of generally valid architectural recommendations for designing benefit-oriented and architecturally flexible software. In contrast, Domain-Driven Design (DDD) lacks the portfolio concept needed by software manufacturers. Also completely unreflected is the organization of teams, although the role of the *domain expert* is described, which comes very close to or even completely corresponds to the role of the customer product manager. For the design of software products, DDD thus only provides good starting points.

Ultimately, the Spotify Engineering Model is also a form of a modernized matrix organizational model. However, this organizational model represents an effective counterproposal to counteract the typical silo formation of a classic matrix organization with functionally structured business units. The model primarily uses the same employee profiles and agile roles such as Scrum Master, Product Owner, Agile Coaches, Software Architects, etc., and relies on agile teams with heterogeneous employee profiles that complement each other and take product responsibility for a clearly defined area within the Spotify platform. Thus, comparable skills are not grouped in functional departments; moreover, there are no classic projects that would require reporting to functional project managers. The matrix of the Spotify Engineering Model is solely focused on the delivery of code to improve the platform. This is the reason why employees are arranged in stable, spatially close teams, in which they work together with various skills and self-organized to deliver great products.

The vertical dimension is the primary organizational structure, which, according to the framework's founders, is perceived as pleasant by employees and allows them to engage willingly and enjoyably in their work time in agile teams in a varied way.

The horizontal dimension represents the most effective methodology for sharing knowledge, tools, and code. The special charm of the Spotify Engineering Model lies—besides a lean and easily understandable organizational model—in the manageable number of recommendations and rules. To what extent the company's success is based on the organizational model—or primarily on the business model—remains open. Numerous companies—mainly start-ups—are already organized according to the example of this framework.

In the end, however, the Spotify framework does not offer a suitable solution in the considered context: With regard to portfolio management of software products and the associated prioritization requirements, the model—without significant modifications—does not seem suitable as such. Portfolio management is not described in the Spotify model. The processes and mechanisms by which prioritization is carried out, or the key figures by which such prioritization is controlled, remain open. Also missing in the considered context is the central operator aspect of an online platform. This circumstance is a significant evaluation criterion for the framework and presupposes complete control over the entire DevOps cycle. However, this is not always given. Nevertheless, the ideas of practical inter-team cooperation can be adopted in particular.

The ART concept from SAFe is variable and ideally combined with the decisive portfolio aspect, making it flexibly applicable to any complex dependencies in software releases. The roles defined with SAFe are not fundamentally new, but they are suitable for supporting software manufacturers in aligning a large number of different teams with a shared mission and vision and ensuring the necessary coordination and governance as best as possible. SAFe generally recommends establishing a Product Owner per team, with Gustavson characterizing the role of the Release Train Engineer as "Chief PO" [15, page 2].

Horlach et al. criticize SAFe for only one aspect, namely the lack of reference to recommended implementation practices within IT infrastructure strategies [1]. At least in the case of medium-sized software companies, it can be assumed that they align themselves with only one IT strategy. Furthermore, the criticism is unjustified insofar as an IT strategy can also be synchronized across several portfolios. However, this crucial point remains open within SAFe—namely the implementation of such synchronization. This aspect plays a decisive role in the present context; this also applies to the aspect of alignment with software product lines, which is not dealt with in detail in SAFe. Nevertheless, essential parts of SAFe can be integrated into an ideal model for software manufacturers.

References

1. Horlach, B., Böhmann, T., Schirmer, I., & Drews, P. (2018). IT governance in scaling agile frameworks. In *Multikonferenz Wirtschaftsinformatik.*
2. Paasivaara, M. (2017). Adopting SAFe to scale agile in a globally distributed organization. In *Global Software Engineering (ICGSE), 2017 IEEE 12th international conference on* (pp. 36–40). IEEE.
3. Evans, E. *Domain language: Tackling complexity in the heart of software.* Domain driven design reference. https://domainlanguage.com/ddd/reference/. The DDD Reference contains a brief summary of every definition and pattern in Eric Evans' 2004 book, plus three patterns that didn't make it into the original book, which Eric now thinks of as part of his understanding of DDD. Accessed 27 Nov 2022.
4. Goll, J. (2011). *Methoden und Architekturen der Softwaretechnik* (1st ed.). Vieweg+Teubner.
5. Spotify. *Unternehmensinformationen.* https://newsroom.spotify.com/company-info/. Accessed 14 Apr 2022.
6. Ivarsson, A., & Kniberg, K. (2012). *Scaling agile @ Spotify with tribes, squads, chapters & guilds* (Oktober 2012). Conference paper. https://creativeheldstab.com/wpcontent/uploads/2014/09/scaling-agile-spotify-11.pdf. Accessed 27 Sept 2021.
7. LinkedIn Profil von Henrik Kniberg. https://www.linkedin.com/in/hkniberg/. Accessed 14 Sept 2022.
8. LinkedIn Profil von Anders Ivarsson. https://www.linkedin.com/in/aivarsson/. Accessed 14 Sept 2022.
9. Schettino, V. J., et al. (2017). Spotify characterization as a software ecosystem. In *Proceedings of the 11th Brazilian symposium on software components, architectures, and reuse* (p. 8). ACM.
10. Statista. (o. J.). *Anzahl der Mitarbeiter von Spotify weltweit in den Jahren 2011 bis 2017.* https://de.statista.com/statistik/daten/studie/297149/umfrage/anzahl-dermitarbeiter-von-spotify/. Accessed 9 Dec 2022.
11. Alqudah, M., & Razali, R. (2016). A review of scaling agile methods in large software development. *International Journal on Advanced Science, Engineering and Information Technology, 6*(6), 828–837.

12. Leffingwell, D., Knaster, R., Oren, I., & Jemilo, D. (2018). *SAFe reference guide – Scaled agile framework for lean enterprises* (1st ed.). Version 4.5. Pearson.
13. Scaled Agile Framework. Website der Scaled Agile Inc. https://www.scaledagileframework.com/about/. Accessed 15 Apr 2022.
14. Adams, B., & Mcintosh, S. (2016). Modern release engineering in a nutshell-why researchers should care. In *Software analysis, evolution, and reengineering (SANER), 2016 IEEE 23rd international conference on* (pp. 78–90). IEEE.
15. Gustavsson, T. (2017). Assigned roles for Inter-team coordination in large-scale agile development: A literature review. In *Proceedings of the XP2017 scientific workshops* (p. 15). ACM.

How to Adapt and Implement a Large-Scale Agile Framework in Your Organization

4

You can adapt a Large-Scale Agile Framework suitable for your organization using the presented methodology or develop it from scratch—for example, for a different problem class. We will introduce you to an approach and explain how this can be achieved based on the current state of research.

In this chapter, we will demonstrate how to proceed when adapting a Large-Scale Agile Framework to be perfectly tailored to the problem classes of software manufacturers. Undoubtedly, other industries have different problem classes, but almost all organizations are more or less strongly software-driven or also develop software independently. To help you answer the question to what extent your organization acts in the role of a software manufacturer, a separate section is dedicated to answering this exciting question and shows you exemplary companies whose IT strategy can be largely assessed from the outside.

The most urgent question in most companies is: "How do we switch to an agile mode as quickly as possible in which the most diverse teams within an organization work together efficiently?"

The question "How organizations act perfectly agile" concerns every organization— differences only exist in the maturity level of the respective organization in this regard.

Involve employees and teams and their needs closely
First, the basic prerequisites in the form of agile teams, roles, and processes must be created within the organization. These organizational changes are partly taken into account by the respective Large-Scale Agile Frameworks; however, fundamental organizational measures must also be taken to prepare for such profound organizational changes. This includes infrastructure issues, such as spatial changes resulting from the establishment of new teams or the procurement of agile software tools and their training for your employees.

S. Block, *Large-Scale Agile Frameworks*, https://doi.org/10.1007/978-3-662-67782-7_4

Introduce agile methodology step by step

The introduction of a Large-Scale Agile Framework—no matter which Agile Framework seems most suitable for your organization—is not a process that will take place in an organization from one day to the next, but rather should be a continuous change process. The introduction of a Large-Scale Agile Framework must go hand in hand with successfully involving your employees in this transformation process within your organization in order to integrate and promote them as best as possible according to their individual abilities.

A proven approach to introducing and adapting a Large-Scale Agile Framework in your organization is presented in the next section with Action Design Research.

4.1   Action Design Research

Action Design Research (ADR) is an agile problem-solving process to create practice-oriented solutions for overcoming the barriers between the tension fields of IT, organizational, and professional domains.

In agile software development, these tension fields regularly exist between domains in companies—e.g., in relation to different domain knowledge. It follows that ADR appears to be a particularly suitable approach to problem-solving in the context of the problem of an agile transformation.

This may seem theoretical and abstract to you at this point due to the terms; however, what ADR can solve for your organization is extremely valuable and certainly well known to you from practice. If you mentally associate domain knowledge with the knowledge "trapped" in the individual departments of your organization and with specific employees, you will immediately sense the challenges ADR can solve for you in your organization.

Methodology

Science and practice are closely interlinked through iterative ADR cycles. The integration of employees from companies into research-based projects enables optimal cooperation with practice-oriented researchers, each addressing a problem existing in corporate practice and leading to viable decisions and a science-based problem solution. The applied ADR methodology follows the guidelines of Sein et al. and is divided into the phases shown in Fig. 4.1 "Action Design Research" [1]. This scientific approach, in which individual theses are evaluated and verified in a solution-oriented manner, can be implemented very practically in any organization. The ADR methodology will also find particular appeal in your organization because everyone will feel included and involved. Rightly so, because that is exactly what ADR effectively implements.

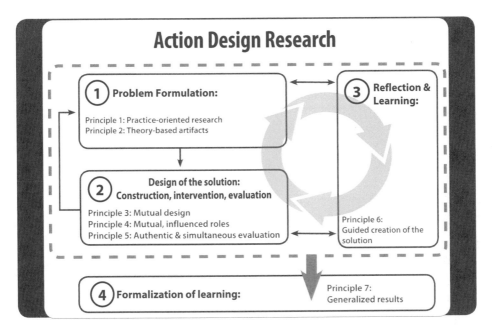

Fig. 4.1   Action Design Research

Phase 1: Problem Formulation

Start your Action Design Research with an initial kick-off event in which you discuss your company-specific problem with stakeholders and concretize the fundamental research questions relevant to you based on this challenge. The defined research questions help you to concretely validate in which areas there is a particular need for change and how you can effectively address this. The approach is science-oriented and proven in practice.

Based on this, define the Opportunity Statement. It is helpful if you present the specific setting of your company in terms of market situation and competition and other relevant factors. Determine 1–2 main responsible persons in your company who can contribute their long-standing practical experience in the context and act as immediate contact persons and sparring partners in the practice-oriented research, development, and validation of the model.

Document the theory-based artifacts resulting from this problem-oriented research activity, ideally in an internal company wiki.

Phase 2: Construction, Intervention, Evaluation

To create truly effective artifacts for relevant problem spaces, an accompanying formative evaluation supports the research and prototyping process.

Thus, the ADR team, with extensive representation of other practitioners from your company, iteratively moves from the initial to an increasingly improved definition of requirements and solution artifacts to arrive at the alpha version of a first model. The *Minimum Viable Product*—the so-called MVP—is such an alpha version in the prototyping of agile software development.

In a further iteration, an improved beta version is created, which should then prove itself in future practical application as agile software artifacts for your company.

In addition to the regular weekly meetings of this agile team, the third principle of mutual design is applied to work together on these prototypes in an authentic and simultaneous evaluation.

Continuously supplement the problem formulation with the insights gained in the formative evaluation. The evaluation results also flow into the as-is analysis.

Phase 3: Reflection & Learning

The learning and reflection process is reflected in the corresponding tasks in this phase:

1. Reflect on the design of the solution artifact.
2. Evaluate compliance with the rules.
3. Analyze the intervention of the results with regard to the defined practice and research objectives.

By examining the originally defined problem from ever new perspectives in Phase 3, a conscious reflection of the chosen theories and the emerging ensemble of individual solution artifacts takes place, which significantly contributes to identifying relevant knowledge for solving class problems. In this process, the research process is continuously adapted based on early evaluation results to reflect the increasing understanding.

With an expert interview, you reflect on a summative evaluation of the design of your solution artifact. Furthermore, you continuously evaluate compliance with the rules established in the process and analyze the intervention of the results with regard to the defined practice and research objectives. The invaluable advantage of this approach is that you ensure that your reflection and learning phase conceptually moves from the creation of a single solution towards the application to a broader class of problems. Consequently, you create not just a science-based solution for a single problem, but one that is equally suitable for a multitude of similar challenges.

Phase 4: Formalization of Learning

The formalization of generalized results summarizes the learnings for your company in a science-oriented and practical manner. In addition to the iterative examination and validation, a final reflection is complemented by a final evaluation aimed at ensuring that the created artifacts are generally suitable for solving similar problems in the class of comparable initial situations.

Accordingly, tasks in this phase:

1. Abstract the learned concepts for a class of field problems.
2. Share the results and assessment with practitioners.
3. Articulate the results as design principles.
4. Articulate learning in light of the selected theories.
5. Formalize the results for dissemination.

How to Successfully Apply the ADR Methodology

You apply this problem space exploration technique of ADR both in the analytical problem analysis and in the context of an evaluation repeatedly. The formative evaluation represents the current analysis for you based on a representative of the processes practiced in your company.

In a second step, in ADR Phase 2, you supplement this with ideal-typical processes and activities that are generally considered useful in the agile environment. This means that the entire knowledge process is accompanied by continuous analysis, reflection, and optimization, as facts are examined from different perspectives and constantly questioned.

The questions that arise in this process help you structure the problem and create a clear overview of the problem situation based on detailed questions.

Start with an Evaluative Analysis into Agile Transformation

For all types of organizations, the following questions regularly arise when prioritizing processes and activities in the agile software release cycle:

Why?	**Objectives:** • What are the strategic objectives? • Why? Are defined objectives still current and valid? • Critical: Commitment (agreement of all parties)
What?	**Problem analysis:** • What is the overarching prioritization? • Review the need for overarching prioritization • What function does local prioritization have? • What types of decisions need to be prioritized?

How?	**Processes and activities:**
	• Organization of decisions
	• Derive the requirements for processes and activities within overarching prioritization
	• How and when do higher-level priorities apply?
	• Identification of overarching decision-making processes
	• Definition and classification of decision criteria
	• Methodology, roles, and processes
	• Collective decision-making/prioritization/coordination processes between agile teams
	• Synchronization of information, decisions, etc.
	• Integrated validation processes
	• Knowledge management
	• How is feedback from customers and internal teams incorporated?
Who?	**Roles:**
	• Who is involved in the decision-making and prioritization process?
	• Domains
	• Roles
	• Teams
	• Organizational forms
	• Who is responsible for which processes and activities?
	• Specialization versus generalization
When?	**Time management:**
	• Critical time: Deadlines
	• Coordination within teams
	• Synchronization of agile teams
	• Release planning and roadmap for software products

4.1.1   Defining Individual Adaptations for a Large-Scale Agile Framework

To adapt an agile framework to the specific requirements of your organization, the requirements must be defined in accordance with the goals of your organization and the needs of your employees and teams.

As part of the iterative reflection, you continuously ensure, with concrete questions and considering current research, which requirements arise for the specific problems in your company.

The following are the requirements for an agile organizational and prioritization model for companies in the role of a software manufacturer; these include, for example, the following processes and activities:

Processes and Activities
• Particularly required for the effective orchestration of various software products are:
  – Transparent product strategy,

- Medium and long-term, cross-product product roadmap,
- Agile product release plan,
- IT security by design.
- The agile model should provide suitable approaches to
  - Support early effort estimation,
  - Avoid misprioritization,
  - Clarify features and release strategies,
  - Serve quality improvement,
  - e.g., through feedback and agile control mechanisms.
- The model should fundamentally be geared towards reducing time-intensive testing efforts.
- For this purpose, the agile model must support small-scale effort definitions that enable more accurate and reliable effort estimation.

4.1.2   As-Is Analysis in the Transformation Process through Evaluation

A very proven method to determine such a transformation process as precisely as possible for your organization is to conduct an evaluation by surveying your employees.

An initial problem analysis facilitates the entry to effectively identify practice-relevant problems and causes: problems can only be solved when their causes are known. Therefore, an evaluation by surveying the employees of your organization is the ideal approach to identify existing problems and acute optimization needs in the context of introducing a large-scale agile framework.

The 5-W questions method is suitable for effective problem analysis. By constantly asking "WHY" problems occur or prioritization and coordination processes are difficult, even initially hidden causes become clear through a constantly questioning as-is analysis. The focus is on finding the cause of the error so that optimizations can be effective.

Easily Applicable Solution Models as a Result of the Formative Evaluation
In the context of a scientific investigation, an evaluation for the as-is analysis typically takes place as a fixed integral part in one piece. Instead of a classic evaluation process, a continuous validation of assumptions and hypotheses appears more suitable in the agile context today. What you then receive are easily applicable agile solution models.

Qualitative Employee Survey—Considerate Inclusion of All Stakeholders
Based on an accompanying qualitative employee survey, you evaluate the current state for your company. The goal of such a qualitative survey in relation to the practical example of developing an agile prioritization model for software manufacturers is to determine how cross-product coordination can be improved in the dimensions of technical framework conditions, professional documentation, and inter-process communication.

In a qualitative survey in the form of individual interviews, you should definitely ensure that employees in various roles are involved. In the practical example, these are, for example, those employees who are relevant for the implementation of software product development. Thus, the survey in the practical example serves both to take into account the needs and wishes of employees and to determine the need for change for optimized process design in software development and the prioritization of requirements and documentation of a software product family.

You conduct the survey informally as a personal conversation. Be sure to use adapted questions if you interview different target groups. Such adjustments are necessary, for example, if some of the evaluation participants do not have in-depth technical knowledge, while another evaluation group has exactly this expertise. Your W-questions prove to be particularly useful for you now, as they help you to identify backgrounds and differing needs in your company. If answers emerge during the survey that are relevant in several sub-areas of the survey, be sure to note this in the written documentation and take these valuable insights into account in your evaluation. In addition to exploring needs, the survey also serves to evaluate previous ideas and any interim results.

Evaluation Participants

The evaluation should definitely include a representative selection of people in relation to your initial problem and the company context. Ask yourself the following questions, for example:

- Which teams/departments/specialist groups are affected or should be involved in the process in the future?
- Which employees are currently facing difficulties in the process?
- Which activities will change?
- How do the changes affect existing processes in the company?
- Which processes have not yet been digitized?
- Which employees and departments need to be involved for what purpose?

If you lack detailed knowledge of these or similar questions in the company context, the evaluation provides your company with valuable insights that correspond above all to the current practice in your organization. When in doubt, interview a few more people rather than foregoing important internal company information. Of course, such a survey, including preparation, implementation, and careful evaluation, involves considerable effort; however, you can be sure that these efforts are worth it and will have a positive impact on the results. Especially when you want to establish new roles such as a Chief Digital Officer (CDO) or new teams in the company, such a survey is of particular benefit.

To illustrate, Table 4.1 "Participants of a Formative Evaluation" visualizes a representative selection of people for an evaluation in relation to the employees and roles typically involved in agile software development.

Table 4.1 Participants of a formative evaluation. (Source own representation—Sascha Block)

No.	Role/Function	Function/Team	Location	Date
1	Company Management	Board/Managing Director	Hamburg	21.09.21
2	Product Management	Product-/Cross-Team	Hamburg	18.03.21
3	Area Management	Product-/Cross-Team	Hamburg	19.03.21
3	Chief Information Officer (CIO)	Product-/Cross-Team	Hamburg	19.03.21
4	IT Consultant	Product-/Cross-Team	Hamburg	18.03.21
4	Product Owner	Product A	Hamburg	17.05.21
5	Service Consultant	Service-/Cross-Team	Munich	17.05.21
6	Product Owner	Product B	Hamburg	18.05.21
7	Product Owner	Product C	Berlin	05.07.21
8	Service Owner	Service I	Hamburg	05.07.21
9	Service Owner	Service II	Munich	06.07.21
7	Software Developer	Product A	Munich	07.07.21
8	Software Developer	Product A	Munich	07.07.21
9	Software Developer	Product B	Munich	07.07.21
10	Software Architect	Product A, B	Hamburg	08.07.21
11	Software Architect	Product C	Berlin	09.07.21
12	Security Expert	Product-/Team-wide	Hamburg	09.07.21
13	UX Design Expert	Product-/Team-wide	Hamburg	12.07.21
14	Support	Product-/Team-wide	Hannover	13.07.21
15	DevOps Engineer	Product-/Team-wide	Hamburg	12.07.21
16	Sales	Product-/Team-wide	Munich	08.07.21
17	Marketing	Product-/Team-wide	Hamburg	10.07.21
18	SecDevOps Specialist	Product-/Team-wide	Hannover	10.07.21
19	Research, Innovation, Presales	Product-/Team-wide	Hamburg	10.07.21

When assembling the evaluation participants, it is also important to ensure that the different agile teams are represented, so that the characteristics and differences regarding agile approaches become clear.

In particular, question—and do so service-/product-wide—whether and what special features and needs the different teams have for agile approaches. Use evaluation to examine in particular whether and to what extent requirements for a higher-level prioritization exist. Your evaluation will then also provide a representative cross-section in terms of the range of tasks and professional functions, enabling you to obtain a balanced overall picture for assessing your organization as a whole.

Empathic Interviews

Empirical research for a new process design—or for optimizing an existing model—should always begin with a deep understanding of the relevant processes and the technical context; for this purpose, interviews with stakeholders are particularly suitable [2, page 39]. In order to gain the most accurate understanding of the different tasks and roles in the agile software development environment, empathic and openly designed interviews should be conducted along predefined questions, so that the mindset of employees regarding agile practices is captured, as well as relevant information on processes, activities, and roles.

Directly applicable and helpful for conducting such interviews are the following recommendations, which are based on the scientific recommendations in the teaching module "Empirical Software Engineering" at the University of Hamburg [3]:

- Avoid yes/no questions
- Formulate open-ended questions
- Do not try to fill silence
- Establish eye contact
- Dig for interesting stories
- Ask follow-up questions
- Show empathy and paraphrase
- Look for extreme experiences
- Continuously ask "Why?"
- Leave room for comments

4.1.3 Survey Design

Ideally, the questionnaire addresses the three areas of everyday work, communication, and agility, covering both different and central aspects of agile software development that are relevant to your company.

Clarify in your survey design, in particular, how you currently prioritize, identify, and document requirements across teams in the company.

The questions in the Everyday Work section serve you for the analysis of existing tasks and processes within and between teams. Essentially, you can use the results of questions 1) to 5) for your team descriptions. With questions 6) and 7), the actual analysis of existing problems and requirements for a prioritization and organization model to solve these challenges begins.

Everyday Work
1) What are your everyday tasks?
   What functions do you take on in software development/in projects?
2) What do you regularly do outside of specific tasks?

3) How do you contribute to software development?
   (e.g., core tasks, specialization, practices, and procedures)
4) How is work progress currently measured, controlled, and visualized?
5) How are decisions made and documented concerning your activities? How and who makes the decisions?
6) What problems do you frequently face in your work?
7) Specific suggestions: What kind of support do you wish for?
   (e.g., in information gathering, communication, specific work processes)

Communication
8) Imagine you have made an important decision that affects the entire team or even spans multiple software products. How do you communicate the decision made or record it? Are you aware of who the recipient of such a decision is or how do you solve this?
9) Do you have the impression that you receive important information too late or not at all?
    O regularly O frequently O occasionally O rarely O never
    If yes: What kind of information? Example situation?
10) What information is repeatedly important to you in your specific position?
11) Have you been able to contribute and implement your ideas so far?
12) What suggestions do you have for improving cross-product documentation? Especially for optimizing the
    – Technical documentation
    – Infrastructure documentation (build management and deploy management)
    – Artifacts for software architecture/technical framework

Agility
13) Do you feel that the software product development is agile enough?
14) Do you see difficulties in the cross-product lifecycle and what are the causes of existing problems?
15) What would you change to improve the lifecycle of cross-product solutions?

4.1.4   Evaluation and Results of the Formative Evaluation

The preparation, implementation, and evaluation of a formative evaluation regularly involve a considerable amount of effort. Make sure that sufficient time and support are planned for this in your company. Careful coordination for implementation is just as essential as transparent communication within the company about this project.

Honest and insightful answers from employees, which are ultimately valuable, will be obtained in the survey if you approach it openly and create trust. Make your goals transparent and easily understandable and take 10–15 minutes before each interview to explain the background and objectives. Make it clear why the person being interviewed is relevant and that the survey is solely for the optimization of their daily work routine, thus automatically helping their company achieve increased success.

In your evaluation, you can then incorporate relevant statements. Mark these, for example, according to the following scheme: [Number of the interviewee, abbreviation of the role, number of the question]; combined sources can be added comma-separated. Verbatim quotes should be marked with quotation marks and italicized. Arrange the statements you have collected for the evaluation in a readable continuous text and thus summarize existing problems for your company and existing practical requirements in an understandable way. If this is advantageous for understanding, you can of course change individual sentences grammatically, but never in terms of content.

Finally, summarize the insights gained from the evaluation and aggregation of the answers of the formative evaluation.

4.1.5   Summative Evaluation

The summative evaluation can, for example, take place within the framework of an interview with experts in the company who are suitable for evaluating the facts and insights collected during the formative evaluation based on their assessment.

The purpose of the summative evaluation is to determine whether the results derived by you and the model established using the Action Research Design appear suitable for improving the overall organization and prioritization. With a focus on the efficient design of software product lines, the optimization of the dimensions of the technical framework, the subject-specific documentation, and the inter-process communication are at the center of such a model.

In agile software development, the optimization of the dimensions of the technical framework, the subject-specific documentation, and the inter-process communication are at the forefront of an agile model in every company. However, it is up to you to determine the specific requirements for your company. The combination of formative and summative evaluation provides you with the best methodology and results that you can ultimately rely on.

4.1.6   Expert Interview

An expert interview takes place in the form of established evaluation theses, which result directly from the model requirements and can be confirmed or denied by the experts. In this case, the denial of a thesis—with regard to the suitability of the generated model artifact for problem-solving—corresponds to its rejection, and the affirmation accordingly to the suitability of the model for problem-solving.

The established theses ultimately reflect and answer your research questions in a measurable way.

With the results of the evaluation, you switch to active practice mode
With the evaluation, you have worked on tangible results that reflect the needs of your employees and teams and determined which new structures and processes are suitable for improving collaboration within the organization and defined goals and results in your organization.

4.2   Consider the Influencing Factors of the Cloud Trend and Virtualization in the Focus of an Agile Framework

With the increasing shift of IT infrastructures to the cloud and with container-based virtualization of applications, the complexity level of IT applications is extended by a new dimension. This increase in complexity in IT scenarios also has a significant impact on the establishment of an agile framework.

Although IT security has always been of great importance for the development and operation of software, cloud security poses different requirements than the protection of monolithic applications in traditionally largely isolated corporate networks.

With the cloud trend, numerous processes and business processes within an organization are also changing. With the switch to the cloud or the expansion of cloud scenarios, procedural and organizational changes within an organization are inevitably necessary. The following section explains the relationships that exist here and the dimensions in which this has a concrete impact.

None of the existing large-scale agile frameworks reflect the specific requirements in the cloud context or with regard to IT security and their effects on the design of an agile framework.

Since there are indeed relevant requirements for this, which are accompanied by urgently needed organizational changes, it is absolutely sensible to reflect on the relationships and effects of certain technologies that are directly related to cloud service models. This includes clarifying questions such as how to implement IT security by design or a zero-trust strategy. Furthermore, the extended protection needs of a container-based software architecture and associated mechanisms such as secret management and components such as a public key infrastructure must be taken into account. REST APIs, the approach of RESTful design, and microservice paradigms emerge as a possible, effective technical implementation. The effectiveness of influencing factors for a clearly visible visualization of information related to IT security and software architecture artifacts and their optimal communication and visualization should not be neglected. The individual sections already reflect the corresponding tasks, functions, roles, and processes that result from this; these are presented once again in the generally valid context of agile teams in Sect. 4.4.

4.2.1 Cloud Computing

Cloud Computing is an IT service model for the demand-oriented use of IT resources from a pool of configurable services from IT hardware and provided cloud applications and basic services for using these cloud resources.

Cloud computing thus becomes usable only through the provided cloud infrastructure—which in turn combines hardware and software. Within cloud infrastructures, a distinction is made between the physical layer and a defined abstraction layer.

The physical cloud layer consists of the hardware resources required to support the provided cloud services. Such cloud hardware does not differ from regular hardware in traditional data centers and includes server, storage, and network components.

The conceptually higher-level cloud abstraction layer, which consists of cloud software, lies above the physical layer. Both levels together realize the essential cloud properties in mutual interaction.

Based on the definition of the National Institute of Standards and Technology (NIST), a cloud model is defined that consists of five essential characteristics and three service models and distinguishes four types of clouds, which differ in terms of cloud deployment [4, pages 2 ff.].

This cloud model consists of five essential characteristics, three service models, and four deployment models:

4.2.2 Cloud Properties

The 5 Essential Cloud Characteristics
1. **On-Demand Self-Services:** A cloud customer can unilaterally and automatically provide desired computing capacities independently as needed.
2. **Provisioning via Internet:** The provided services are available over the internet and are scalable through standard mechanisms.
3. **Resource Pooling:** The computing resources of the cloud provider are provided from a pool of IT resources and services and can also be shared by multiple customers. Based on a multi-tenant model, these resources are dynamically assigned as various physical and virtual resources and reassigned as needed by the cloud customers. Although a customer may perceive a location-based perception, a cloud customer generally has no precise control or knowledge of the exact location of the provided resources. Even if defined cloud services can be limited to a cloud region, a country, or a state as a physical cloud resource, there is no control or claim to select a specific hardware in the sense of a defined Configuration Item (CI) artifact at any time.
4. **Rapid Elasticity:** Cloud capabilities can be elastically provided and released. This cloud property includes the option for customers to use freely definable rules for

automatic capacity expansion, enabling horizontal and/or vertical scaling as needed. To the cloud consumer, the available features often appear unlimited and can be used in any quantity and at any time.

5. **Measured Service:** Cloud systems automatically control and optimize resource usage based on intelligent measurement functions at an abstraction level suitable for the type of service (e.g., storage, CPU utilization, bandwidth, and active user accounts). Resource usage can be monitored, controlled, and reported online, providing transparency for both the provider and the user of the utilized cloud service.

4.2.3 Cloud Service Models

Different service models are also defined for cloud environments, which in turn have concrete effects on the agile processes within their organization.

1. **Software as a Service (SaaS):** The cloud consumer has the option to use the cloud provider's cloud applications, which are based on a cloud infrastructure. Access to the provided applications is usually from various client devices either via a thin-client interface, such as a web browser, or through a program interface (API). The SaaS customer does not manage or control the underlying cloud infrastructure, including network, servers, operating systems, storage, or the provided application features. Even though the software services are customizable and configurable, the source code and the basic technologies used regularly remain hidden.

2. **Platform as a Service (PaaS):** The capability provided to the customer is to deploy, in the cloud infrastructure, applications created or acquired by the customer, which are supported by the platform provider using programming, libraries, services, and tools. The consumer has control over the provided applications in PaaS and may also have permissions for configuration settings for the application hosting environment. In no case does the PaaS customer manage or control the underlying cloud infrastructure, including network, servers, operating systems, or storage resources.

3. **Infrastructure as a Service (IaaS):** The capability provided to the consumer is the provision of processing, storage, networking, and other basic data processing resources. The IaaS customer is able to independently provide these resources to deploy and run any software on these resources, including operating systems and any applications.

   The consumer does not manage or control the underlying cloud infrastructure but has control over operating systems, storage space, and deployed applications; and regularly has limited control over selected network components to use them in the sense of, for example, host firewalls.

4.2.4   Cloud Models

With the background of the previously presented cloud properties and cloud service models, different cloud models have evolved, which have other characteristics in terms of the provided cloud infrastructures and deployment strategies.

Private Cloud

The cloud infrastructure is provided for the exclusive use by a single organization comprising multiple cloud users. A private cloud can be owned by the organization itself or by a third party, or it can consist of a combination of both.

Whether the operation and management of a private cloud take place within or outside the premises of the respective organization is secondary. What is more important is how the authorization model of such a private cloud regulates and logs access, as these central aspects of a cloud architecture are directly related to the integrity of data and are therefore highly relevant for compliance with data protection requirements.

Community Cloud

The cloud infrastructure is provided for the exclusive use by a specific community of consumers who have shared concerns (e.g., mission, security requirements, policies, and compliance considerations). The community cloud can be owned by one or more organizations, belong to a third party, and be managed and operated by a single organization or a community, and such a community cloud can exist within or outside of buildings.

Public Cloud

In a public cloud, the cloud infrastructure is made available for open use by the general public. The public cloud can be owned by a company, an academic or governmental organization, or be in shared ownership. Physically, the cloud infrastructure is located in the premises of the cloud provider. Amazon AWS, Google Cloud, and Microsoft's Azure Cloud are among the largest and most well-known public cloud providers.

Hybrid Cloud

In a hybrid cloud, the cloud infrastructure is a composition of two or more different cloud infrastructures (private, community, or public) that remain separate entities but are connected through standardized or proprietary technologies to enable data and application portability.

Multi-Cloud

The multi-cloud, on the other hand, does not represent its own cloud model and does not extend the five cloud models by a sixth cloud model, but merely represents a cloud usage consisting of any combination of the five classified cloud models.

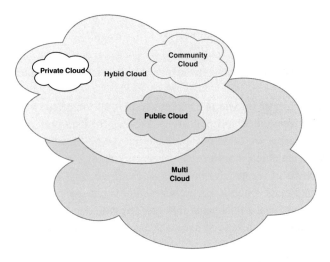

Fig. 4.2 Cloud Types

Figure 4.2 "Cloud Types" visualizes the coexistence of the various cloud models in a shared, virtual infrastructure:

Impact of Cloud Models on Agile Structures
While the cloud term is often vague and generally used for cloud scenarios, many organizations in practice already use mixed forms of multi-cloud scenarios.

It is important to be aware of this small but significant difference, as it has many fundamental implications for basic IT operations, IT security, and IT governance. Impacts arise, for example, specifically for data protection and, of course, also with regard to the IT security of cloud applications.

A hybrid cloud, for example, exists in conjunction with a network in an organization's internal data center connected to, for example, cloud services from Google Cloud and/or connected AWS cloud services. These cloud scenarios are already widespread and typical cloud representatives.

In many cases, the technological change, with the migration of IT into cloud scenarios, takes place without simultaneously addressing the organizational adjustments that are so essential for organizations in the required manner. If important aspects of IT security are neglected or inadequately considered, serious security risks have already arisen not infrequently.

Technical Infrastructures with Impact on Data Protection and Legal Framework Conditions
Each cloud usage has special characteristics in data processing, and the cloud models always represent different protection areas for which a specific security concept becomes relevant as soon as these cloud zones are used.

Various aspects of data protection come into play here—for example, the technical implementation of the legally anchored "right to be forgotten" for consumers. Security officers and the new role of data protection officers must not only be named in person and function but must also be actively involved in the technical implementation with direct practical relevance.

From the perspective of software development, it is all too often overlooked who the components come from and what implications this has for data protection and IT security. Emergency concepts are often not available but are absolutely necessary to remain capable of acting when damage or threat situations occur.

Especially in terms of security for multi-cloud environments, which consist of public, private, and hybrid clouds, a public key infrastructure is indispensable. With such technical solutions, organizational adjustments are always required at the same time, which can effectively ensure that the prescribed access protection and the functionality with connected support processes are equally guaranteed.

When data is moved from one data room to another data room—and this is regularly the case with cloud scenarios—different requirements arise with regard to data protection.

On the one hand, this requires technical mechanisms that meet this requirement, as well as organizational measures that are optimally coordinated with them. At the same time, however, these technical infrastructures also always have an impact on legal foundations and agreements between the respective cloud operator, the cloud contract partner as a direct cloud user, and the users as immediate cloud users.

4.2.5 Virtualization & Containerization

Cloud computing uses virtualization technology because of the cost-efficient advantages it offers, such as payload-oriented hardware and energy use, automated error detection, consequently improving the quality of software, and increased flexibility and easier manageability.

Virtualization

Virtualization enables the shared use of resources of a single physical instance by multiple users and organizations. The virtualization concept is thus essentially a **technical agility principle** that consists of dividing the physical infrastructure of computer and network resources into smaller, reusable, and more portable and flexible units. The advantages lie in the efficient use of resources and the effective operation of parallel systems in an isolated environment.

Hypervisor

The hypervisor, also called Virtual Machine Monitor (VMM), is a software as a central component of every virtualization concept, which enables the emulation of the underlying hardware resources and infrastructure. VMM creates the illusion of multiple running machines on the same underlying hardware such as CPU, memory, NIC, and hard drive, enabling a variety of applications running on different operating systems [5]. The hypervisor is executed on the host computer, and each encapsulated VM is referred to as a guest computer (Guest-OS).

There are two different types of hypervisors:

Type 1 Hypervisor: Uses a direct connection to the hardware infrastructure, e.g., HyperKit (MacOS) or Hyper-V (Windows).
Type 2 Hypervisor: Runs as an application on the host-OS and thus has no direct connection to the hardware infrastructure, e.g., VirtualBox or VMWare.

Figure 4.3 illustrates the difference between "Hypervisor Type-1 and Type-2 based on Bernstein".

Containerization
The technology of containerization is the alternative to virtualization. Containerization involves encapsulating software code and all necessary dependencies in an isolated container [6].

The bundling of software in containers simplifies the automatic deployment of software services in the cloud and on heterogeneous systems, as a virtual operating system and file system are executed on the integrated, native system. This significantly simplifies the development process across the phases of development, testing, integration, and deployment, as it allows the developer to provide software that is platform-independent and highly portable.

Docker
Docker is one such containerization solution. By now, Docker has firmly established itself as the base technology for containerized operation and deployment of applications due to its ease of use.

The once-created, virtualized container already provides an isolated layer for automated quality assurance tests with its virtualization layer. With the right approach, these containers can be more easily restricted to protect against unauthorized access than programs running on a native platform.

The robustness of applications also increases with the containerized operating environment, as each container serves as an isolated sandbox for the programs contained within and protects the underlying system from being affected by applications from other environments.

Thus, containerization allows many containers to run in parallel on a single system without affecting each other.

Figure 4.4 "Docker Container versus Virtualization" compares the different virtualization principles.

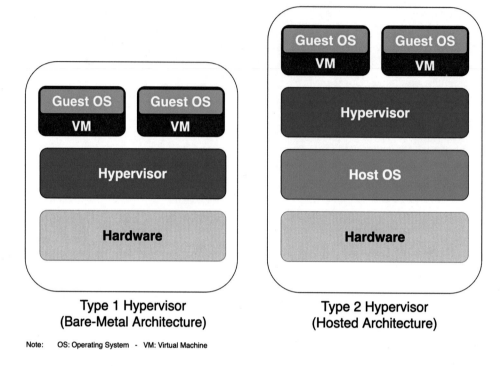

Type 1 Hypervisor
(Bare-Metal Architecture)

Type 2 Hypervisor
(Hosted Architecture)

Note: OS: Operating System - VM: Virtual Machine

Fig. 4.3 Hypervisor Type-1 and Type-2 based on Bernstein

The Docker Daemon in the Docker container concept corresponds to the layer of the hypervisor of a virtual machine. The Docker Daemon runs as a service in the background on the host OS and manages—as a middleware component—everything required for the operation and interaction in the data flow with Docker containers.

The Docker Daemon communicates directly with the host OS and organizes all required services and data for the container in the process. The Docker Daemon also ensures a clean separation in the layer concept with the goal that each container is isolated from both the host OS and other containers.

Container Orchestration

With further mechanisms and tools, containerized applications can then be scaled much more easily and thus offer a demand-oriented agile solution for performance adjustment.

The management of a large number of containers then requires a reliable solution for so-called container orchestration.

Long ago, the former niche technologies of container solutions around Docker and the orchestration tool Kubernetes have proven themselves in numerous projects and established themselves as a standard, thus making agile deployment of software something completely ubiquitous.

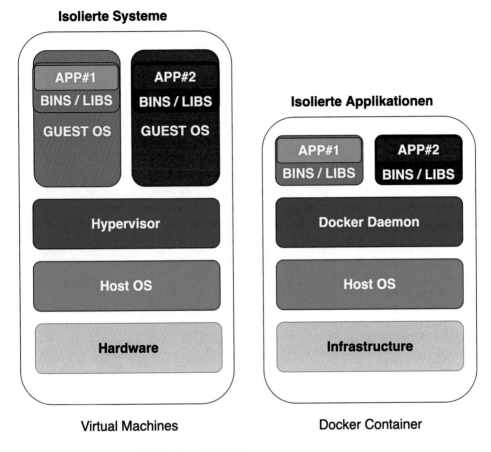

Fig. 4.4   Figure 18 Docker Container versus Virtualization—Sascha Block

Kubernetes—The De Facto Standard for Container Orchestration
One such orchestration solution is Kubernetes, which, as an open-source tool, handles the deployment, scaling, and management of containerized applications. Although Docker also offers an orchestration solution with Docker Swarm [7], Kubernetes is considered the most widely used orchestration solution in professional environments according to a survey from the "State of Cloud Native Development Report 2021" [8]. The CNCF report is of high relevance, as more than 19,000 developers worldwide were surveyed between November 2020 and February 2021. More than 3800 survey participants answered questions about the development of backend services and the technologies they use. The spread of container-based deployments has been increasing ever since; more than a year has passed since this survey, which is already a relatively long period for evaluating technology trends. Many existing software releases have since been replaced

by new release versions. However, basic technologies do not undergo rapid change, especially since the selection remains limited. Those who read the report closely will notice that Kubernetes technology is still in an evaluation stage in many projects; the shift towards the cloud, along with the associated topics of containerization, is thus in full swing in the vast majority of organizations. It is certainly worth considering to what extent the CNCF is influenced by economic interests in its statements, as each project involves very high investment sums and correspondingly high profit expectations. But even under this aspect, the CNCF remains an excellent starting point for evaluating technological solutions against each other.

Risk of Incomplete Knowledge of Container Technologies
An interesting statement comes from the CTO of the CNCF, Chris Aniszczyk:

> *"The discrepancy between the use of containers (93%) and the use of Kubernetes (96%) has steadily increased over the past year. There seems to be a growing gap in understanding that these technologies are essentially a complete package. What's fascinating is how quickly Kubernetes has evolved from a niche technology to such a ubiquitous technology that people don't even know they're using technologies built on top of it, as the value for end-users has shifted upwards."* It is worth pausing at this point in the technical context: Of course, there is a significant risk in using technologies that are not fully understood. This is an important insight and an excellent transition to the next section and the relevance of knowledge about software architectures and IT security.

In the context of large-scale agile frameworks, it is a central point of high relevance to anchor technical knowledge in organizations and to disseminate the right information and facts. Despite all collaboration tools, effective mechanisms are needed to identify and record relevant knowledge. This, in turn, requires the necessary time frame, patience, and all the necessary support.

4.2.6 Relevant Bodies for Establishing Internet and Cloud Standards

Since container orchestration has become an established standard in software development and deployment of software releases, and the interoperability of cloud technologies represents an important characteristic for software architectures, it is advantageous to regularly obtain information from first-hand sources. The following standardization bodies are highly recommended for this purpose:

Open Container Initiative (OCI)
The Open Container Initiative is an open initiative with the defined goal of creating open industry standards for container formats and container runtime environments [9].

The OCI has existed since June 2015 and was founded by Docker and other leading companies in the container industry. Companies such as Amazon, Google, Cisco, Apple, SUSE, Microsoft, and many other strong partners participate in the OCI and contribute their requirements and expertise.

The Open Container Initiative Community sees itself as a technical open-source community. Therefore, the tech initiative is working intensively on the further development and establishment of standards for container formats and container runtime technologies.

Currently, two specifications are in the focus of the standardization committee:

- Container Runtime Specification (Runtime-spec) and
- Container Image Specification (Image-spec).

Transparency first The Technical Oversight Board (TOB) is the technical supervisory body of the OCI and is responsible for managing conflicts, violations of procedures or policies, and for all cross-project or overarching issues that cannot be resolved through the decision-making body for OCI projects. The TOB is also responsible for adding, removing, or reorganizing OCI projects. Of course, all specifications are also published on GitHub [10].

Cloud Native Computing Foundation (CNCF)

The Cloud Native Computing Foundation (CNCF) serves as a vendor-independent body for cloud standards. The CNCF hosts cloud projects at different maturity levels and is thus a central point of contact for learning about and evaluating cloud technology trends and the important components of the global technology infrastructure. To this end, the CNCF brings together the world's leading developers, end users, and providers and organizes the largest open-source developer conferences. The CNCF is part of the non-profit Linux Foundation.

The projects differ in their maturity level: The most advanced stage with a high maturity level is currently formed by the 16 graduated projects, which include the Container Runtime containerd, the Coordination & Service Recovery services CoreDNS and etcd, the Service Proxy envoy, the Logging solution fluentd, the Container Registry Harbor, the Application Definition & Image Build HELM, the Tracing solution JAEGER, the Scheduling & Orchestration solution kubernetes, the Service Mesh LINKERD, the Security & Compliance solutions Open Policy Agent and TUF, the Monitoring service Prometheus, the Cloud Native Storage solution Rook, and the Database solutions KV and Vitess [11].

33 projects are currently assigned to the Incubating status. And 68 more projects are currently still in the Sandbox stage, thus showing the lowest technology maturity level. Before committing to a technical solution as an organization, it is strongly recommended to check the official project status through this body before backing the wrong horse...

Internet Engineering Task Force (IETF)

The Internet Engineering Task Force aims to improve internet technologies by creating high-quality, technical documents and guidelines that influence the way people design, use, and manage the internet [12].

Members who develop technical specifications for the committee have many years of technical expertise. The documents of the IETF are therefore of high technical quality and are created based on network engineering principles and established standards.

When the IETF takes on the protocol responsibility for a protocol or function, it is responsible for all technical aspects and properties of the protocol.

The standards are created based on the technical judgment of the participants on defined topics, based on practical experience in implementing and applying these highly relevant specifications.

In principle, anyone can become a part and active member of the committee. The entire circle of technical experts is made up of voluntary participants, and anyone who wants to contribute to "making the internet better" is encouraged and welcome.

Working Groups of the ITEF

For effective standardization, the ITEF is divided into working groups, which are shown in Table 4.2 "Working Groups of the Internet Engineering Task Force (IETF)".

All relevant protocols, security standards, and frameworks, such as OpenID Connect (OIDC) for secure and standardized Internet technologies and thus also for cloud technologies, are supervised by the IETF; so you should definitely consider the recommendations and standards of the IETF in the context of your software architecture.

4.3 Software Architecture & IT Security as an Integral Part of an Agile Framework

Modern cloud architectures and virtualized operating environments are highly heterogeneous and complex systems, based on distributed systems and consisting of a multitude of components with countless functions, always relying on software.

Basic principle of responsibility in handling sensitive data

In all of this, the basic principle of responsibility in handling sensitive data applies. At all times, sensitive data such as personal data, personal health data, intellectual property, or financial transaction data must be identified, i.e., technically cleanly classified, in order to define the appropriate security levels and standards in data transfer based on this.

Then, an appropriate security configuration is carried out, with adequate protection levels for the classified data. With this approach, a high or even very high level of protection for sensitive data can be ensured.

Table 4.2 Working Groups of the Internet Engineering Task Force (IETF)

ITEF Working Group	Specialization
Internet Engineering Steering Group (IESG)	Internet Steering Group for Technology The Internet Engineering Steering Group (IESG) is responsible for the technical management of IETF activities and the Internet standards process
Internet Research Task Force (IRTF)	Internet Research Task Force The Internet Research Task Force (IRTF) promotes research work that is important for the development of the Internet by setting up targeted, long-term research groups that deal with topics related to Internet protocols, applications, architecture, and technology
Nominating Committee	Nominating Committee The Nominating Committee, or as it is commonly called, the NomCom, is responsible for reviewing open positions of the IESG, IAB, and IAOC and nominating a candidate for each
Tools Team	The IETF Tools Team is a group of volunteers from the IETF community that develops tools to support the work of the IETF itself
Internet Architecture Board	Internet Architecture Committee The Internet Architecture Board sets the long-term technical direction for Internet standards and ensures that the Internet continues to grow and evolve as a platform for global communication and innovation
Directorates	Directorates IETF Directorates, composed of experienced IETF participants, often serve as advisory groups for the work of the IETF
IETF	The IETF Trust was established to acquire, hold, and maintain intellectual property and other property used in connection with Internet standards
IETF Systers	The IETF Systers program provides women with the opportunity to network with peers from all areas of the Internet Engineering Task Force and the Internet Research Task Force

4.3.1   IT-Security-by-Design: Software Architecture & IT-Security

How can IT security be anchored as an integral component in an organization as a bundle of various activities and technical protective measures when IT systems are regularly highly complex and these almost always consist of countless individual components, basic technologies, and frameworks? The artifacts of software architecture—with an integrated IT security architecture and its communication within the organization—play a central role in this.

Software architecture as a technical and process-oriented agile software design process for all stakeholders

In practice, it is extremely challenging to ensure IT security in every individual component as well as overall—i.e., in the interaction of components through their interaction and data flows—permanently. That is why it is so important to map the **software architecture** together with the determined requirements as best as possible—and with direct reference to IT security. The software architecture documentation is an especially important tool for all stakeholders, largely detached from role and function. These artifacts are indispensable for, for example, software architects, IT security specialists, and all stakeholders within software development itself. This is not only about the technical detailed documentation for IT specialists but also about easily understandable process documentation for all stakeholders.

IT-Security, software architecture, and software documentation complement each other

Starting from the definition of requirements, the documentation of ongoing software development, the recording of architecture decisions and their implementation status, security-relevant facts about IT architecture and the clear identification of data worth protecting play a central role. The aim is to maintain an overview of an increasing number of API endpoints or to clearly record technical debts in the IT architecture, with the goal of closing these vulnerabilities as quickly as possible.

Software architecture is the supporting foundation of every IT solution, regardless of the extent to which hardware components—which in turn also rely on software building blocks—play a role. No one would dispute this. Nevertheless, software architecture is still neglected in many projects. IT security ultimately becomes possible only on the basis of a solid and gapless software architecture documentation.

IT-Security-by-Design

The earlier IT security requirements are taken into account, the more cost-effective their consideration will be. You will benefit immensely in favor of high software quality and avoiding unnecessary costs if you involve your IT security specialists early on and establish agile processes in which **IT-Security-by-Design** is taken into account in a practical manner.

The approach *IT-Security-by-Design* is based on the idea of considering IT security requirements already in the initial design phases [13, page 87]. Even if it may seem uncomfortable because IT security requirements increase the overall requirements and efforts, maximum IT security remains a MUST criterion, so these security guarantees must not only be fundamentally included at a defined point in time, but should also be incorporated as early as possible to keep costs minimal and ensure security standards right from the start.

Subsequently raised requirements are—see also section "Process models, frameworks, and standards"—proven to be significantly more complex and costly [14, pages

71/72]. If security requirements are incorporated as early as possible, the overall project duration is also reduced. If IT security-relevant functionalities can be directly integrated into prototyping and these features are testable and verifiable in early phases, resource-intensive changes can be avoided.

A pragmatic approach to effectively integrate security-relevant aspects and make IT-Security-by-Design a reality is the implementation of the Zero-Trust strategy.

4.3.2   Zero-Trust Strategy

Associated with the increasing use of cloud services and the resulting challenges in terms of IT security and privacy protection are fundamental aspects such as identity theft, data protection breaches, data integrity, and data confidentiality. This makes trust management for cloud computing, microservice, and API-based architectures indispensable.

Precisely because cloud computing services are provided from remote and globally distributed data centers and we cannot exercise direct control from within our organization, except for taking technical measures, there is a need for a suitable strategy to protect any data; the Zero-Trust concept offers proven solutions for this purpose.

Establishing trust based on the Zero-Trust strategy
A **Zero-Trust strategy** is a conceptual model for highly protected IT architectures and offers conceptual protective measures in the form of technical best practices to ensure trust in sensitive environments based on technical protective measures and procedural trust steps in organizations [15]. Figure 4.5 illustrates the "Zero-Trust Strategy" with its basic functionality based on the components in reference to Mehraj/Banday.

4.3.3   Protection Principles and Their Technical Implementation Based on Zero Trust

Let's take a closer look at the individual measures of the Zero-Trust strategy with reference to cloud strategies and their effectiveness in terms of IT security:

Identify data and access
A Zero-Trust strategy is based on the basic principle **"never trust, always verify"**.

This security model assumes that only users, devices, data, applications, and services operating within the security boundaries of an organization should be trusted after successful user AND device authentication.

Such a security strategy must also ensure that every system and each individual entity is verified for their identity before granting access to anyone requesting a connection to its resources. Consequently, such a trust check occurs every time a user attempts to

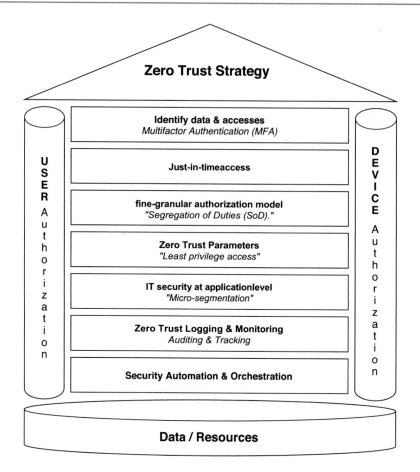

Fig. 4.5 Zero-Trust Strategy—Representation based on Mehraj/Banday.

interact with the system, classifying the entire network traffic as untrustworthy. These two principles are, so to speak, the cornerstones and can be technically implemented using multi-factor authentication.

Multi-factor Authentication (MFA)

The principle of multi-stage authentication (MFA principle) requires more than just a single authentication method to verify the user's credentials. Instead of relying solely on a password, multi-factor authentication may, for example, require a user to also enter a secret code sent to an email address or a mobile phone number that only the user should have access to.

"Prevent data breaches, automatically comply with GDPR"

By implementing technical measures, the Zero Trust model virtually automatically contributes to preventing data breaches caused by the exploitation of privileged credentials, by banishing the concept of trust from an organization's network architecture. This is achieved through **micro-segmentation of the network** with fine-grained control of user access, thereby preventing unwanted access, which is often lateral in system architectures, i.e., allowing access to connected systems. Another very effective protection mechanism of the Zero Trust model is aimed at quickly withdrawing trust from both individual entities and a system component. The **Zero Trust strategy** thus realizes a strict approach aimed at maximum IT security.

Just-in-time Access

The **just-in-time access** is based on the idea that no user or machine identity should have permanent, constantly available access to an important resource. Instead, the identity is verified each time a connection is established. Likewise, the authorization to access a resource is automatically removed after the connection has been established and the data transfer has ended. This ensures that the identity requesting access undergoes the required security checks each time. This is technically implemented through the mechanism of time-limited secrets, so-called tokens, and technology specifications such as OAuth 2.x or Open ID Connect (OIDC).

Based on the classification of data, sensitive data flows in the networks between the individual data transfer interfaces are specifically monitored, and authorized access, as well as unauthorized access attempts, are logged. Since data flows can regularly be directed in multiple directions simultaneously and should always be optimized, this principle leads to the definition of micro-networks. Minimal data flows are then also the basis for the implementation of fine-grained permissions.

Fine-grained Permission Model & Segregation of Duties

The principle of separation of tasks and responsibilities—also known as Segregation of Duties (SoD)—reflects that no person or device should have complete access to all important systems or data of a company. If this were the case, a potential attacker who gained control of the security data of that person or device would have unrestricted access to all areas of the company network.

Examples of overly broad access include network firewalls and virtual private networks (VPNs). They isolate and restrict access to technology resources and services, but once access has been gained, one is considered trustworthy by default. If access in cloud models were still limited to this model, potential attackers would only have to overcome these hurdles to gain complete control of system landscapes and exploit access to all data.

Another important aspect of the separation of responsibilities is that no person should hold multiple roles, especially not in the critical parts of the software release pipelines. For example, no developer should have access from the test to the production environment or be able to expand their privileges without appropriate supervision.

Accordingly, fine-grained authorization models must be implemented, which usually operate on the basis of microservices, but in any case ensure that only the actual minimal required permissions are granted.

The fine-grained role-based authorization concept also reflects the fact of accepting security restrictions within the architectural concept, that a frontend can never be controlled in detail per se. Even implemented protective functions regarding frontend manipulation have limited effectiveness, so that a trustworthy protection level can only be achieved through the interaction of all individual protective measures.

Role- and permission-based processes

The fact that applications are increasingly being run in containers requires role- and permission-based processes in all agile teams. Increased sensitivity in handling sensitive data is also essential during the development, deployment, and production of software artifacts and complex applications.

Zero-Trust Parameter: Least privilege access

In practice, the separation of tasks is achieved by assigning each user a role with the least access rights (Least privilege access), which means that each user or device within the network can only access the most important resources they need and nothing else. This has the advantage that if an attacker successfully gains access or control of a user's login credentials or device from outside, this access is limited to this isolatable environment, reducing the potential security risk. This principle is closely related to the previously explained mechanisms of the fine-grained authorization concept and the separation of tasks and responsibilities.

Microsegmentation

The Zero-Trust model also utilizes microsegmentation. By segmenting services, the company's IT environment is divided into security zones. Separate authorization is required for access to each of these zones. This is a proven method that significantly minimizes the likelihood of an attacker "jumping" from one part of the network to another to access and compromise more sensitive data.

Auditing and tracking through logging & monitoring

Regular audits and proper reviews of IT security ensure, among other things, that the required security standards of the minimum necessary protection level are always met. This includes, for example, current network protocols with encryption standards adapted over time. However, auditing is not just a random check, but an agile, ongoing process. In order to arrive at a meaningful tracking of possible abnormal occurrences, so-called incidents, or to be able to confirm with a clear conscience that only authorized access takes place, every connection and activity in the network must be recorded based on log files. This generates a large amount of logging data, which can only be evaluated automatically due to its volume.

Within the monitoring process, these log data can provide insights into unusual activities in the network, such as a verified and possibly compromised identity. It should be noted that detecting a compromised identity is not a trivial matter. On the one hand, the existing data protection regulations must be observed, and these regulations prohibit—in combination with the implementation of Zero-Trust rules—any content-related insight into data worth protecting.

Thus, the abstraction levels of log data, along with user reports, are often the only clues to identify compressions. Random checks complement the approach to suspected cases of compromise.

An IT security solution requires corresponding legally compliant, anonymized session data (Session Data) so that in legitimate control situations it can be precisely analyzed which actions were performed by which user with which authorization in a session. This approach using logging and monitoring is not only very useful for forensics but can also be used as evidence for reporting in corresponding security audits.

Security Automation & DevOps Orchestration

The automation of deployment processes plays an important role for agile frameworks and the integration of practical IT security principles for two reasons: In order to enable automation policies and security automation at all, individual processes must be apparent. For this purpose, countless individual data flows must be aggregated and mapped.

In doing so, a profound understanding of technology is required, which regularly involves familiarizing oneself with new tools and data flows. While complex data flows have previously taken place predominantly within monolithic applications, this paradigm is gradually dissolving not only through microservice architectures but also because the Zero-Trust concept requires precisely this detailed understanding and knowledge of individual data streams within and outside our organization.

The necessary tools to implement this are, on the one hand, Git systems and container solutions that encapsulate our components. Release strategies, including extensive test management, then reflect the interaction of our software components and map the meta-level of data flows. Only on these infrastructural foundations can tasks be automated across the entire cloud platform or even outside the cloud.

4.3.4   Secret Management

Secret keys, or simply secrets, are digital secrets worth protecting that exist within a company's networks and beyond. The need for protection extends to traditional corporate networks—which are generally easier to protect—as well as the emerging cloud environments.

A secret is a key-value pair that grants access to information, APIs, and services to a specific user or group of users.

With such secrets, sensitive information such as configuration files and source code can also be protected. A fundamental IT security requirement is that source code never reveals unprotected secrets.

With the versioning of source code, secret protection also extends to resources shared with other developers and web-based repositories. At this point, there is an additional need for a solution to manage sensitive secrets.

Secrets include credentials such as:

- **Passwords**
- **Usernames and database identifiers**
- **API keys**
- **SSH keys**
- **Certificates**

4.3.5 Extended Protection Requirements for Virtual Container Environments

Especially for a cloud computing environment, security challenges must be overcome that are associated with the specific cloud infrastructure. As previously shown, cloud-based services are inevitably closely linked to the technologies of virtualization and containerization of an IT landscape. An extended level of protection extends to these containerized environments, in which sensitive information in the form of so-called **Secret Keys** or **Secrets Keys,** is located.

Protection requirements for containerized applications
When applications are operated in containerized environments, these secrets must be injected into these applications as environment variables across countless hosts in distributed container landscapes. The injection of these secrets into the container environment occurs at build time, so that the secrets are only accessible at runtime, with authorized access.

Key Management in the Context of Agile Frameworks
In the context of agile frameworks, key management of such secrets is not directly considered. Rather, the management of keys and cryptographic key material is indispensable in the context of implementing IT security. In the role-based authorization concepts— on which the permissions granted by Secret Keys are based—there is another important security concept that must be implemented directly when establishing an agile framework for your organization.

4.3.6 Key Management & Cryptographic Protection Measures

Verified information and proven methodology for key management with many details are specified, for example, by NIST [16,17]. The Federal Office for Information Security (BSI) also adapts its guidelines on cryptographic procedures and regularly updates recommendations on key lengths and IT security [18]. The recommendations for implementation in your organization should initially be considered in the following aspects when implementing:

- **Guidelines for cryptographic key management;**
- **Practice for managing cryptographic key material;**
- **Specification of security services in the context of software architecture** especially regarding the use of cryptography, algorithms, and key types that can be used;
- **Definition** of necessary **organizational processes** with direct **connection to emergency management;**
- **Definition of update regulations.**

Lifecycle of Cryptographic Protection Mechanisms
Secrets are regularly generated based on cryptographic functions and encrypted in the same way. Cryptographic methods for protecting sensitive data are software artifacts. These can become obsolete and ineffective just like hardware, or only guarantee an insufficient level of IT security protection.

The estimated time span during which data protected by a specific cryptographic algorithm in combination with the key size is referred to as the **security duration of the algorithm.** During this time, the algorithm can be used both for applying cryptographic protection (e.g., encrypting data) and for processing the protected information (e.g., decrypting data), although the period for applying the protection may be shorter than the security duration of the algorithm (see figure).

Security Lifecycle of an Algorithm: The algorithm used here MUST provide adequate protection for the sensitive data throughout the entire lifecycle of the algorithm, i.e., the period for which the use of this protection method is considered secure [17, page 60]. In Fig. 4.6, the "Lifecycle of cryptographic protection measures based on the NIST classification" is shown. Relevant in the context of agile frameworks is that mechanisms are in place in organizations where regular audits ensure the effectiveness of cryptographic methods.

Establish Agile Protection Measures for Secrets
In addition, you should ensure that agile mechanisms are in place for your organization that, on the one hand, verify the assumptions and prerequisites at regular intervals and check the implementation.

Fig. 4.6 Lifecycle of cryptographic protection measures—Sascha Block—Own representation based on NIST classification

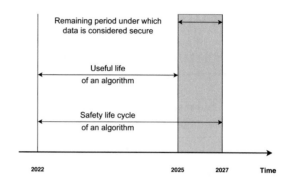

Implement Crypto-Agility

Consequently, there is also a need for us to be able to regularly or, if necessary, easily adapt our protection mechanisms. All of this requires sophisticated secret management mechanisms that must be an integral part of an agile framework as defined protection measures.

It is widely claimed that these crypto functions—which contain a key pair generation rule—are also worth protecting. The logic behind this follows the assumption that if a potential attacker knows the rules by which we create usernames or key pairs, the attack protection would be significantly weakened.

Kerckhoffs' Maxim as an Important Cryptography Principle

Rather, Kerckhoffs' maxim still applies—a principle of cryptography dating back to 1883 and originating from Auguste Kerckhoff:

> *"It must not require any secrecy and*
> *can fall into the hands of the enemy without harm."*
> *La cryptographie militaire 1883—Auguste Kerckhoff* Applied to cryptographic methods and principles of IT security, Kerckhoffs' principle means that it must be irrelevant whether a potential attacker knows an algorithm implemented in IT systems. It follows: If the attacker knows the crypto algorithm and the cryptographic method still effectively protects the secret protected by it, both the secrets are protected, and the applied cryptographic method can be considered secure.

This also implies for cryptographic methods: All crypto functions may be publicly known as long as the secret key—the so-called Secret Key—is effectively protected. Kerckhoff's principle is therefore based on the protection of cryptographic keys, not on the protection of cryptographic algorithms or crypto functions. This important fact once again underlines the central point of how indispensable the protection of any secrets is.

Virtualization & Microservice Architectures Require Sophisticated Secret Management

Containerized microservice architectures with widely distributed individual components and countless API endpoints require, in addition to certificate-based end-to-end encryption, a sophisticated platform solution for managing countless secrets distributed across the microservice architecture.

The management of secrets aims to centralize the management of multiple secrets that may be distributed across several IT projects and countless software components. These secrets must be protected both at the location of secret storage and during transmission. In this context, endpoints worth protecting must be taken into account in all phases of the DevOps cycle—i.e., throughout the entire lifetime of a secret. Environments worth protecting include the local development environment, automated build, staging, and production environments. With the automation of individual phases in the software development and delivery process, the importance of protecting sensitive data increases. With the introduction of an agile framework, these essential security aspects must be combined with improved security in the form of easily enforceable DevSecOps principles.

Secret rotation and limiting the validity of secrets

A proven protective measure for this is automatic rotation of secrets, complemented by the definition of a time-limited validity of these access mechanisms. Only when a system effectively protects valuable secrets with technical protection mechanisms and agile business processes are in place that implement and live these protection mechanisms can established IT security be spoken of.

In terms of security, the most important improvements that advanced secret management offers are encryption, revocation, rotation, and Identity and Access Management (IAM) of secrets. Rotation and revocation are also an important part of the automation increasingly used in modern software development processes. Integrating the management of secrets with third-party services for proxy access to other platforms and sharing secrets among multiple clients is another use case that can boost a development team's productivity.

Consequently, this security requirement results in the scenario of using a central platform for managing and rotating secrets. Such a secret platform is connected to a role-based user concept that takes into account both internal users of an organization and external users. With the function of a central secret safe, all existing secrets rotate throughout their lifetime, as long as these secrets are valid and grant access as the only existing and central storage for secrets worth protecting. In this secret safe, all secrets required by each individual application are stored, such as database passwords and API keys.

The automation of build processes is architecturally connected to the use of this platform for managing secrets. It is a MUST criterion that the sensitive credentials are not stored in plain text in a version control system like a GitLab or GitHub repository, so access to the credentials must occur from the temporary environments during the runtime of a build process. These practices enable secure, automated builds of software releases at any time. In a containerized architecture, the build automation phase also includes authentication with the secrets management platform, retrieving the secrets, and injecting them into the containers, the so-called "secret injection."

4.3.7 Public Key Infrastructures

A **Public Key Infrastructure (PKI)** is, according to the definitions of NIST, the architecture of an organization with the technology, practice, and procedures that, in combination, support the implementation and operation of a certificate-based cryptographic system with a public key. This includes the framework for issuing, maintaining, and revoking certificates for public keys [19].

As a PKI framework, such an infrastructure encompasses the services responsible for generating, distributing, controlling, and deactivating public key certificates. Such a framework establishes the necessary technical components as well as all required organizational processes to ensure that certificates and keys are used to protect data on a permanent basis, based on defined security policies.

The PKI thus consists of critical infrastructure components with central functions for access control and must be taken into account when implementing an agile large-scale agile framework. Agile processes for this infrastructure must ensure digital certificate management and reliably generate public-private key pairs with technical processes. Service-oriented, digital processes, based on the basic services of digital signature and authentication, ultimately enable critical and indispensable reliable business and security requirements.

The protocol standard already defined in 2004—based on X.509 Public Key Infrastructure (PKI) certificates, as defined in RFC 3280—is designed for use on the Internet [20]. Certificates as trust anchors in the World Wide Web, cryptographic methods for encryption and secure transmission of data are the central subject of IT security measures.

The PKI is also based on the principles of role-based access control and encryption and thus becomes an indispensable tool for platforms, networks, and cloud structures for managing these secrets in need of protection. A PKI simplifies the handling of a large number of clients as a central building block. In addition to the protective function of a protocol-based, encrypted network communication, a PKI adds further security levels and thus enables the overall security of an IT system.

4.3.8   Microservice Architectures

With the ongoing cloud trend, applications designed as microservices are increasing in number and distribution day by day. The evolutionary precursor to microservices is the applications in the form of monoliths. The **monolith** forms an inseparable unit—as a "large whole"—within an IT system. A monolithic architecture does not follow an explicit division into subsystems, the so-called components. This architectural approach of monoliths is in direct contrast to a distributed IT system, which also includes microservices.

Just like their monolithic ancestors, microservice applications must comply with enterprise-wide constraints regarding compliance, security, performance, etc. Authorization, i.e., controlling which individuals and machines are allowed to perform which actions, is a fundamental security issue that requires new solutions in a microservice world, as requirements regarding performance, availability, and even where authorization is architecturally enforced, change fundamentally.

Microservice Definition

Microservitization is a development towards the transformation of services and components into **microservices,** meaning highly fine-grained and autonomous services, in order to isolate previously bundled program functions through functionally limited microservices that then interact via standardized interfaces [21].

Properties of Microservices
- Atomic microservice architecture, i.e.
  - granular services, i.e. minimal service definition,
  - focused on a single task,
  - aligned with a limited context,
  - autonomous,
  - independently deployable,
  - loosely coupled services.

This design pattern connects the underlying software architectures with some fundamental consequences. Microservices require—in contrast to a monolithic architecture—an increased monitoring effort by default, as it is necessary to ensure that the multitude of microservices distributed in different cloud environments communicate with each other and forward corresponding information objects. Microservices thus require appropriate real-time monitoring. This obligation is, at the same time, a valuable advantage in the operation of an IT application, with the additional layer required for monitoring with role-based access control, increasing the complexity of the software architecture.

Basic Recommendations for a Good Microservice Architecture

Taibi and Lenarduzzi have summarized the following practical recommendations for the design of microservice architectures [22, page 2]:

1. To avoid timeouts that cause service requests to be unable to connect to the microservice, timeout values should be used so that calls and potential time overruns due to the unresponsiveness of services are avoided from the outset. With connected monitoring and appropriately defined Service Licence Agreements, the availability of the service must then be restored as quickly as possible.
2. Microservices should share connected modules and software libraries, so that existing dependencies are kept to a minimum.
3. Each microservice API must be versioned, and at the same time, it must be ensured that service consumers do not direct their service requests to outdated API versions.
4. Mega-services, i.e., oversized services that bundle multiple functionalities, should be broken down into individual microservices.
5. Shared persistence, i.e., the shared use of data by multiple microservices, regularly causes problems when parallel data access is not prevented.
6. Data should not be exchanged directly between different microservices; rather, the data flow must always be directed via APIs, and each microservice may only process the data it needs for its limited functionality.
7. The design of service interfaces must follow a higher-level design pattern that reflects all microservices and must not be done separately for each service in a separate manner.
8. Hard-coded IP addresses and ports in microservices can lead to errors and hinder adjustments when the network infrastructure changes, and are contrary to the flexibility of microservices.
9. Services that are directly accessible and connected to each other should not be made accessible via an API gateway layer and should not be directly connected to each other. To simplify the connection of microservices and support the monitoring of individual microservices, authorization issues should always be delegated to the API gateway. The authorization configuration should be managed centrally through changes to the so-called API contract by the API gateway. The API gateway is responsible for providing the content for the various consumers and ensures that only the required data is provided.
10. Easy maintainability and optimal interoperability can be ensured by using current technology standards.
11. The use of too many different communication protocols regularly leads to disruptions that make microservices unusable.
12. Even if individual teams are regularly responsible for individual microservices, this must not result in a team-driven microservice design that dominates the microservice architecture.

13. Microservices must be able to operate independently of each other; otherwise, only the creation of a distributed monolith is achieved.
14. Continuous tests must be established and always aligned with current test cases; under no circumstances should only static tests be aligned with a transient and outdated data world.

Microservices in Relation to the Structure of Agile Teams and Deployed Technologies

From these recommendations, it follows that suitable synchronization processes between teams must ensure that corresponding cross-team definitions exist and are applied. Used technology standards must be known across teams.

Microservices have a direct impact on the structure of agile teams and thus direct relevance for a Large-Scale Agile Framework: Since microservices enable independent deployment, small teams can work on separate and focused microservice services, using the most suitable technologies for their task, which can then be deployed and scaled independently of each other.

An organization-wide error culture must ensure that in the event of errors—which may result, for example, as side effects from one or more microservices, a calm and prudent, mutually constructive error elimination always takes place.

Taibi and Lenarduzzi conclude that by observing the above points, the majority of potential errors can already be avoided from the outset, and the role of software architects in interaction with agile software teams is of great importance.

When breaking down a monolith into microservices, much of the process involves identifying independent business processes that can be isolated from the monolith, not just extracting functions into various web services. The connections between microservices, including connections to private data and shared libraries, must also be carefully analyzed.

4.3.9   APIs, Resources, and Dynamic IP Addresses in Cloud Networks

Application Programming Interface (API) means "interface for application programming". APIs are the elementary building blocks and the countless hubs for data; APIs are also worth protecting in the context of possible cyber-attacks. API gateways provide the appropriate protection mechanisms. An API enables access to endpoints where different services usually grant access to databases in the form of defined database queries. Hardware status and control of graphical user interfaces, for example, the control of apps—the smartphone applications that have become indispensable to us today—are unthinkable without APIs.

An API can be viewed from at least two perspectives:

API from a Code Perspective

An API consists of code, which is why the technical view from the perspective of computer science is inevitable.

API in a Business Context

On the other hand, APIs have a significant impact on every data-based process, shaping the respective processes with the connected business logic, so that an API is usually not only relevant for a single context. Only in the interaction of various agile teams do the relationships relevant to API design become apparent, which then result in the technical implementation. With the realization of microservices, APIs become slimmer, are easy to read, and can be used quickly and versatilely with the correct implementation.

The second part of the book presents tools and methodology for creating an appropriate agile API documentation.

4.3.10 APIs and REST

In the context of cloud architectures and/or microservices, REST plays an important role. Roy Fielding coined this "Representational State Transfer architectural style", or REST, in his dissertation as a hybrid architectural style that derives from several network-based architectural styles and combines them with additional constraints that define a uniform HTTP protocol-based web interface [23]:

REST Constraints
- Client Server
- Statelessness
- Cacheable
- Uniform interface
- Layered systems
- Code on demand

Protected Resources and API Design

APIs are therefore always about uniformly defined interfaces for exchanging data and protecting resources. Protection mechanisms must be designed in such a way that only protected access via web technologies using exposed **Uniform Resource Identifier (URI)** is possible for exclusively authorized requests.

Within an agile organization, there is not only a widespread understanding and security awareness that resources are fundamentally trustworthy and worth protecting, but also a set of rules in the form of a role-based authorization concept. The information about who can access the resource when and under what conditions defines processes that always involve a large number of different stakeholders and ultimately result in the API design.

4.3.11 Quality Characteristics of Microservices and Web APIs

For Web APIs and microservices, certain quality characteristics have emerged that are crucial for a good microservice architecture, these are:

1. **Reusability** and
2. **Flexibility**

The reusability is in turn positively reflected in optimal usability. The usability and requirements for ergonomics of human-system interaction are defined according to Part 11 of DIN EN ISO 9241-11 [24].

In concrete terms, this means: Only if an API is easy to use or learn and can simultaneously meet the defined requirements for mapping the required use cases as a service consumer, does this microservice actually provide a real added value to an organization.

Interoperability as an Essential Quality Feature

Interoperability is an essential quality feature for software components, such as microservices and specified API interfaces, to fit together, i.e., to be interoperable with each other in terms of data exchange. Interoperability must consider any changes due to new requirements or possibly necessary error corrections. This can have negative consequences for service consumers and thus worsen interoperability. Therefore, this should already be taken into account within a DevOps strategy through agile software/service release management; Git repositories play a central role in this.

Mutual Features for Interoperability

Figure 4.7 shows the mutual "quality features for interoperability and their impact on the reusability of software artifacts".

Table 4.3 "Quality features for interoperability and their impact on reusability" explains the individual quality features of software and distinguishes their significance in the context of interoperability and reusability of software artifacts from each other.

The mutual relationships underline the importance of cross-team communication and corresponding quality assurance measures. Using (partially) automatable deployments and testing procedures, concrete quality characteristics can be defined step by step and applied as test criteria.

4.3.12 RESTful API

Regarding definitions for RESTful API design, properties are defined that play an important role in the architectural pattern of REST APIs. Even though these requirements alone do not yet represent a microservice implementation, they already form the essential foundations for it:

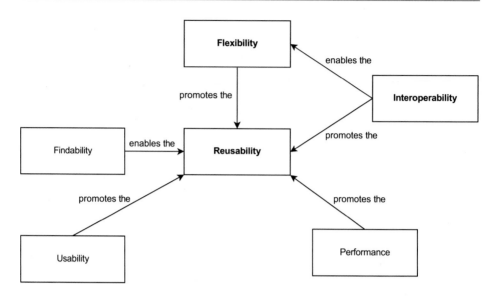

Fig. 4.7 Quality features for interoperability and their impact on the reusability of software artifacts—Sascha Block

Table 4.3 Quality features for interoperability and their impact on reusability

Feature	Requirement
Discoverability	• provided, machine-interpretable documentation A machine-interpretable documentation with **defined syntax and semantics** is crucial for easy discoverability of an API. Only in this way can the functionality offered by an API or a microservice be effectively used. An API developer portal with documentation aimed at software developers is highly recommended. In addition, additional semantic technologies and languages can be used, such as **Resource Description Framework (RDF),** see W3C specification [25]. **RDF is a standard model for data exchange on the web.** RDF has features that facilitate the merging of data, even if the underlying schemas differ, and it particularly supports the development of schemas over time without having to change all data consumers. • Compliance with naming conventions
Interoperability	Unlike the usability of a web API, interoperability focuses on the technical perspective and thus the integrability by service consumers. A web API should ideally not impose any requirements on the technologies used by the service consumer. In addition, when changes are made to the web API due to internal or external factors, care must be taken to ensure that existing service consumers can continue to interact with it without compromising interoperability. • Stability in focus over time • Evaluation of technologies in terms of lifecycle, simplicity, proven effectiveness, etc.

(continued)

Table 4.3   (continued)

Feature	Requirement
Performance	• efficient resource utilization • Abstraction of application-related requirements (functionality from the perspective of users, the insured)
Usability	• use proven methods • adherence to naming conventions *By adhering to established conventions for naming resources, representations, and Uniform Resource Identifiers (URIs), consistency increases, which has a positive effect on usability and findability. Consistency in software development is reflected in the simplicity with which an API can be derived. This makes APIs easy to learn and quickly usable. Higher consistency also reduces the documentation effort for an API.* • reference to the represented domain • meaningful feedback on errors • presence of up-to-date documentation for software developers The documentation of an API contains both information on its use and meta-information, such as the name and all attributes used in the API, as well as an introductory description text that explains the context of use. The documentation must also focus on the description of the correct API usage, significantly increasing understanding and preventing potential errors in API usage in advance, including defined preconditions. Three types of documentation specifically for software development can be distinguished: 1. reference documentation 2. workflows 3. tutorials • meaningful feedback on errors Errors in the use of an API can never be fundamentally excluded, but can only be reduced with the help of provided information on usage. However, errors in web APIs, unlike in the case of more easily testable local APIs, cannot be analyzed using a debugger or similar methods, since the underlying implementation is not under one's own control and usually cannot be viewed. **Therefore, the analyzability of any errors through meaningful feedback from the service is an important quality aspect.** The error analysis focuses on the analysis possibilities of the service consumer, with the help of which they can find and possibly fix the cause of the error without communication with the service provider, provided the error does not originate from the service provider. For this purpose, **meaningful error codes must be defined by all parties involved—including third parties.** From the perspective of IT security, it is worth considering which details are communicated externally, as every API naturally always represents an interesting attack vector for potential attackers… However, this must not be understood as an excuse for saving meaningful error messages, but requires the additional effort to define how error messages are communicated in different directions. If users can only report errors in the sense of a 404 classification, error search and elimination are significantly more difficult. If the same users report an X53B error with a limitation of an internally classified component, this will only have a positive effect on their service quality!

Table 4.4 REST definitions resource and representation

Term	Definition
Resource	A resource is a **uniquely addressable and conceptual assignment to one or more entities,** not depending on the time of instantiation. An entity can basically be anything with which a service consumer wants to interact, see RFC2396 [26].
Representation	A representation is a **state description of a resource that does not require a specific data format.**

- Design of RESTful APIs that follow defined design paradigms,
- distributed services, i.e., distributed services within a (cloud) service network,
- not every service within this service network necessarily has to be a microservice.

Table 4.4 "REST definitions resource and representation" explains the computer science-related distinction between resource and representation and at the same time illustrates the role of services/microservices as consumers of data.

Boundary conditions for uniform REST APIs

An architectural style always defines corresponding boundary conditions (constraints) for architectural elements in order to achieve certain system properties, such as easy extensibility or scalability. The following boundary conditions have been established for RESTful APIs:

Table 4.5 "Requirements for RESTful API Design" lists the four requirements for the compliant implementation of a REST API with their respective boundary conditions.

REST Layer Model with Reference to RESTful Services

Each REST API can be classified into four different technical layers. Figure 4.8 "Hierarchical Layers REST API" illustrates the individual layers in which REST APIs encapsulate corresponding functionalities.

Each level has specific properties of REST, while the levels below are each a subset of the upper levels.

Table 4.6 "Layer model of REST APIs" explains the different architecture layers of an API in the corresponding level classification.

Specification of resource-oriented web APIs

For the specification of resource-oriented web APIs, various specification languages now exist, such as Web Application Description Language (WADL), OpenAPI (originally Swagger), RESTful API Modeling Language (RAML), or API Blueprint.

Table 4.5 Requirements for RESTful API Design

Requirement	Boundary Conditions
1. Identification of Resources	• is done by **at least one URI,** i.e., by means of a compact **string for identifying an abstract or physical resource** A URI consists of a scheme and a scheme-specific structure, with the scheme determining how the scheme-specific structure is constructed and interpreted [26]. To find out whether multiple URIs address the same resource, however, further domain-specific knowledge is required, which is why a fundamentally solid documentation is referred to again at this point
2. Manipulation of Resources through Representations	Once a resource is identified, **interaction with the resource** is possible. To manipulate the state of a resource, the service user transmits the desired state using a representation to the resource, which receives this representation and then changes its own state In principle, multiple representations can exist for a resource, for example, to map different use cases
3. Self-Descriptive Messages	All necessary information for understanding the response or request should be contained in the message itself or at least somehow linked to it. A message is defined in this case by the message header with any **meta-information** and the **message body with a corresponding representation**
4. Hypermedia as Engine of Application State	Hypermedia as Engine of Application State (HATEOAS) is a component of the REST application architecture that distinguishes it from other network application architectures. With HATEOAS, a client interacts with a network application whose application server provides information dynamically via hypermedia Standardized REST definitions enable a software design that is durable and promotes independent development of the software

4.3.13 Conclusion and Relevance of APIs in the Context of Large-Scale Agile Frameworks

APIs play a special role in microservice architecture, as the functional scope of individual APIs—according to the previously defined criteria—is significantly more granular than in monoliths or other architectural patterns.

This results in—which must also be taken into account within an agile framework—a significantly increased number of APIs and increased administrative effort in API management.

Frontend-oriented service approach…

The more APIs are understood from the perspective of a frontend-oriented service approach, the greater the benefit to users and thus to your organization. Consequently, APIs are increasingly bundled as products and supplemented with a product owner

Fig. 4.8 Hierarchical Layers
REST API

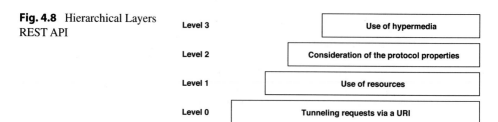

REST Level	Explanation

Table 4.6 Layer model of REST APIs

REST Level	Explanation
Level 0	At level 0, the **services are classified** that have only one URI and where the entire interaction is controlled via the message body of the corresponding application layer protocol. Well-known examples are services according to the WS* specifications using Simple Object Access Protocol (SOAP) with HTTP. All requests are defined in Web Service Description Language (WSDL) and instantiated in the form of Extensible Markup Language (XML) in the message body
Level 1	Based on level 0, at level 1 the **URI is divided into several URIs and the concept of resources is introduced** Each URI thus refers to a resource, which then serves as an endpoint for interaction
Level 2	With level 2, the **correct use of the application layer protocol** is finally focused. For example, only idempotent (in computer science, a piece of program code that produces the same result when executed multiple times in a row as when executed once is called idempotent) and **side-effect-free methods** should be used for a read operation, e.g., the GET method in HTTP Level 2 thus plays an essential role in error analysis
Level 3	The third and final level 3 requires the use of hypermedia. Then, hyperlinks between resources should be used for navigation, and all the semantics necessary for interpreting the resources and hyperlinks should be contained in the representations of the resources. Only if the service considers and uses the principles of hypermedia can and should it be called a **RESTful Service**

assignment, ensuring that APIs always provide basic business functions for frontend-oriented service operations.

…for a wide range of heterogeneous devices
Since the provision of APIs is now regularly carried out for a wide range of different devices, it is all the more important to consistently observe the framework conditions outlined above. With a multitude of highly heterogeneous frontends such as millions of IoT devices and a sheer variety of countless smartphone devices and different operating system environments, user expectations and the level of complexity continue to rise. A large-scale agile framework can only meet this challenge if it provides effective mechanisms for the efficient merging and aggregation of these properties.

Because APIs are such important and central building blocks in any IT architecture for the reasons described, it is particularly important within the context of a large-scale agile framework to establish mechanisms that ensure a large number of agile teams can work on different APIs in parallel. It is crucial to establish standards at a higher level and to communicate them permanently between the involved agile teams.

4.3.14 Service Mesh & Agile Microservice Architectures

As soon as we follow a microservice architecture and use a multitude of different API endpoints to expose countless services to various user groups via internet technologies, the design pattern of the service mesh is suitable for implementation.

Using a Service Mesh to Implement a Zero-Trust Strategy
In terms of IT security, the architectural pattern of the service mesh also offers certain advantages, as the security-relevant aspects of the zero-trust principle can be implemented particularly well and at the same time all the advantages of cloud services come into play.

With the cloud trend and hybrid cloud scenarios, IT systems are no longer limited to fixed IP addresses, but transform into dynamic networks with constantly changing, dynamic IP addresses. From a technical perspective, this presents various challenges with implications for emergency scenarios, network management, and IT security.

Therefore, effective processes are needed to ensure that IP addresses and endpoints worth protecting are secured and monitored at all times.

A service mesh is a very young design pattern that is suitable for solving exactly these challenges for Platform as a Service (PaaS) and cloud architectures.

Reusability of Required Basic Functionality
With a service mesh, service outsourcing takes place in such a way that required basic functionalities do not have to be reinvented, implemented, and configured again and again, and also not with different technologies, but rather a comprehensive configuration is available for all services.

Above all, the network management for all incoming or outgoing requests from any services:

- **both internal network requests,** of the internal services we consume,
- **as well as external network requests,** i.e., those services we provide externally.

With each application that is not part of the process, a new proxy configuration is also required, which manages each individual incoming and outgoing network request for us. Since it lives outside the service, the proxy configuration is thus by default portable and agnostic, and can therefore support any service that is compatible with the provided language or the framework of the service mesh itself.

Service-Oriented Architectures with Direct Reference to Agile Organizational Forms

The IT security-relevant aspects of the zero-trust principle can be systematically implemented with this architectural pattern and help to design small-scale, service-oriented APIs at the same time. In the course of IT security-relevant requirements, there are often various misunderstandings between the agile teams involved, especially the further away they are from technical IT security topics. The efforts to design fine-grained authorization concepts and carefully defined group rights have direct effects on data protection aspects, IT security, organizational and technical cuts that go beyond the architectural design. A close orientation along defined user stories and customer journeys is just as important as reflecting this seemingly more technical aspect in the agile framework that your organization has established. Connected support processes, for example, require defined visibility that is oriented on the one hand towards legal requirements, but on the other hand is suitable for covering effective support routes in various directions. The later these effects are considered within an organization, the more complex the implementations for covering these requirements will be.

4.3.15 Improving IT Security Based on OWASP Guidelines

The Open Web Application Security Project—or OWASP Foundation for short—is a community that works to improve the security of software through numerous open-source software projects, events, and guidelines. The OWASP regularly publishes and updates its Top 10 lists of currently threatening security risks to raise awareness among IT managers and software developers about security.

The OWASP Top 10 for web applications represents a broad consensus on the most important security risks for web applications. Insecure design was a newly defined security category in 2021, focusing on risks associated with design flaws. Security-by-design is to be established through increased attention to real threat models, the use of secure design patterns, the establishment of IT security standards in architectural design, and the application of reference architectures [27].

Are you already using established security standards for mobile applications and a comprehensive testing guide to align organization-wide processes, techniques, and tools with the security testing of mobile applications? Have you defined comprehensive sets of test cases for your software and apply them regularly to ensure reliable, consistent, and complete results for increasing your IT security?

Benefit from the free IT security knowledge of the OWASP community and establish guidelines such as the OWASP Mobile Security Testing Guide [28] in your agile software development processes.

4.3.16 Penetration Testing/Pentesting

In contrast, there is the approach of classical pentesting, in which IT security is analyzed according to predefined security criteria. Penetration tests involve a controlled attack on a predefined environment, such as software, an app, or a network, to assess its security. The results of such pentests are evaluations with detailed test results in the form of explanations and reports with recommendations for action for the test object, which was analyzed and evaluated at a specific point in time.

The German IT industry association bitkom explicitly welcomes in its position paper on the proposal for a regulation on digital resilience for the financial sector (DORA) that *"testing methods" such as "penetration tests" and "red team" tests" are provided for in the proposal. The proposal states: "The competent authorities shall identify the financial institutions that are to carry out threat-based penetration tests in a manner that is appropriate to the size, activity, and overall risk profile of the financial institution and the scope of these tests."* [29, pages 2/3].

Traditionally, pentesting often takes place at a later stage and serves as a demonstrable seal of quality in many organizations. Undoubtedly, pentesting is a useful protective measure, but it offers no guarantees that software solutions are permanently or currently secure, which requires agile mechanisms. A possible agile solution approach that takes this into account in the sense of IT-Security-by-Design is presented in a separate section and within the agile prioritization model for software manufacturers.

Nevertheless, the static and purely time-based pentesting, which is often carried out with the motivation to obtain a security certificate, currently still accounts for a significant proportion of the **security checks** taking place. In the course of increasingly frequent attacks on **security vulnerabilities such as the recent log4j** [30], IT security cannot and must not be limited to occasional pentests.

The Federal Office for Information Security (BSI) has assessed the vulnerability in the Java library Log4j as extremely critical and, as a result, published a cyber security warning at the red warning level [31].

The preparation and typical procedure of a pentest is explained in a separate section in this chapter.

Pentesting aims to identify vulnerabilities in IT systems and processes, assess the associated risks, and initiate appropriate countermeasures. In contrast to Vulnerability Scans, the results of a pentest are much more detailed and, due to manual work, more extensive and precise in the outcome of the vulnerability analysis.

Possible starting points and scenarios for effective pentests:

- Simulation of a stolen company laptop for privileged access to the corporate network
- missing hard disk encryption?
- unsecured passwords/password safes?
- two-factor authentication?

Continuous pentests are essential to ensure effective IT security; using tools and methods of real attackers, internal and external pentesters analyze vulnerabilities under realistic conditions.

Objectives of a penetration test
- Demonstration of the vulnerability of IT systems/inventory (status analysis)
- Optimization of IT security
- Prioritization of protection mechanisms
- Testing of reaction mechanisms
- Penetration tests for compliance reasons
- Reduction of the costs of a vulnerability management program

Phases of a penetration test
Phase 1—Preparation
Phase 2—Information gathering and evaluation
Phase 3—Assessment of information/risk analysis
Phase 4—Active intrusion attempts
Phase 5—Final analysis

It should be taken into account that the phases of a pentest do not strictly follow a linear sequence, but rather individual events from the respective phases merge into events of the other phases. This is precisely why it makes sense to integrate these phases into the security phases of a Large Agile Framework as well.

Phase 1—Preparation of a pentest
- Determination of objectives
- Definition of target systems
- Definition of approach
- For external pentesters: Contractual agreement between the company and pentest

In particular, the following questions need to be clarified:

- Which test tools, malware, botkits, etc. are permissible?
- Are Denial-of-Service (DoS) attacks allowed? Are internal company processes defined in response to DoS attacks, and are employees trained and authorized to make decisions accordingly?

- Does the testing procedure allow for the physical or digital destruction of IT systems and thus test the effectiveness and efficiency of backup procedures?
- Are social engineering methods included in the pentest, and how extensive are they? (Is extortion, lying, or illegal entry into the company allowed to test the effectiveness of security measures?)
- Who contacts the cloud provider (deputy regulation!) and registers the test there should also be part of the contract.
- For cloud tests: Is the consent of the cloud provider available? (required!)

Phase 2—Information gathering and evaluation
- Information gathering within the company and from third parties
- Use of scanning tools such as port and vulnerability scanners
- Development of an overview and documentation of system and software architecture
- Use of Metasploit scanning and auxiliary modules

Important: The more knowledge the pentester has about organizational structures, employees, and IT systems of the company, the greater the likelihood of uncovering security gaps.

Phase 3—Evaluation of information/risk analysis
- each evaluation is based on the criteria defined in Phase 1
- Consultation and coordination with system managers

Phase 4—Active intrusion attempts
- active use of identified vulnerabilities
- Damage assessment and evaluation
- Use of exploit code with stress tests for systems

Phase 5—Final analysis
- Documentation of findings and uncovered security gaps
- Recommendations for action to eliminate uncovered security gaps
- if necessary, divided into management and IT reports with technical details

For pentests of cloud environments, it is particularly the side paths and almost never the direct attack on the cloud infrastructure that reveal security gaps.

Variety of mobile devices and IoT devices
With the steady increase in numerous mobile devices and countless IoT devices and their practical use in service-oriented scenarios, networked connectivity goes hand in hand, and vulnerability to attacks increases rapidly.

It is clear: The importance of IT security continues to increase and is already indispensable. So how can we improve the quality of software, optimize functionality, and at the same time take security aspects into account?

4.3.17 Recommendations for integrating IT security as a fixed component in an agile framework

IT security must therefore be an integral part of every software architecture and its agile model. All agile teams must understand the integral software architecture aspects in context and their impact. In this way, all stakeholders actively take into account the associated requirements of a comprehensive IT security strategy and ensure that these requirements are taken into account early on in all software-based processes and connected organizational workflows.

> *"IT security is the control and quality seal of digitization and should be included in the pricing of digital products and services for every company from the outset."*

Improve software quality and reduce costs
Under these conditions, a positive side effect can be automatically achieved: The quality of software increases and costs for IT and software are significantly lower because aspects relevant to IT security are taken into account directly during development. Both goals are much easier to achieve if these requirements are firmly anchored in the software architecture through IT security-by-design and incorporated using agile prototyping.

Resolve legal framework conditions and IT security using agile prototyping
Legal framework conditions—such as software-side regulations in favor of tightened data protection, which in turn are accompanied by increased IT security—can also be directly implemented using agile prototyping.

Especially now in the age of digitization and due to the Corona pandemic, this is painfully apparent. Where digitization projects are initiated with great effort, teams from different organizations regularly come together. Communication about software architecture plays a central role here, as it is at the heart of creating every digital solution.

Specifically improve communication within and between agile teams
How is it that numerous software projects do not achieve the desired progress or even fail completely? A major factor in this is poor communication. Each of us has experienced this at some point. The reasons for this are regularly diverse. In the worst case, communication is completely omitted and important information does not even flow into the solution process.

Fig. 4.9 Software library as the Achilles heel of a digital infrastructure. (Source: Sascha Block)

But even if parties from different teams blindly trust each other and the exchange of information about software architecture is lacking or insufficient, problems are pre-programmed that stand in the way of successful digitization.

Figure 4.9 "Software library as the Achilles heel of a digital infrastructure" caricatures such a fragile architecture: The symbolically depicted existential dependence on a single software library represents an enormous risk, especially if this library is not under one's own control and must therefore be understood as the Achilles heel of such a digital infrastructure.

In this context, a solid software architecture documentation and targeted communication about the software architecture are at the center, as they form the basis for designing and implementing software solutions. This is an extremely important point, as the software architecture is relevant beyond organizational boundaries, especially when external parties are involved in the implementation of digital strategies. All too often, however, the truly important facts remain undocumented, are not communicated at all or inadequately, but continue to play a central role in the architecture of complex software solutions, completely unimpressed by this.

Pragmatic architecture documentation with collaboration tools and Git repositories
The good news is that agile frameworks with their mechanisms are particularly suitable for breaking up these paradigms and achieving demonstrable results in improving communication. The agile approach offers effective mechanisms to dissolve mistrust and

fears and to strengthen mutual trust in communication in all directions. These are crucial factors when it comes to ensuring functioning communication—also about the software architecture. The architecture of software and its documentation regularly has far-reaching effects. The relevance of software architecture documentation extends far beyond the teams directly involved in software development. Support processes, organization-wide quality management, and communication with customers and partners are equally affected.

An example of what such software architecture documentation can look like with the collaboration tool Atlassian Confluence is shown in Fig. 4.10 "Software architecture documentation with the collaboration tool Atlassian Confluence".

Pragmatic architecture documentation becomes manageable through the use of various tools such as collaboration tools, which also act as versioning tools, as well as technical code and deployment documentation based on code versioning tools, primarily Git repositories. It is essential to always establish the cross-connections, which often have a significant positive influence on cross-team communication of various stakeholders, e.g., in the form of links. Only if easy access to information is guaranteed for all participants, can quality goals and "informative satisfaction" be realized across teams. We will introduce you to these agile tools, the methodology, and the necessary infrastructure in the second part of the book.

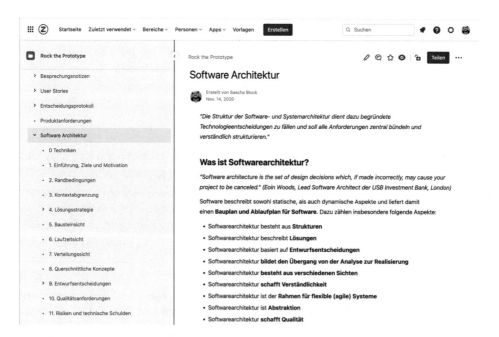

Fig. 4.10 Software architecture documentation with the collaboration tool Atlassian Confluence. (Source: Sascha Block)

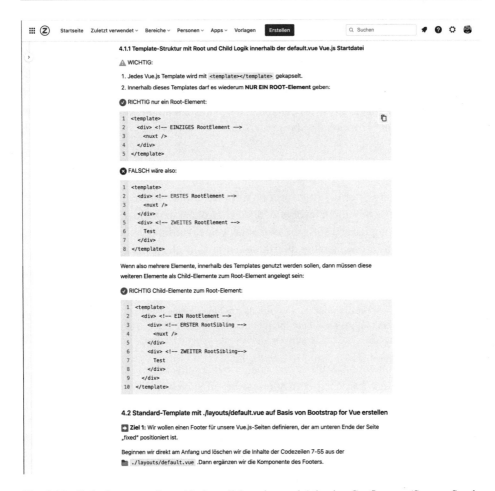

Fig. 4.11 Code documentation with the collaboration tool Atlassian Confluence. (Source: Sascha Block)

Confluence is now also well-suited for documenting code, as illustrated in Fig. 4.11 "Code documentation with the collaboration tool Atlassian Confluence".

Many projects lack meaningful, visualized architecture artifacts
Are all these artifacts well documented and graphically visualized in your projects? A well-designed and formally correct overview diagram and precise flowcharts usually have more expressive power than countless words and numerous meetings.

Are your teams trained in the routine creation of these invaluable artifacts? Is the necessary time frame and importance given to architecture documentation, and is there a functioning interaction within prototyping and is all this connected to a threat model-based pentesting?

Step by Step to the Detailing of Software Architecture Artifacts

Clear recommendation: Start with simple representations and develop these representations step by step through an increasingly refined and detailed process. With this approach, you will obtain different representations that are practically useful for different recipients and purposes due to their varying levels of detail.

In Sect. 7.5 "Pragmatic Software Architecture Documentation" in the second part of the book, we present corresponding best practices.

Living a Culture of Error—Eliminating Fears, Mistrust, and Lack of Communication

Live a healthy culture of error! Any form of software is fundamentally not error-free by default, but requires a minimum level of defined control and protection mechanisms.

The more technologies and software components are interlinked, the greater the likelihood that IT systems are vulnerable. For these reasons, mechanisms are needed to firmly anchor IT security in an agile framework.

> *"IT security must be an integral part of your agile model!"* It is essential that you protect your software and especially your data as best as possible against potential attackers. Access to data and documents must also meet the requirements of data protection and data security in the digital world, even over long periods and across system changes.

Even if error-free operation is the actual goal, we can only achieve it step by step. The goal of error-free and hardened software can be effectively achieved through testing, testing, and more testing. Different testing methods and methodology complement each other in this process.

The prototypical approach in an agile model supports the IT security-by-design approach and ultimately realizes a healthy culture of error in the close collaboration of all agile teams and towards hardened software.

In the agile interplay of software teams with software architects and IT security teams, regular tests support fast release cycles as well as functioning, good communication between the teams. Specialized IT security teams effectively complement this with their security-oriented mindset and forensic methodology. No team should have to evaluate its own work quality, but always another team. A healthy culture of error increases effectiveness as well as smooth communication, and well-documented software artifacts are part of the whole.

Establish Agile Mechanisms Based on Defined Security Rules

In order for you and your organization to benefit from the effectiveness of these technical possibilities of a *Secret Management Solution,* you must align agile mechanisms based on defined security rules in parallel with the protection measures technically configured in the IT systems and establish these processes with and among all stakeholders. This includes appropriate awareness training at all organizational levels. This is not an easy task, especially since this is a protection mechanism that you must regularly train and repeat. Only if "fire protection measures" are well known AND effective firefighting tools are available to trained employees at all times, can fires be effectively fought or not occur at all. You should always keep this image in mind when dealing with IT security in your organization.

1. Maximum Security from the Start: Data Protection & IT Security Already with the Definition of Requirements
IT security and data protection can be integrated into the early stages of the DevOps processes, and not just at the very end of the **Software Delivery Pipeline.**

IT security—including the requirements for data protection, with the integral demands of integrity and confidentiality—are thus already part of our quality requirements and are implemented as early as possible and then verified in the form of tests with the results (meeting the requirements OR insufficient: must be improved immediately). In this form, tests are carried out iteratively, i.e., regularly repeated and then firmly established as part of the software development/delivery process.

Just as continuous integration of software enables a "left shift" by accelerating test and feedback loops to discover errors earlier in the process and improve software quality, DevOps processes can include automated security tests and compliance.

2. Automate IT security in your processes
With increasing automation of tests and processes, there is a lower risk of introducing security flaws due to time constraints or human error. Automated tests are more efficient and cover more areas at a higher frequency. IT processes thus become more consistent and predictable. If a defect occurs, it is easier to locate and fix more quickly through automated error messages.

3. Establish continuous integration through IT security tools
By using security tools, particularly with an end-to-end automation platform and DevOps tools that encompass development, deployment, integration, testing, operation, and security, we gain transparency and control over the entire development cycle of systems. Increased IT security can be achieved through automated pipelines in the stages of development, testing, and operation by creating a closed process for testing and monitoring with corresponding IT security status reports that gradually encompass more and more systems and data flows.

4. Close security gaps immediately!
Security breaches or vulnerabilities can never be 100% ruled out; the crucial factor is a rapid response capability to solve the problem immediately. SecDevOps reduces the lead time to a minimum so that patches and updates can be developed, tested, and deployed more quickly. In addition, meticulous tracking of error configurations with DevOps tools significantly simplifies and accelerates the state of all monitored applications, environments, and pipeline stages.

If the exact version status of an application with all components in its environment is known and even provided in a containerized form, it is also possible to quickly determine the component of the application that needs the update, identify the instances that require attention, and roll out updates in a faster, more consistent, and repeatable deployment process. The majority of the workflows required for this are automatable.

5. Make Compliance & IT-Governance transparent and easily understandable for everyone
It is essential to enable everyone in the company, not just the IT department, to ensure requirements, compliance, and IT governance. DevOps focuses on streamlining processes throughout the entire pipeline to ensure consistent development, testing, and release practices. DevOps tools and automation can be configured to empower developers to be self-sufficient and "get their work done" while simultaneously ensuring access controls and compliance automatically. As a solution to the growing "shadow IT" phenomenon, many organizations use an internal DevOps service to provide appropriate development and testing environments with shared repositories, workflows, deployment processes, etc. This allows each involved agile team on-demand access to the appropriate infrastructure (including production) while access control, security measures, release points, and configuration parameters are automatically anchored centrally to avoid configuration drift or inconsistent processes. Furthermore, it ensures that all instances in all environments, whether development, quality assurance, or production, are identified and tracked and that they operate within predefined guidelines and can be monitored and managed by the responsible teams.

6. Design Source Code & IT Systems to be revision-proof
Both the source code and the respective system environments must be considered in a security concept. By creating manageable systems that are consistent, traceable, and reproducible—i.e., revertible to an initial state—it can be proven who has access and who made which changes when.

7. Monitoring & easy generation of status reports
Monitoring with easy-to-generate status reports is essential for evaluating and monitoring the security status. To achieve this, automated processes must be established, which also ensure the additional advantage of consistency and availability at any time.

Predictable events should—connected to the threat model—deliver results in the form of occurring actions, notifications, info state, and test outcomes. In this way, the security process is automatically logged and documented for security audits.

Ideally, DevOps extends across the entire pipeline, ensuring traceability from code changes to release. Automating build, test, integration, deployment, and release processes allows access to a wealth of diverse information that can be used for various purposes in very detailed logging. This simplifies auditing, enables various security protocols and compliance reports, all of which can be created on-demand and fully automatically.

8. SecDevOps enables higher IT security and adaptable services towards customers
SecDevOps allows organizations to achieve speed in establishing and adapting services without compromising stability and governance. Security and compliance controls are an integral part of DevOps processes and include requirements for data protection and IT security. By successively implementing DevOps processes that incorporate best practices and recommendations from BSI and OWASP for IT security from the outset, an effective and adaptable security layer for applications and environments is established. The gradual expansion of SecDevOps measures ensures the best possible security and governance in the long term, in a rational, efficient, and proactive manner.

9. Establish Threat Modeling to effectively counter threats!
The most effective method to ward off threats is to proactively identify, assess, and counter these recognized threats with the available resources before they occur. The next section details how this can be achieved.

4.3.18   Threat Modeling

A **Threat Model** represents both technical risks and potential threats as well as business risks in IT systems. Through the case-specific and thus targeted user-oriented perspective, the modeling of different threats and risks (Threat Modeling) represents a particularly effective form of risk identification, risk classification, and risk assessment. Ultimately, the Threat Model is an indispensable basis for risk analyses, penetration tests, and any other type of internal security analysis within the scope of IT compliance.

Protection Objectives
Various protection objectives are distinguished for IT security, which abstractly describe the security goals pursued in a process, system, or similar. A system can also demand the guarantee of several protection objectives. Table 4.7 "Classification of IT-Security Protection Objectives" explains the background and purpose of each protection objective to effectively anchor IT security in organizations.

The protection objectives listed above must be ensured across all components and also in cloud environments or when using third-party solutions, and must be designed in compliance with GDPR. In this context, the operator of an IT system is responsible for providing evidence of meeting these protection objectives. However, what is even more important nowadays is that you earn the trust of your users with your digital services and communicate trustworthily who stores and uses which data when, where, and how. In the coming years, there will be an increasing trend for these rights to be enforced on the consumer side. These rights have been demanded by users for a long time; therefore, those who have already aligned their IT services with these customer-centric needs are acting more foresightedly and wisely.

Table 4.7 Classification of IT Security Objectives

Protection Objective	Explanation
Confidentiality	The protection objective of confidentiality (engl. confidentiality) is ensured when an unauthorized subject cannot access the information to be protected. To ensure this protection objective, a system or data transmission must ensure that the information to be protected does not leak out. This protection objective is often implemented through *access rights,* so that unauthorized persons do not receive read rights for an object. For data transmissions, *encryption* is a suitable method to achieve this protection objective.
Availability	For the protection objective of availability (engl. availability), it must be ensured that a request for information or a service by an authorized subject can be served within an acceptable time. To ensure this protection objective, sufficient resources such as computing time and storage must be provided and control over these resources must be protected to prevent impairment.
Integrity	To ensure the protection objective of integrity (engl. integrity), the data to be protected must be protected against unauthorized and unnoticed manipulation. For locally stored data, this protection objective can be achieved by restricting write access for unauthorized subjects. For data transfer over an insecure network such as the Internet, manipulation can only be prevented by increased security mechanisms. For example, *cryptographic hash values* ensure that manipulation of the data is detected by the recipient, so that the manipulated data is not further processed.
Authenticity	For the protection objective of authenticity (engl. authenticity), the **identity** of a subject must be **ensured.** This means that the subject must prove that it is what it claims to be. This is done in an *authentication process,* in which, for example, a user authenticates themselves to a system using knowledge (knowledge of a password), possession (chip card, digital certificate), or biometric properties (fingerprint, iris features). For data transmissions, this protection objective must additionally ensure that the transmitted data has been "freshly" generated and is not a replay of an old message.
Non-manipulable	The protection objective of being non-manipulable (often also referred to as binding or non-repudiation and in Engl. Nonrepudiation) ensures that actions that have been executed on a system cannot be denied afterwards by the subject who performed these actions (traceability of transactions). This protection objective is particularly relevant for all business-related transactions or in connection with data protection. Digital signatures, for example, can be used to achieve this.

Thinking through risks and threats using questions and scenarios
When considering IT risks and potential threats, it is useful to ask questions like the following:

- How can an attacker change the authentication data?
- What is the impact if an attacker can read the user profile data?
- What happens if access to the user profile database is denied?

Threat Modeling Activities
Each threat modeling process is based on a structured approach that is divided into the following activities:

- **Identification** and **Modeling** of risks and threats as a "Use-Case",
- **Classification** of the risk/threat,
- **Assessment** of the risk/threat in terms of the extent of damage in the event of an incident,
- **Deriving recommendations for measures** to eliminate or reduce risk,
- **Monitoring the implementation,**
- **Continuous optimization.**

Threat Model as a Jira Board
The entire threat modeling process is—for example, within a current app project focusing solely on native app development, specifically related to a developed iOS app and/or Android app—represented in the form of a **Jira Board as a Threat Model.**

The logic of such a Jira board threat model with the individual processes can be designed as follows:

1. Each risk is recorded as a Jira ticket, **issue type Threat.**
2. In the **summary,** the risk is briefly and easily understandable, e.g., "weak certificate signatures".
3. The risk is specified with **the description.**
4. The **priority** (lowest, low, high, highest) indicates the urgency to eliminate the risk. Since the priority is often not assessable in advance, the specification is not defined as a mandatory field.

Risk groups in a threat model
The risk groups correlate with the protection objectives but are presented here as a threat, i.e., a specified risk.

The IT security framework presented by Bryant and Saiedian has proven effective in identifying IT security alerts in relation to expected behaviors that are conducive to conducting security investigations in a methodical manner [32].

In Table 4.8 "Classification of IT-Security Risk Groups," the different risks according to the STRIDE classification [33] are explained, which were reflected and expanded by the BSI in a security profile for a SaaS collaboration platform [34].

With the use of cloud or equally exposed APIs, the security architecture in the context of cloud management must be considered. It is important to note that with the individual layers of a cloud-based security architecture, the security services of the cloud provider also become the responsibility of the organization. Therefore, manipulation and privilege escalation are particularly important. The STRIDE classification is suitable for effectively detecting classified attack patterns and initiating appropriate countermeasures without delay. With protection and countermeasures linked to this classification, almost all attack patterns for the access and delivery layers can be covered, as cloud access

Table 4.8 Classification of IT-Security Risk Groups

Risk Group	Explanation
Spoofing identity	An example of identity forgery is the illegal access to and use of another user's authentication information, such as username and password
Tampering with data	Data tampering means the malicious alteration of data. Examples include unauthorized changes to persistent data, such as those stored in a database, and the alteration of data flowing between two computers over an open network, such as the Internet
Repudiation	Repudiation threats are actions that deny users the execution of an action without other parties having a way to prove it otherwise—for example, a user performs an illegal operation in a system that lacks the ability to track the prohibited operations Nonrepudiation, i.e., undeniable, refers to a system's ability to counter repudiation threats
Information disclosure	Information disclosure threats involve the disclosure of information to individuals who should not have access to it—for example, the ability of users to read a file to which they have not been granted access, or the ability of an intruder to read data on the transmission between two computers
Denial of service (DoS)	Denial-of-service (DoS) attacks deny service to valid users by making the service—usually a web server—temporarily unavailable or unusable through a targeted network attack. Defense against certain types of DoS threats is achievable with various protective measures and strategies—such as load balancing—to improve system availability and reliability
Elevation of privilege	In this type of threat, an unprivileged user gains privileged access and thus has sufficient access to endanger or destroy the entire system. Elevated privilege threats include those situations where an attacker has effectively penetrated all system defense systems—e.g., firewalls—and has become part of the trusted system itself, a dangerous situation

always takes place only via these two cloud architecture layers. Consequently, every agile organizational model to be established must be able to capture these real existing threats and define responsibilities along individual experts and specialist teams in order to use effective mechanisms that are capable of responding quickly and independently to respective cyber threats.

Priority levels of risks/threats
Each row of the Threat Board represents the priority level of a risk.

The row-by-row representation in the Threat Model graphically illustrates this prioritization, accordingly, from top to bottom:
Determine priority levels for risks/threats:
Highest priority (highest)
High priority (high)
Medium priority (low)
Low priority (lowest)

Risk classes: Damage extent of risks/threats
In order to meaningfully assess and prioritize risks, an evaluation of the expected damage risk in the event of the occurrence of the respective risk or threat is necessary.

The six columns serve the function of prioritizing individual risks and use the following status:

Define damage extent of identified risks/threats:
- not prioritized
- low risk
- medium risk
- high risk

With the Threat Modeling, we have introduced an approach that allows you to include accompanying penetration testing in your agile framework.

The prototypical approach presented in the book offers you the direct opportunity to involve an IT security team right from the planning and implementation phase.

4.3.19 As early as possible to agile deployment & automated tests

Agile deployment realizes the concept of continuous delivery, i.e., the ability to frequently deliver software features to customers and then continuously learn from the real-time use of the software by the customer.

As early as possible and agile deployment has become so attractive because the potential for even shorter feedback loops has been recognized. From a quality assurance perspective, we should definitely align our software development as early as possible towards the earliest possible agile deployment.

This ensures that we test our software development with the deployment environments in the environments where we want to operate our software later. This, in turn, means that we orient the test platform as close as possible to the production environment to avoid errors and deviations.

What deployment goals do we have here and what is the purpose of agile deployment?
A) Monitoring and optimization of quality processes
B) Automated execution, control, and logging of software tests
C) Automation of quality and deployment processes/release processes

With the transition from traditional software development, characterized by slow development cycles, with only quarterly or, at worst, annual release cycles and a waterfall-like interaction mostly between stakeholders from product management, product development, system testing, and the customer, a gradual change to an agile organization usually takes place, which is oriented towards the approaches of research and development. Typically, non-agile organizational forms can be recognized by the fact that customer feedback processes are not or not sufficiently integrated into the product, service, and software development process.

Deployment obstacles: Too large teams, strict planning phases, lengthy release cycles, no or insufficient feedback loops
There are usually classic organizational forms with classic department structures and regularly much too large project teams. Responsibilities are roughly divided into disciplines such as system architecture, design, and testing. Development takes place sequentially with a strict planning phase at the very beginning of each project. Delivery to the customer usually takes place at the end of the project, and only then can customers provide feedback on the received software functionality. Likewise, such organizational forms lack any agile deployment with prototypical character or feedback-based testing methods.

Olsson et al. have identified barriers to agile transformation and aligned them with a stage model that is oriented towards continuous deployment of software [35]:

Maturity Level 1: First steps towards an agile transformation
The next step in the development of the organization is that individual teams adopt agile practices, but still adhere to a central control for specifications and product management, up to system verification. So, the traditional software development model is still predominantly used. This can often be recognized by the fact that short feedback loops with the customer are missing.

Maturity Level 2: Continuous Integration

An organization that pursues a **continuous integration** strategy has successfully introduced practices that enable frequent integration of development performance, with daily builds and rapid handover of release changes. This maturity level already includes (partially) automated builds and (partially) automated tests. Humble and Farley define continuous integration as a software development practice in which team members integrate their work frequently, resulting in multiple integrations per day [36].

Only the ability to automate test cases, integration of software libraries and packages, release builds, etc., enables teams to test and integrate the updated code artifacts daily and feature-oriented. With this maturity level, the required time from idea to actual implementation in software is noticeably reduced. At this point, both the connected software development teams and system validation work according to agile practices. This includes specialists for user experience and usability as well as IT security.

Maturity Level 3: Continuous Deployment

In this phase, all practices of the second maturity level are applied so that service and customer-oriented functionalities are continuously realized in short intervals through software releases.

Furthermore, continuous customer feedback is implemented, which is based on learning from validated information and data on the use of the software by users and customers in a real usage context. This means that verified insights are already incorporated into the elimination of errors and optimizations are only implemented if there is an expectation that they will provide added value for the customer.

At this stage of development, marketing, R&D, product management, and customers are all involved in a fast, agile cycle of software release development.

Maturity Level 4: Continuous adjustments based on the latest requirements

The fourth maturity level realizes the stage of immediately responding to customer feedback and results in the actual and immediate provision of software functionality as a means of experimenting and testing with respect to all aspects of real customer needs. With this agile maturity level, the deployment of software is considered as a starting point for any further prioritization of functionality rather than as the delivery of the final product. With this maturity level, quality processes are continuously monitored and optimized. Regular software tests are (partially) automated and are carried out with documentation.

The agile deployment strategy leads us straight towards (partially) automated testing procedures.

What do we need to do to achieve automated testing?

1. Evaluation and definition of the build tools, test frameworks, and tools to be used
2. Definition and setup of the test environment and test strategies for manual testing as well as for test automation

3. Definition and monitoring of our Continuous Integration/Continuous Deployment pipelines

To implement these capabilities, it is recommended to follow the best practices presented in the second chapter and to use established DevOps tools, which you will gain a comprehensive insight into at the latest in the DevOps periodic table.

Understanding maturity levels as evaluation stages to be passed through
The knowledge and conscious consideration of maturity levels is of particular importance when an organization is striving to become more agile. Each maturity level takes time, and the individual maturity levels are to be understood as evaluation stages that cannot be skipped but must be taken one at a time. Each organization will be shaped by different experiences on its journey, and it is also important to understand that there are often multiple ways and tools as solutions to the goal. Best practices and science-based recommendations for action can, however, be understood as gentle suggestions that often make things easier for those involved and prevent frustrations.

Positively understand that optimizations will always be necessary in the future
Furthermore, all stakeholders within the organization understand that an agile software development process can never reach a final result at any point in time because future adjustments will continue to take place and will always be based on the latest requirements. Lastly, optimization and error correction are based on a positive feedback and error culture, and every effort is based on cooperative collaboration.

4.3.20 DevSecOps

Efforts to integrate security into DevOps have led to the DevSecOps paradigm, which can prove to be a real challenge in practice.

DevOps leads to DevSecOps
In particular, with the careless use of various DevOps tools, including the use of cloud-specific development tools or, for example, the improper or careless use of container tools, the need for developer-centric tools for testing towards application security increases. This includes specific tools designed for continuous testing and practices to harden IT security during the development and operation of software.

DevSecOps and agile team structures
DevSecOps goes beyond automation, continuous integration, and deployment processes, as it specifically involves IT security specialists with the goal of hardening software. With the establishment of security practices in DevOps routines, the collaboration between different teams automatically intensifies, which has a direct influence on the

agile organizational model. As soon as critical systems, objectives, risks, and evidence for IT security have to be provided and managed during development, DevSecOps plays a particularly important role. After implementing security into the DevOps toolchain, the more extensive DevSecOps work only begins. Within the agile organizational structure, behavioral changes must be brought about alongside established security processes to create a security culture. The special DevSecOps role has established itself in many ways as a practical solution proposal to effectively minimize risks with a targeted task focus.

The DevSecOps tool truffleHog

An example of such a tool is the analysis program truffleHog [37], which is designed to search Git repositories for seemingly hidden secrets and thus automatically dig deep into the commit history and branches of software releases for the IT security specialist. The analysis program, which is available as a free version under the GPL-2.0 license, uncovers hidden secrets in the code that were usually accidentally transmitted at different stages of development.

Threat modeling and code reviews are also considered DevSecOps practices.

4.3.21   Code Reviews

Code reviews are part of the quality assurance process and also part of the development lifecycle.

With a code review, we check whether conventions are being followed and systematically test software for its error-free operation.

Approach to Code Reviews

In order to review program code, the exact functionality of the code must be clear as a result of a review. The reviewer thus uses the basic principle of validating hypotheses, meaning they verify whether the programs really do what I, as a reviewer, would have thought and expected beforehand?

It is precisely with this verifying approach to code reviews that code reviews gain important significance in terms of error analysis or in the identification of unwanted side effects.

At the same time, it becomes clear why it is considered that no programmer should review their own code, because as the creator of a code fragment, this very question of what a code fragment should fulfill is predetermined from the outset. The analysis is inherently limited by implicit knowledge, and the result is accordingly one-sided...

When program fragments—be it through creative inspiration—or through analytical approaches from a different perspective with unexpected input values or deviating behavior are confronted, it often leads to surprising and equally undesirable results.

Using Frameworks to Practice Code Reviews

Good starting points for code review exercises are frameworks. Most open-source frameworks are excellently documented, so that numerous sources for task assignments of foreign code can be used within agile software teams, which are unknown to the code reviewer. Such exercises are even more effective when the code review is prepared by another team member, so that the code confronted with the code reviewer in the analysis actually represents a completely foreign code artifact.

For example, many software developers use the Java Spring Framework, but how many developers really know the framework internally and in the interaction of its components? What happens in the individual steps in a program fragment and in a module and in the interaction of the numerous components?

Getting Familiar with Foreign Code is a Very Common Requirement

In a code review, we want to understand what we are applying in terms of code, we want to understand what the programmers were thinking when creating the software. The review of foreign software artifacts is suitable for improving one's own skills and is extremely useful in getting familiar with foreign code in ever shorter periods of time.

Getting familiar with foreign code is a very common requirement because foreign code artifacts are constantly being used in software development, be it as part of the open-source environment or from outsourced contract artifacts.

4.3.22 Pair Programming

Pair programming is a form of collaborative learning; two programmers work together to achieve a common goal. Preston confirmed in his study the advantages of the pair programming methodology in terms of effectiveness and in the analysis of critical properties that successful collaborative learning approaches must fulfill in order to be considered as such [38].

Classic Approach to Pair Programming

In the classic pair programming approach, one programmer takes on the role of the "Driver" and, as the code editor, is responsible for writing a program draft on a computer, whiteboard, or simply on paper [39].

The other partner takes on the role of the so-called "Navigator" and fulfills several tasks at the same time. One of these tasks is observing the work of the "Driver" in terms of tactical and strategic errors; these can be syntax errors, typos, and calling the wrong method. Strategic errors occur when the implementation or design of the driver will ultimately not achieve its goals. The Navigator is the strategic, far-sighted thinker of the programming pair. Since the Navigator is not as deeply involved in the design, algorithm, code, or testing, he or she can more easily adopt an objective perspective and has greater degrees of freedom to think about the strategic direction of the work. In collaboration, both act as a team and are constant brainstorming partners for each other. As an effective pair, they continuously discuss alternative approaches and solutions to the problem.

Pair Programming as a Team Building Measure & Perfect Training Method
Pair programming can also be used ideally as a team-building measure or to learn or train code conventions, algorithms, or a specific technique.

Working in pairs or as a team often increases motivation. Together, for example, it is easier to define the result of more readable comments or to gain a better technical understanding, such as how components should ideally be architecturally connected to represent a specific behavior.

In pair programming, the community idea counts with the goal of bringing improvements for oneself, the team, and a common solution.

Pair Programming and Code Reviews
Pair programming is particularly practical in terms of code reviews, as programmers should never look at code from programs they already know when analyzing errors.

Knowledge Exchange, Improving Competencies, and Having Fun Programming Together!
The benefit of pair programming lies not least in the exchange of knowledge, improving competencies, and of course, the fun of programming should not be neglected!

4.3.23 Logging & Monitoring

With the establishment of DevOps and the implementation of a series of practices to accelerate a software development process aligned with the DevOps cycle, the logging of software activities, known as logging, takes on an important role.

Logging from the Perspective of IT Security and the Requirements of KPI-Oriented Monitoring
From the perspective of IT security and with the goal of (partially) automated deployment, appropriate logging is required in order to build a corresponding monitoring system that can assess effectiveness levels as well as security-relevant aspects in real-time. While we will address the requirements of KPI-oriented monitoring in a separate chapter, it is important to consider at this point in the context of setting up effective logging which data we can technically collect, what efforts are associated with it, and what value these logging data will have for us in terms of meaningful monitoring.

Not all logging data is equally valuable to us
Almost every component is technically capable of generating countless logging data. In connection with logging data, it is always necessary to question the time interval for

which this data has any significance. Against this background, logging is often limited to ensure appropriate data protection.

Reconciling logging and IT security requirements
Some security requirements are diametrically opposed to these restrictions. Often, however, both requirements can be reconciled; for example, through appropriate data protection concepts, documented IT security processes based on the four-eyes principle, and by applying the consistent premise of not collecting data en masse blindly, but only when there is a specific need and appropriate occasion, such as in justified threat situations.

Evaluating various logging sources
Sources for logging data include, for example, various types of software repositories containing historical, communication, bug, and runtime information that are relevant for optimization and should be used for systematic analysis.

Effectively supporting software development & IT security with logging policies and tools
All of this is done with the aim of supporting software development—including IT security—by providing policies and tools for the development and maintenance of high-quality logging code.

So far, there are only a few guidelines and tools for creating high-quality logging code. The current application context of log analysis is very limited in terms of feedback for developers and correlation with usable telemetry data.

We want to support the IT operations side by enriching the context of log analysis through systematic estimation of code coverage across log execution and in-depth problem diagnosis through correlation of logs such as traces and APM data.

Approach to integrating a practice-oriented logging mechanism
Starting with a systematic analysis of commit logs from software repositories, which aims to filter and analyze relevant descriptions from bug reports, a list of code commits can be systematically created. With this practice-oriented approach, we gain valuable information about existing problems in the logging code.

Four different components of logged logging code
In software repositories, there are basically four different components of logged code:

1. The object of log logging
2. Detailed explanatory information artifacts, the so-called *verbosity level*
3. Static texts
4. Dynamic content

All of these four components can be changed separately, using different revisions. An effective logging approach requires automatically localizing changes that lead to errors based on the change lines. We need a logging mechanism capable of identifying existing problems and localizing them based on applied code fixes.

Once such a benchmark dataset is available, an exploratory study can be conducted based on this data to evaluate the effectiveness of various existing tools for detecting logging code problems.

Test Environments and Test Devices
Especially with regard to data protection considerations and the development of corresponding expertise, usable test environments and test devices are required to build effective data analyses and to verify the implemented analysis processes. When establishing agile processes, it is important to consider which teams and product owners will take on these tasks and how the individual agile teams can be best involved.

4.4   Agile Teams, Roles, Tasks, and Processes

Agile software development in teams requires a shift towards DevOps and thus requires new teams, roles, tasks, and processes; these will be presented in detail in the following section.

The classifications listed apply across the board and should be considered largely independent of the individual Large-Scale Agile Frameworks. If a Large-Scale Agile Framework defines its own roles, tasks, and processes, the explanations of the respective Large-Scale Agile Framework should be consulted.

To ensure the broadest possible practical relevance, the team and role descriptions are based on proven team constellations and processes that should be applicable in most medium-sized companies. Especially in the IT sector, individual job profiles vary in part or entirely in their title and are largely comparable or even identical despite different designations, only through the defined functions and areas of responsibility as well as required skills.

Agile Teams:
In addition to agile software development teams, many other, very differently specialized teams are regularly involved in the development of existing software solutions:

- Agile Software Development Teams
- Frontend and Usability Technologies
- System/Manufacturer Test
- IT Security & DevSecOps Teams
- Technical Documentation
- Infrastructure Services

- Sales
- Research, Innovation, and PreSales
- System Integration
- Support
- Product Management
- Marketing and Content Teams
- Legal & Data Protection Experts

Agile Roles
Various specialists take on different roles in software development within agile teams. The typical representatives with very different specializations within the teams are:

- Product Owner
- Project/Team Leaders(**)
- Software Architects
- Software Developers
- Software Engineers
  - DevOps Engineers
- Service/Maintenance Officers

Note(**): Agile concepts typically avoid roles that already indicate a management or leadership function in their designation.

Tasks and Processes
The tasks and processes are either team-specific and tailored to the respective agile team or have a **cross-functional function.**

Cross-functional means that the role coordinates corresponding tasks and processes between different teams or assumes a coordination function between the different teams.

4.4.1 Agile Software Development Teams

Roles
Product Owner, Project/Team Leader, IT and Software Architect, Software Developer/Software Engineer, Product Manager, IT Security Specialist, QA Engineer

Tasks
The initial and ongoing development of technical software solutions is organized in specialized development teams, with assignment at the Product Owner level. Within the scope of software development, these teams are also responsible for developer tests, which are largely automated.

The type of technical architecture and detailed process documentation is also in the hands of the product-specific development teams.

Processes

The *Product Owner* of an individual software product is responsible for the product strategy and aligns it with the cross-product strategy of product management. In the case of software specialists, a predominantly technical and product-oriented perspective can be assumed within the scope of software product development. For complex software products, the *Project Manager* assumes a temporary and the *Team Leader* a permanent management function, which includes organizational and personnel responsibilities. This includes project controlling, writing status reports, defining and describing work packages, employee management, and cross-project and cross-site communication.

The focus of *Quality Assurance Engineers* is on protecting, monitoring, and ensuring the product quality of an organization. The central task is to establish a quality assurance process that meets the current requirements and objectives of the organization. At the same time, this process must provide software, service, and product teams with a solid foundation to ensure the availability and stability for stakeholders and end customers is consistently reliable. In this context, the *Quality Assurance Engineer* performs functional tests that reveal existing problems or insufficient usability. These specialists are also significantly involved in service/product development, as they are well acquainted with defined quality characteristics. The QA Engineer selects suitable test approaches depending on the requirements, such as behavior-oriented, technically based test procedures, or tests based on acceptance criteria. Very often, approaches from various test procedures are combined. For the Product Owner, the role of the QA Engineer is a very important support.

The *Software Architects* are responsible for the technical and professional software architecture. They coordinate this with other software architects and all stakeholders in such a way that no disadvantages arise from a specific software architecture in the interaction of numerous and different software components or, for example, for a specific software product constellation in the future.

The six activities depicted in Fig. 4.12 "The six main tasks of software architects" based on "Hruschka/Starke" interact with each other and usually require continuous adjustments, which are best implemented agilely. Clarifying requirements and constraints: Insufficient, incomplete, or defective requirements need to be clarified, with the minimum prerequisite being the subset of architecture-relevant requirements. Based on the requirements and constraints, structures for data processing and cross-sectional concepts are to be designed. Subsequently, software architects accompany the implementation and communicate and evaluate the software architecture.

The *software developer* deals with concrete implementation tasks and is an expert in a range of specific technologies and methods required for the provision and use of software products. This includes development-specific resources such as development tools, third-party software and frameworks, the software architecture, and the connection of

Fig. 4.12 The six main tasks of software architects based on Hruschka/Starke

software products to internal and external software modules and IT systems, as well as the team-internal agile approach.

A product owner and their deputy are the designated contacts for the *maintenance* and support of a software product.

4.4.2   IT Security Teams

Roles
IT Security Specialist, Pentester, Sec-DevOps, IT Security Consultants

Tasks
The *IT Security Specialists* pursue the hardening of any software components and systems and ensure their ongoing monitoring. With this focus, IT specialists independently accompany all ongoing processes within the organization in both a consulting and implementing capacity. In doing so, IT security specialists implement the establishment of security standards and ensure their compliance through appropriate policies.

Processes

With their IT security-focused expertise, security specialists support software and IT architects in an advisory capacity, organize penetration tests, and ensure in collaboration with agile software teams that technical debt is eliminated as quickly as possible or at least that appropriate protective measures are in place during the transition phase to prevent damage. IT security specialists thus also have a veto right when it comes to putting software, services, or releases into production. Likewise, IT specialists advise on contract design, for example, when service contracts require cooperation with third parties. Their goal is also to establish system-wide test environments and enforce access rights to source code.

The security tools used are partly very specific depending on the system environment, partly generally applicable, so that, for example, BSI or OWASP recommendations can be implemented. The IT security-oriented logging and monitoring is thus to a large extent the domain of the IT security teams.

4.4.3 Implementation of Legal Framework Conditions and Data Protection

Even though requirements for legal framework conditions and data protection generally automatically flow into software, organizations benefit in the medium and long term from targeted influence through a separate requirements management for this area.

Complex IT scenarios—especially when they are increasingly located in cloud scenarios and thus open up their service scenarios towards the web and mobile applications—require effective data protection and IT security concepts that meet the legal framework conditions. Only recently, the effects of the Privacy Shield ruling have unsettled numerous companies [40].

Data protection is based on the classifications defined under IT basic protection, which make it possible to evaluate data in the dimensions of confidentiality, integrity, and availability and to assign them to the corresponding protection requirements categories [41].

Roles
Data Protection Officer, Information Security Management (ISMS) Officer, ISM Teams, IT Law and Data Protection Experts

Tasks
Under the leadership of the organization's Data Protection Officer, the teams are primarily responsible for ensuring and maintaining the data protection of the personal and sensitive data entrusted to them within the organization. Specialists in this area ensure compliance with legal framework conditions, organize IT certifications and standardizations according to ISO standards, provide IT security awareness training, and perform

administrative tasks. In the area of IT law and data protection, full lawyers cooperate with the technical teams to achieve their goals.

Processes
Using various approaches, potential integrity violations are analyzed and proactively prevented through rules and measures implemented within the organization. In addition, the creation of emergency plans with respective instructions for individual employees is the responsibility of these teams. Through close cooperation with IT security specialists, processes are evaluated by simulating potential threats using threat models for the organization and IT processes.

4.4.4   Software Product Management/Service Management

Roles
Team Lead Product Management, Product Manager, Service Manager

Tasks
The overarching product-service management works in close cooperation with the members of the agile software product teams and takes on the task of cross-product coordination in particular.

Processes
Product/Service Management prioritizes requirements and resources, is responsible for resource planning and coordination, as well as the expansion of the product/service portfolio. With a future-oriented approach, Product/Service Management has the visionary task of establishing a long-term, strategic product/service vision. As an escalation point, Product/Service Management mediates both externally towards the customer and internally—primarily between the team leader, product/service manager, and software architects.

4.4.5   UX Teams: Frontend Design, Usability, and User Experience

Roles
Team lead, Project manager, Usability experts, Usability engineers

Tasks
The frontend and usability team standardizes the interfaces in software products and provides technical solutions to the product/service teams. A uniform operating concept ensures that graphical elements in the interfaces have a consistent appearance and processes are similarly designed; the developer can fully concentrate on the subject matter

during product development. Technically, the developers use appropriate interfaces developed from one or more offered frameworks. By using frameworks agreed upon among the teams, it is avoided that product/service-specific solutions dominate the frontend design, and usability teams can manage and be responsible for uniform user flows for all connected development teams.

Processes

The usability engineers maintain the constructed usability frameworks and take on the developer role in the team. Usability experts do not need to perform developer activities but methodically monitor the constructed components.

For this purpose, it is necessary for these team members to question the professional context of the users. This ideally happens in direct dialogue and by observing the users during work and while using the software.

Qualitative interviews with users have also proven to be effective. Mockups and discussions with customers are very helpful in creating user-friendly operating concepts for individual software solutions.

4.4.6 Quality Assurance and Testing Procedures

Roles
Team lead, Software testers

Tasks

When creating software, the responsible team is in charge of establishing and implementing tests, such as a system test and the testing of individual components. The team specializes in quality assurance using various testing procedures and establishes the corresponding testing methods within the entire software creation process. The team members do not necessarily know the software products to be tested from the inside but test the software with various tools from the outside. The challenge with testing procedures is the complex interaction of the various product/service components.

Processes

The so-called "smoke test" is one such testing procedure and ensures that the basic functions of the application run smoothly in the form of automated surface tests. A software tester checks daily whether the smoke tests, usually carried out outside regular working hours, such as at night or in the early morning, are successful for all supported version combinations of the software products. In case of test errors, these are logged and forwarded to the product/service development teams via ticket. After the successful completion of the testing procedure, the software goes live on the test systems.

The team leader ensures the quality of the testing procedures and must maintain an overall view of the active testing procedures so that all relevant areas are tested as far as possible. Each product/service team can use its own testing procedures with separate test data. In higher-level rounds, agile teams should strive to exchange their experiences and harmonize testing procedures with each other as far as it makes sense.

In the form of integration tests, these are also partially product/service cross-cutting tests.

4.4.7   Technical Editing

Roles
Technical Editors

Tasks
The team composed of technical editors is responsible for software documentation, usually for external stakeholders. In this context, these documentation specialists cooperate with software architects to create a unified internal documentation. Typically, the translation process for multilingual documentation is also located within such a team.

Basically, there are two types of different documentation artifacts to distinguish: First, the documentation in the form of online help, which every software manufacturer is legally obliged to provide, and second, the creation of installation manuals or marketing material such as product/service flyers. Furthermore, the technical editing department generates graphics, tutorials, etc., and serves as a technical-focused proofreading service for other departments, e.g., marketing. Since online documentation now often leads to various web-based service artifacts, workflows from internal wikis, such as Confluence systems, towards publicly accessible websites are suitable. FAQs and other service artifacts are also integrated and continuously updated in this way. All service artifacts have both external and, to some extent, purely internal character.

Processes
It makes sense to establish a clear assignment of employees at the product/service level. This assignment of technical editors to product teams usually arises from factors such as strong company growth and requests from project teams.

Documentation creation usually takes place through proofreading release notes and can follow traditional workflows: If working with change requests or problem reports, release notes have proven to be effective; these are written in advance by the developers and proofread by the project management of the respective product team from the release date onwards, i.e., a review is carried out with regard to terminology and comprehensibility. It is highly recommended to use a single-source publishing procedure to ensure that surface texts (properties) are uniformly designed and appear correspondingly in release notes and documentation. This also makes it easy to write uniformly and generate a comfortable online help from a single source of truth. It should also be ensured that generated output formats are cross-platform and do not cause any unpleasant surprises in different languages. For this purpose, the use of a so-called translation memory is absolutely sensible. This also allows for defining connected workflows, such as a quality assurance process for mockups.

4.4.8 Infrastructure Teams

Roles
Teamlead, Infrastructure Engineer

Tasks
These teams provide established infrastructure services within the company. The differentiation between an infrastructure team and a DevOps team is that no ongoing operation is maintained and coordinated; the service offerings are focused on hardware and tools for software development. The services include both consulting and usable software artifacts. Specifically, these are, for example, deployments of systems such as

- Confluence and Jira
- GIT repository server
- Build environments
- Etc.

Supporting this, the team drives technology topics forward through developed visions, e.g., by adding technologies such as Kubernetes or Docker as technical abstraction layers for hardware.

Processes
The work progress can be controlled, for example, using a timeboxing approach. Requests are tracked in the form of incoming tasks in Jira. The services defined via Jira tickets are successively processed by the infrastructure engineers. To bundle competencies, it is recommended that individual team members specialize in about three technology topics each, so that they complement each other in their different skills. In addition, this ensures that all required services can be provided at any time. With the help of Jira, the team leader continuously analyzes where exactly problems exist and topics "get stuck". The documentation of knowledge on technology topics is done in the Confluence wiki. A status round serves to review individual tasks and check their status for delays. Typically, such processes are scheduled weekly and take place once a week as a *"Weekly"*.

4.4.9   DevOps Teams

Roles
DevOps Engineers

Tasks
The **DevOps Engineer** is a specialized DevOps expert who combines the already established roles of Build Engineer, System Administrator, and Tool Developer.

Why a DevOps Engineer?
The reason for introducing the role of the DevOps Engineer is the consistent merging of different disciplines and a recurring shift of various responsibilities.

With a focus on **automating various development processes** and optimizing the **pipeline,** the DevOps Engineer plays a higher-level role. They bring together the previously mentioned roles and embody a responsibility that acts as an active communicator for the implementation of selected **DevOps approaches** on the developer side as well as in IT operations.

Through the approaches to be implemented, not only is a **faster release cycle** aimed for, but the end customer is also brought more into focus through approaches from the **User-Driven** Design area.

Processes
The 16 task areas of the DevOps Engineer:
Based on the scientific study *"Who Needs Release and DevOps Engineers, and Why?"* will provide a more in-depth definition of the **role of the DevOps Engineer** in the following. The results of the study show that the following **16 areas of responsibility** can be assigned to the role of the DevOps Engineer [42]:

1. **Integration:** Source Control Management (SCM), including branch and merging strategies for parallel software development and support through SCM tools such as GIT.
2. **Build System:** Techniques and tools for generating and packaging source code and program files into delivery units, e.g., using software solutions like Ant or Maven.
3. **Continuous Integration:** Management of tools for automated quality assurance based on defined events, for example, using tools like Jenkins. A specific application example: After each change that developers deliver via commit to the corresponding test scenario, the delivered code fragment is automatically tested on a dedicated build/test server. This area of responsibility also includes tagging and storing the built artifacts in repositories such as JFrog or Nexus.
4. **Environment/Infrastructure:** Defining and managing the system environments and infrastructure involved in software development (e.g., servers, VMs, and containers,

as well as any hardware and network components to be configured) for implementing different staging activities, such as development, software testing, operation on the staging environment, and productive live operation (Dev, Test, Staging, Production). This includes coordinating with other roles and areas of responsibility.

5. **Execution and Planning of System Tests:** The DevOps Engineer supports the implementation of development-specific test scenarios and advises on their planning. It should be noted that test definition is only worthwhile and sensible for longer-term and more complex projects, as extensive time is required for defining specific test scenarios and their mapping in the system test.

6. **Delivery/Release:** Setting up and maintaining the pipeline for software deployments and software releases, both for existing and new projects.

7. **Operation Monitoring:** Monitoring and controlling the production environment and proactive error correction.

8. **Problem Diagnosis:** Diagnosis of errors and undesired system behavior occurring after a release. It is important to note that as detailed error images as possible with timestamps and precise descriptions should be available for problem localization.

9. **Version Upgrades:** Upgrading existing production environments to newer release levels, possibly using techniques such as Canary Deployment or Rollback.

10. **Pipeline Optimization:** Optimization of the various activities of the release process with a focus on Continuous Delivery.

11. **Scripting:** Scripting and automation of manual release engineering tasks, typically using scripting languages such as Bash, Python, or PowerShell.

12. **Communication:** Ability to promote active dialogue within the team. Targeted exchange of information through both formal and informal discussions, social networks, internal wiki, and custom documentation, as well as via email and other communication media.

13. **Coordination and Planning:** Support of release planning, for example in the form of a release roadmap or the temporal definition of development cycles. This area of responsibility requires strong coordination skills in relation to other team members such as developers, external database administrators, or IT service providers.

14. **Non-release related activities:** Engagement in further development-related activities such as system design, easily understandable system architecture, or the design of test scenarios.

15. **IT Security:** Necessity to establish a release-related and maximum security-oriented infrastructure and security-oriented processes. This also includes IT security training, company-wide uniform standards for data protection, and related training and education.

16. **Cloud:** Knowledge and implementation of cloud-based technologies and processes for build, test, and deployment environments.

4.4.10 Sales—The distribution of products and services of your organization

Roles
Account Manager, Sales Representative, Service Account Representative

Tasks
Sales is responsible for the offer and sales process and takes care of all customers, whether you act in the role of a software manufacturer or sell software-supported products and services. The assignment to customers—in the case of software product or SaaS offerings, these are licensees—is usually divided among individual account managers but can also be clustered into any other units.

Processes
In customer support, the account manager is the first point of contact. For existing customers, they are on an equal footing with the customer product manager. For software products, the customer product manager ensures that customers receive offers for their inquiries about individual product/service and feature extensions. For change request inquiries, this task includes coordinating the offer design with product management. For pure license sales, the sale usually takes place according to the specifications of an internal company price list. When commissioning software-related services, the coordination of efforts and deadlines with team colleagues is required. Likewise, regular meetings with customers must be organized and conducted.

Public tenders typically take place in close cooperation with the respective service/product manager. Sales significantly shape the contract management, for example, in the form of contract details for Service Licence Agreements (SLA) and coordinate these with product management.

4.4.11 Research, Innovation, and PreSales

Roles
Technical Consultants

Tasks
Technical consultants conduct purposeful research on technical issues from developer practice; they test new frameworks, technology standards, APIs, or tools and explore and test new or modified procedures or processes. In this way, such a team actively contributes to promoting innovation within the company. In addition, such a team can take over or proactively support the accompaniment of tenders and support the pre-sales process in the context of providing technology-related information and proofs-of-concept.

Processes

In this role, the team members act as a technical support function—through consulting and coaching—as a link between the software development area and affiliated teams such as product management or individual software teams. Technical consultants are typically also commissioned by individual software development teams to evaluate specific technical issues or to bring about objective decisions if discrepancies exist between different teams regarding technology preferences.

The following procedure appears particularly proven in practice:

As soon as the team has developed and evaluated an alternative procedure, it is discussed internally within the company or openly with customers. After two rounds of discussion on an internal discussion platform, the optimized process technology is then defined as a mandatory standard for all products or services. Product improvements are implemented as quickly as possible using this approach.

4.4.12 System Integration

Roles
Team Leader, Integration Engineer

Tasks

A system integration team is responsible for integrating software products into heterogeneous IT landscapes. In the case of software license product customers, as well as server/cloud applications, there are often extremely customer-specific IT systems that ultimately demand the same benefits from software but have significantly different requirements regarding the operating environment.

For complex software products consisting of numerous individual components, integration at the licensee may include "meshing" the individual components on behalf of the specific requirement specification into a customer-specific individual solution. In this case, the members of an integration team not only take on a function in relation to technical issues but also have functions in the professional context in practice.

Processes

In the preparation phase, the integration engineer clarifies all integration-related questions and checks whether all associated prerequisites are met, e.g., whether the technical infrastructure is in place. In addition, the team members ensure that the contact persons on the customer side are familiar with the subject matter required by the commissioned software services.

If the integration of software takes place on-site at the licensee, software products in heterogeneous IT systems often do not work directly "out of the box." Thus, software integration is always very complex, technology-specific, and regularly requires intervention at the code level. Shell scripts are primarily modified or created in this process. This often involves API connection to a customer-specific IT infrastructure in addition to pure software configuration. Different IT skills are required for dealing with middleware; these usually include: Unix, Java, and specific knowledge of server systems, connected network infrastructure, middleware technologies, shell scripting, handling XML, XAML, and JSON files, creating configurations, executing queries at the database level, setting up a database, e.g., in Oracle, understanding the functionality of TLS, knowledge of software code functionality, and knowledge of adjacent software components operated by licensees in parallel with the marketed software license products.

A customer-specific implementation often also includes extensions through individual programming.

Following an on-site integration, aftercare topics are again in focus: These include application monitoring, patching, and performing updates, integrated into ongoing operations.

Software projects often have a project duration of more than half a year. Usually, several software projects run in parallel, and each individual project is in a different project status.

As a result of their activities, the team members of an integration team are an essential link for software developers by passing on information about real customer-side process flows and licensee feedback, which arises during integration assignments, to the software development teams.

If a software defect—the so-called *bug*—requires a change request, communication with product management should also take place. Regular exchange between all involved teams is also recommended.

4.4.13 Support Teams

Roles
Team leader, Support staff

Tasks
The primary function of the support team is to provide first and second level support for customers. Support requests are usually received by most support teams via email, telephone, and increasingly via chat and social media. To ensure the best possible support in critical areas, an effective all-round support aims for a 24/7/365 support concept. To establish these high-quality standards in smaller companies—without an underlying call center mode—a service model with on-call support hotline for processing and resolving support requests is recommended, at least for critical software products or software-based services.

Some support teams also handle the service of software deliveries for provided products and solutions and their organization, such as through a download and service portal.

Processes

As part of support management, a support team regularly manages personal data of customers and companies, often organized through a dedicated helpdesk system or a central CRM system. Ideally, service and license management is organized in a central system. If the support also manages a web-based customer portal and provides extended service in the form of product downloads and documentation for its customers or licensees via customer login access, the support team is also responsible for the associated service tasks.

To resolve support requests, support teams often still use very specific support databases. Many companies are now moving to the use of external cloud solutions such as Atlassian Jira Service Desk, especially since Jira and Confluence are already extremely widespread and, due to the almost identical user interfaces with Jira and Confluence, are already largely familiar in companies that use Atlassian.

The support process is conducted via email and connected online portals. After opening a service call, the support system automatically records the processing status for the support staff and guides them through the service process based on further information. Data is checked for completeness and, if necessary, followed up with the service customer. The ticket status changes within different statuses such as "interrupted" until the requested information—e.g., screenshots or log files—is available. Subsequently, problem analysis takes place; if the first level support cannot solve the problem, the ticket goes to the second level support or switches to other teams, such as system integration or software development teams.

For specific software product teams, it is advisable to define special service representatives. In any case, all support processes with all details—such as technical environment details—must be comprehensively documented so that it is always traceable for everyone—including the customer!—who currently "wears the hat". Internal software development—whether focused on digital services or software products—also benefits from perfect error documentation and analysis. Communication with the customer and internal teams should be clear, comprehensible, and easy to understand for all parties involved. If foreign language support is to be provided, it should be well organized how translation processes are defined. Ideally, such foreign language processes should always be organized directly through the support team to maintain a consistent external appearance.

4.5   Getting Started with Design Thinking & Prototyping

In this section, you will learn how to practically combine techniques from design thinking with prototyping to get started agilely.

Design Thinking is a creative, multi-stage development process for developing innovative solutions. Design Thinking aims to determine the needs of a user as precisely as possible by considering the conventional problem detached from its previous context.

Eliminate prejudices and entrenched procedures

Prejudices and entrenched procedures are eliminated as much as possible so that all people involved in the Design Thinking process are open to new solutions. Iterative processes—as they underlie Design Thinking—thus combine openness to results with problem-solving [43, pages 14/15].

In this context, Design Thinking is considered a scientific method. The idea of Design Thinking was initiated in the 1970s by David Kelley; the creativity methodology has been popular since the beginning of the 21st century. The design agency led by Kelley, which consistently relies on Design Thinking, has already filed well over 1000 patents and won hundreds of design awards by this time.

Table 4.9 "Phases and associated methods of the Design-Thinking process" lists the phases and methods of Design Thinking defined by Gerstbach, which ideally complement agile projects methodically to incorporate new ideas and approaches for creative solution design.

With the digital age, design thinking is increasingly being considered in the agile development of software prototypes. This is closely linked to a science-oriented approach, but at the same time is highly practice-oriented. The reason for this is as follows: The combination of design thinking with prototyping is about creative solution approaches and their formulation as a thesis. These theses are subject to continuous testing with prototyping by verifying the assumptions made regarding their truth content. We thus generate test cases, which we then examine to see whether our assumption turns out to be true or false. This basic principle is a methodology that is very close to computer science.

No matter for which area a new innovative solution is to be created, the same design-thinking process is always used. This process is not linear, but unfolds its effectiveness through repetitions [43, page 65]. It is precisely this iterative approach that can be very well anchored with the prototypical approach in a large-scale agile framework.

4.5.1   Prototyping and Rapid Prototyping

Prototyping refers to the production of software in the form of repeated presentations of this software, with the maturity level of the software solution advancing with each presentation. Prototypes serve to better understand requirements [44, pages 760 f.].

Prototyping is therefore particularly suitable for successively approaching a problem solution and is therefore also used as a method in various process models—including design thinking. Figure 4.13 "Iterative Prototyping Model" illustrates an iterative prototyping model, with the finished software product being, for example, a published stable release with new functionality. Due to the regular involvement of stakeholders through continuous feedback in the development process, prototyping serves the client on the one hand to reduce project risks due to misguided software development, and on the other

Table 4.9 Phases and associated methods of the Design Thinking process. (Source: Gerstbach—"Design Thinking in Companies")

Phases of the Design Thinking process:	Methods:

Phase 1:
Observation
	• **Analysis** of processes through observation
	• **Empathic interviews,** through personal conversations and inquiries
	• **Research:** Gathering information from various sources
	• **Detailed immersion:** Why?
	    1. What do people say?
	    2. What do they think?
	    3. How do they feel?
	    4. How do they act?
	• **Persona profiles**
	• **Productive meeting** (informal conversation)
	• **Story and Capture**
	• **Empathy Map**

Phase 2: **Definition of the problem field**	• **Point of View:** Developing a deep understanding of the person and their problem space • **PoV fill-in-the-blank:** Why? [User] wants [need] because [surprising insight] • **PoV analogy** • **Insight Cards** • **Concept plan** • **Critical Reading Checklist**
Phase 3: **Generating ideas**	• **Word association chain** • **Sticky note method** • **6-3-5 method** • **Collective notebook** • **Scamper technique** • **Idea menu** • **Decision matrix**
Phase 4: **Experimenting**	• **Drawing boundaries** • **Actively building empathy** • **Building a prototype** • **Feedback conversations**

hand, a prototypical approach in software development is expected to deliver the end result that most closely meets the expectations of the user group.

Rapid Prototyping is an accelerated form of prototyping, which applies to prototypes in the context of Industry 4.0, such as 3D printing, as well as software prototypes [45, page 40]. Rapid prototyping aims to support the project progress, especially in the early phases of the development process, with particularly fast and cost-efficient generation of prototypes [46, page 202].

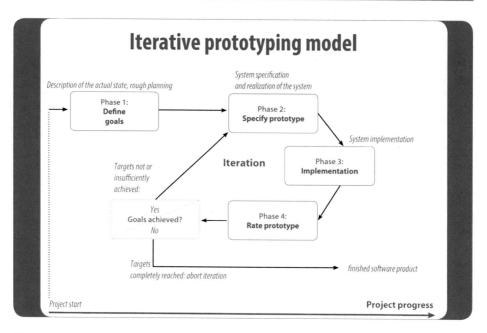

Fig. 4.13 Iterative Prototyping Model

The danger of rapid prototyping lies in the fact that the underlying structures may soon "burst at the seams" due to insufficiently defined requirements and necessitate refactoring or redesign [47, page 708].

Types and Dimensions of Prototyping

Prototyping can be further differentiated: Basically, horizontal and vertical prototypes are distinguished.

While *horizontal prototypes* consider various aspects of a system—such as its functionality and usability—in the form of navigation concepts, *vertical prototypes* are primarily focused on the technical aspects, such as the underlying system architecture.

Vertical prototypes thus consider all system levels (layers) of a system, including data management. Horizontal prototypes, on the other hand, are suitable for providing a broad view of a system by, for example, visualizing the complete user interface concept. Therefore, mockups, for instance, are considered horizontal prototypes. In doing so, horizontal prototypes deliberately exclude architectural implementation details. This makes horizontal prototypes particularly suitable for introducing stakeholders to the basic functionality of a system. This allows clients to assess at an early stage whether a planned system is suitable for solving the intended task in the desired manner. Vertical prototypes—often also known as feasibility studies (English: Proof of Concept)—represent the levels of technical implementation of a system and thus reflect all system layers. Vertical prototypes clarify uncertainties regarding a planned implementation and are therefore suitable for early assessment of the functionality of a planned system. Typically, vertical prototypes evaluate database schemas, optimize algorithms, or attest to the reliability of a system. Vertical prototyping also tests critical runtime requirements by checking agreed response times and predicts the total effort for realization as accurately as possible [48].

Furthermore, *throwaway prototypes* are distinguished from *evolutionary prototypes:* While throwaway prototypes serve to capture a situation as quickly as possible and provide a low depth in terms of the reproduction accuracy of a depicted scenario, evolutionary prototypes are much more detailed. Even though an evolutionary prototype strongly resembles the final product, it is usually focused on a particular aspect of a system and represents it as accurately as possible [49, pages 52/53].

The similarity to the finished software product is also due to the fact that the evolutionary prototype approaches the final product with each iteration stage in its development process. Both prototyping types are conceivable for both vertical and horizontal representations.

In terms of formalization, prototyping can be assigned as a constructive method with predominantly qualitative characteristics [50, page 112].

In order for prototyping to comply with the structured approach still fundamentally required for software development, it is recommended to consider proven process models from the field of software engineering.

4.5.2   Prototyping Phase Model

Pomberger and Pree define a multi-level ***prototype-oriented phase model*** for software engineering, which is divided into *requirements* or *system specification, platform conception, system architecture,* and a subsequent *process of application dynamics in practice;* see Fig. 4.14 "Prototyping Phase Model according to Pomberger/Pree". In a subsequent validation part, *system tests* in the form of expert surveys and based on usability tests lead to a further improvement of the prototype in further iterations [51, pages 26 ff.].

The risk of premature refactoring due to insufficiently defined system specifications can be effectively countered in the prototyping process by first creating an architectural design for technical prototypes to determine the quality characteristics of the planned system at an early stage [44, page 760].

Products and basic technologies in the introduction phase, about which the project team has no profound experience with the technology, reinforce the decision in favor of a prototypical approach. Also, the fact that defined project phases in the waterfall model are run through exactly once hinders learning in the testing of new technologies during the execution of a project. The most serious disadvantage of waterfall-based IT projects is that the user sees and tests the resulting software very late in the project. If requirements were misunderstood by the project team or the project customer could not properly formulate their needs, changes are very expensive, as large parts of the project

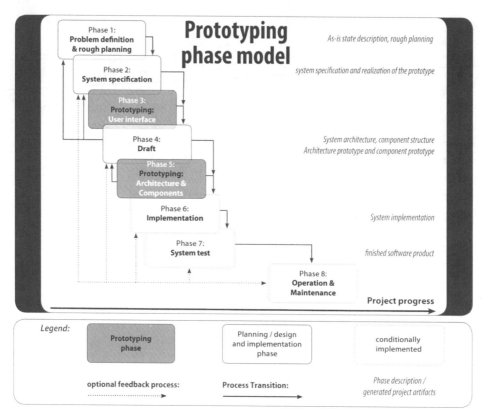

Fig. 4.14 Prototyping Phase Model according to Pomberger/Pree, own illustration Sascha Block

have to be repeated. Change costs during the project are therefore an important aspect in choosing a suitable approach model [52, page 346].

4.6   Aligning Overarching Agile Process Phases with a Prototypical Approach

With the previous section, we have already moved to a prototypical approach with the prototyping phase model and thus into a shaping activity mode. Here, the results of your evaluation on prototyping are specifically incorporated.

In a higher-level view, three overarching process phases are relevant within an agile approach model, which regularly repeat in this form in agile software development:

Phase 1: Requirements gathering and idea generation
Phase 2: Prototyping and consulting process
Phase 3: Testing and summative evaluation

4.6.1   Phase 1: Requirements gathering and idea generation

Due to a required pragmatic agile solution approach for everyday practice—with a strong focus on prototyping—the following process elements appear suitable:

- (Moderated) Brainstorming
- Research
- Empathic interviews
- Persona profiles

Phase 1, Step 1: Initial Project Meeting
Every project starts with a project pre-meeting with the stakeholders; in this appointment, the conversation partners from usually different departments describe their direct and/or indirect client role and the project goals desired from their point of view.

A quote, as exemplified in the following examples, is ideally suited to summarize the stakeholders' expectations:

> *"Essentially, the goal is to create a flexible feedback channel for all employees in the medium term, in order to provide relevant information in the short term." or*

> *"Currently, the idea is for the new content team to provide concrete ideas and content that we want to use on all communication channels. We want to find out with you how well this approach works in practice."*

Phase 1, Step 2: Internal Brainstorming/Research/Initial Project Customer Meeting
After the kick-off event, in the form of the project pre-meeting, it makes sense to use the remaining time for your own preliminary considerations, research, and an internal brainstorming with a deliberately objectified perspective.

Independent research by the client provides valuable information, for example, on existing internal company problems that objectified third parties perceive more clearly.

Phase 1, Step 3: Brainstorming
In a further follow-up appointment, it is a proven method to invite everyone to a joint brainstorming session and effectively combine the external view of the project team with the internal company view of the stakeholders.

For example, define different user groups as users of a software application, a service, or an app together with the stakeholders, such as:

- Customers of Product/Service A
- Customers of Product/Service B
- Prospects
- ...

For a more precise definition, persona profiles are suitable for determining the exact needs and problems in the customer and/or workday.

In a joint brainstorming session, the suggestions of the stakeholders can then be combined with the ideas developed by the project team in advance, discuss the ideas, and roughly group them thematically.

An established method here is to allow each participant to freely assign five priority points to topics and ideas that are considered particularly important for project success or an interesting app. Based on this, it is easy to vote on the topics to be implemented as the main focus of a planned application in the further course.

Phase 1, Step 4: Final Coordination with Stakeholders

Following the brainstorming and the acceptance of the project charter, the results are documented, digitized, and structured. Based on this, initial templates for user stories and persona profiles as well as, for example, a simple project Kanban board are created.

In addition, the basic project work organization is set up with appropriate collaboration tools so that project reporting can already begin.

Subsequently, the work assigned to Phase 2 can begin, which is visually sketched with an initial pen-&-paper prototype, with which UX design the application is oriented with the first prototype to be implemented.

The objective of such a meeting is to learn about the compelling and secondary expectations for the potential future application. In the spirit of an empathic customer-oriented approach to increasing benefits, acute problems, e.g., from the perspective of a department, are also addressed in order to be able to examine them for application-based solution approaches. In addition, support needs for further project work, e.g., in the form of an early employee survey, are announced, contact persons are determined, and stakeholders are sensitized to previously identified project risks—especially with regard to the necessity of user-oriented, interesting features.

In corresponding meetings, processes can be identified that should be supported or digitized. What is technically feasible and what should be implemented must always be closely examined in consultation with the stakeholders. The goal for their next meeting is then already the presentation of an MVP.

Phase 1, Step 5: Empathic Interviews

Empirical research for a new product design as well as a software application should always begin with a profound understanding of the relevant processes and the technical context surrounding the product; interviews with stakeholders are particularly suitable for this purpose [53, page 39].

In order to gain the most accurate understanding of the different requirements, empathic and openly designed interviews are particularly suitable for learning more about the needs of users, their everyday challenges, as well as the mindset of various user groups, for example, regarding the use of new technologies or information from the corporate context.

The open conversation with employees from various company areas also offers the opportunity to introduce the project team with its members and each of them within their respective project role, and at the same time is the best opportunity to initiate direct contact with the users themselves.

Documenting the interviews allows for a professional conversation-analytical data analysis, which remains available for methodical evaluation and for internal company purposes if necessary [54, page 338].

In separate sections of this book, you will learn all the details you need to conduct empathic employee interviews and receive suggestions for developing suitable questions and creating corresponding questionnaires.

Phase 1, Step 6: Persona Profiles
Based on the conducted interviews and in the context of ongoing feedback rounds with other stakeholders and users in different roles, persona profiles can be created. *Personae* represent stereotypical users and embody their different goals, behaviors, and characteristics that are relevant to the product to be developed [55, page 39].

Specific design goals can be determined much more purposefully using selected persona profiles by comparing goals and assigned priorities of interviewed persons and recording general and easily understandable matches in a persona profile [53, page 26].

In the context of software applications, personae should be developed based on the information obtained in the survey, as well as their respective roles as future users of an application. On the one hand, this approach already provides valuable insights into different requirements, such as frontend design, and on the other hand, you also sketch your software architecturally by outlining at least rudimentary authorization rules within the application. Thus, the resulting personae, the software design, and future application scenarios reflect relevant user properties visually and easily understandable.

4.6.2   Phase 2: Rapid Prototyping and Consultation Process

The insights gained from the analysis of users and context are translated into personae and scenarios. By using personae, relevant user profiles are incorporated for the application, while scenarios describe the work with the new system from the user's perspective [49, page 23].

The respective application scenarios, which are incorporated into the stakeholder surveys, provide a solid foundation for the design of a use-case model or individual user stories. Typically, this modeling process is specified in a second step with regard to the system's behavior according to quality requirements and framework conditions [56, page 7].

For complex requirements and long-term projects, it becomes clear at this point at the latest in terms of agile rapid prototyping that quality assurance processes should not be dispensed with. The user stories thus flow not only directly into the design of the prototypes but also into the later testing and debugging. In favor of the agile prototyping approach, it is recommended to use a formative evaluation for the qualitative strengthening of software products and to prioritize user-oriented requirements on the part of the stakeholders. The aspect of IT security should also not be missing in any software project at present; we also provide valuable practical recommendations for this in part 2 of the book.

Phase 2, Step 1: Pen-&-Paper-Prototyping

An initial prototype should already be created very early on, directly at the beginning of the project, in the form of a pen-&-paper prototype after joint brainstorming with several stakeholders. Such a pen-&-paper prototype then serves as the basis for further requirement definitions in all subsequent discussions with stakeholders. This early hand-drawn design typically already outlines essential core functions that can then actually be found in the later implementation of a software application, at least in a slightly modified form.

Often, the simplest variant of an actual pen and paper drawn prototype is sufficient. Equally helpful are digital tools that provide an easy-to-use construction kit and directly offer templates for smart phones or even specific iPhone models as a basis. In addition to the Draw.io tool presented in the second part of the book, the POP—Prototyping on Paper—app is suitable for the uncomplicated creation of a first pen-&-paper prototype, which is available for iPhone and Android and makes it easy for all participants to create vivid app prototypes in no time, see Fig. 4.15 "App POP—Prototyping on Paper".

The app offers tangible advantages over classic pen-&-paper types:

- uncomplicated handling, easy to learn,
- prototypes are directly in digital format and can be easily distributed,
- many templates directly usable,
- the app can be used by everyone in parallel, so that several prototypes can be created and presented simultaneously,
- prototypes can be easily extended to mockups,
- app available for iPhone and Android.

A prototype created within a few minutes with the Pop app is shown in Fig. 4.16 "Pen + Paper Prototype".

Phase 2, Step 2: First Prototype & Technology Kick-off

Now, the direct software development begins with the initial development of a runnable prototype using the technologies and software components planned for the project. To do this, focus first on one or two central requirements and work with your agile teams to create a usable prototype for the corresponding functions.

Already in this early design phase, it will become apparent whether the development environment used proves to be an effective prototyping tool, as the rudimentary design of a software application should be as easy to create in the design process as a pen-&-paper draft.

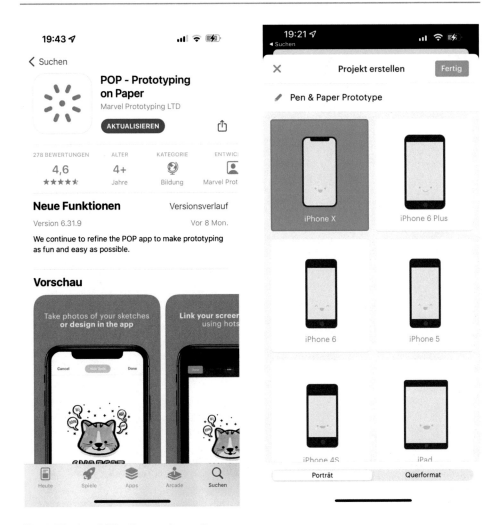

Fig. 4.15 App POP—Prototyping on Paper

By separating the development version and the released version, you can also generate runnable prototype versions that you can evaluate separately from each other, while functions still in development are withheld in a developer variant.

The invaluable advantage that results from accompanying version-based surveys of users is valuable insights that flow directly into the UX design and application logic!

In Fig. 4.17 "Development environment of an iOS app in Xcode", the development environment Xcode provided by Apple for iOS apps is shown with an iOS app in the early development phase.

Fig. 4.16 Digital Pen+Paper
Prototype. (Source: Sascha
Block)

"Prototypical development offers countless advantages…" Feedback discussions with the
later user groups, which you conduct as part of the qualitative target group survey, thus
always focus on logically completed development stages. This fact contributes significantly
to the fact that the prototypical software application is predominantly perceived as a usable
software product and less as a prototype. But that's not all; in addition, you appreciate your
users, continuously build trust in the new software—which is particularly important when
using new technologies as a key success factor—and avoid faulty and expensive misdevel-
opments. Last but not least, you establish a test and error management for software optimization together with your users.

Phase 2, Step 3: Minimum Viable Product (MVP)
The Minimum Viable Product—or MVP for short—is a special prototype with an exploratory character [57, page 49]. The concept of an MVP offers excellent opportunities to
test ideas and hypotheses in early stages, but requires an early focus on essential functions. A good MVP generally serves to answer the questions of whether a product is suitable for problem-solving and whether customers are willing to pay for it. To ensure these
properties, the MVP must meet certain requirements, as illustrated in the figure below
[58, page 2].

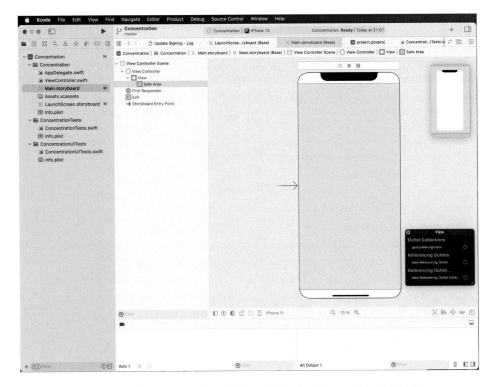

Fig. 4.17 Development environment of an iOS app in Xcode. (Source: Sascha Block)

While the degree of fulfillment for the "functional" property should still be around 100%, the degree of fulfillment for the properties of reliability, usability, and pleasant usability decreases progressively. Often, the term "minimum" as part of an MVP is misunderstood to justify the inadequacies of an MVP.

Figure 4.18 "Diagram MVP—Requirements for a Minimum Viable Product" based on Olsen illustrates how the degree of fulfillment of an MVP is related to its properties and what minimum requirements therefore apply to this prototype.

Although it is true that an MVP is deliberately limited in terms of its product maturity, what is passed on to customers with an MVP must be in a balanced ratio to the entire defined value proposition [59, pages 89/90].

In order for an MVP to be suitable for providing a reliable answer as to whether later development effort justifies the associated costs, a sufficiently high quality standard and degree of fulfillment must already be achieved in order to generate a perceptible added value for the project customer. This is generally fulfilled if the MVP meets the product requirements shown above in approximate percentage.

The following requirements exemplify and illustrate how requirements for an MVP can be classified:

Fig. 4.18 Diagram
MVP—Requirements for a
Minimum Viable Product.
(Source: Sascha Block—Own
illustration based on Olsen)

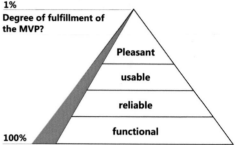

- Runnable iOS application
- News functions consisting of news area with detailed view and news overview
- Simple contact function with defined contact person in the company
- Rudimentary, "dummy-like" representation of the service area without real content
- User guidance via a menu for switching between functions (implemented in parallel as a menu bar and start screen)

For such a concrete milestone of an MVP, a clear date can then be set in the course of the project, at which these requirements have been successfully implemented. Such a date is not a target specification, as is usual in waterfall projects, but rather a milestone of success for the respective project teams.

Phase 2, Step 4: Development of the Funky Prototype
With the Funky Prototype, the development of a final software product begins. The Funky Prototype aims to identify and combine the most successful and significant findings of the previous iteration stages [60, page 253].

From a user's perspective, the Funky Prototype creates a "completely mature software product that is also fun to use."

For this iteration, feedback functions with the following specifications for the Funky Prototype can be defined for an app, for example, in addition to the requirements already defined in the MVP:

- Function for submitting app feedback and app rating
- Subscribable push notifications for personal user notifications and release news
- Service screen with contact details for defined contact persons
- Functional optimization of the user experience

From this, more classical MVP requirements can be distinguished, which fulfill obligatory mandatory functions before the go-live of an app due to system-related specifications—such as those of an app store—or due to legal framework conditions, but ultimately do not inspire users, but are simply necessary.

To test the acceptance of a prototype, elaborate identification procedures that require multi-factor authentication are certainly an obstacle; nevertheless, such mandatory requirements should be introduced iteratively within a sprint at an early stage so that neither a Go Live is prevented nor security risks are posed. This naturally includes the mandatory terms of use and privacy information, which must be integrated simultaneously and in combination with appropriate opt-in procedures.

The focus of the Funky Prototype is therefore on functionality and less on the user's perception of design. As this development stage progresses, a sophisticated prototype with a detailed level of resolution is already available.

The date of the milestone for the Funky Prototype is an important target date and should be duly acknowledged by all stakeholders.

Phase 2, Step 5: Functional Prototype
The Functional Prototype of a typical Design Thinking project is the precursor to the final prototype and should thus provide an extrapolation possibility for the end result. In addition to functional aspects, design solutions must now also be considered and tested. While the number of prototypes decreases, the focus on a few application aspects increases, and their level of resolution continues to increase [60, page 254].

In contrast, the requirement for the final prototype is that the final product—be it a material product, a business model, process, or service—is as tangible for the customer in its most important elements as if it were real. Thus, the final prototype provides all essential information regarding the subsequent commercial development.

For an app, the following requirements for the Functional Prototype can be defined as examples:

- Interface integration with another service, e.g., connection of service forms, such as handling returns via DHL, Hermes, or other used external logistics service providers,
- Adaptation to the corporate design,
- Legally compliant recording of used functions for statistical purposes and debugging.

4.6.3   Phase 3: Test Management and Summative Evaluation

The testing phase is an important process phase to provide a software as a mature application to users. For this purpose, it is recommended to extensively test the final prototype already at the end of phase 2 in order to keep the error rate as low as possible during this phase.

If the previous prototypes are only used internally within an organization, ideally additional internal test groups can be added. Content providers, such as a marketing or HR department, can start the extensive and final testing phase from a user perspective by providing content. In this context, it is particularly important to ensure that the test persons are trained to create appropriate error messages based on predefined test cases.

There are now various agile tools that specify test scenarios with all conceivable error constellations as precisely as possible for developers based on predefined specifications so that they can implement error correction without further inquiries. Only in this way is it possible to effectively identify and correct technical errors.

License issues should be cleared early on by appropriate inquiries with involved test persons and departments. An early release for all programs connected in the testing phase is therefore highly recommended; this should be done in close cooperation with the IT department or the respective support teams.

Usability Tests

Usability is defined in Part 11 "Guidance on Usability" of the ISO 9241-392 (2015) standard as "effectiveness and satisfaction in achieving specified goals for users in specific application environments." [61]. According to this definition, in a best-case planning, three analyses should be planned and carried out to measure software usability and evaluate improvements:

- The properties that the software must fulfill in a specific context,
- the process of interaction between user and product, and
- the effectiveness and degree of satisfaction resulting from the use of the product.

To determine these factors, users should test the software according to specific guidelines. Similar to a survey, usability tests would be conducted using questionnaires or interviews as field trials—i.e., outside of test environments and laboratories—[62, page 25].

For this purpose, a representative sample of employees within the target group would be asked to test the user interface of the software according to specific guidelines. Subsequently, the test subjects would be asked about the usability they perceived and the benefits of the respective function.

A simple submission of quantitative feedback, via integrated feedback functions in the software, web forms, or supplementary test tools, simplifies and improves the test results.

For more information on effectively connecting additional test groups for usability tests, see the section on Friendly User Tests.

4.6.4   Notes and Recommendations on the Prototypical Approach

The presented prototypical approach must always be adapted specifically to the requirements of the project. The approach is particularly applicable to exploratory projects. Fully specified and defined requirements from the beginning would require a less extensive anticipatory evaluation and collection of ideas and needs. Depending on the finality of the product specification, a vertical prototype for clarifying technical questions should be implemented instead of a horizontal one. The approach also appears less effective if it is not possible to effectively involve the customer, as they ultimately need to support decisions based on feedback from employees.

To apply the described approach, sufficient methodological competence in the areas of requirements elicitation, preparation of interviews/surveys, and independent requirements specification is also necessary on the part of the involved project teams. Large teams should supplement the approach with defined internal decision-making processes.

With a parallel work of a large number of agile teams on a common prototype, the organizational efforts for coordination and support of the individual agile teams and stakeholders increase. To efficiently utilize multiple teams, capacities and concepts for task distribution and technical merging of designs would need to be added.

Organizations that have been strongly hierarchical up to now can benefit greatly from training agile project methods; prototypical and exploratory approaches are particularly well suited for this purpose. If there is no interest and openness towards the methods used, this can make it particularly difficult to involve the customer. Comprehensive project reporting obligations and requirements for a waterfall-like project planning in advance also tend to be contrary to the described approach.

For projects with a high budget, the risks must also be assessed differently. As a result, the proposed extension of the shown approach to include appropriate risk management is recommended and precise project controlling is also necessary.

In summary, prototyping and design thinking are ideally suited to establish digital transformation in a novel, agile organizational form and to connect all teams, organizational units, and stakeholders in an exploratory manner. All participants will experience the prototypical approach together, which strengthens cohesion within the organization and clarifies visions and goals of an organization, making them not only visualized but also applicable and tangible through the prototypes.

References

1. Sein, M. K., et al. (2011). Action design research. *MIS Quarterly*, pp. 37–56.
2. Cooper, A., et al. (2014). *About face: The essentials of interaction design* (4th edn.). Wiley.
3. Maaley, W. (2017). *Vorlesungsunterlagen zum Modul Empirical Software engineering—Software requirements—Requirement elicitation methods* Stand 09/2017. Universität Hamburg.
4. Mell, P., Grance, T., & National Institute of Standards and Technology. *The NIST definition of cloud computing*. https://csrc.nist.gov/publications/detail/sp/800-145/final. Accessed 10. Jan. 2022.
5. Smith, J. E., & Nair, R. (2005). The architecture of virtual machines. *Computer, 38*(5), 32–38.
6. Bernstein, D. (2014). Containers and cloud: From LXC to docker to kubernetes. *IEEE Cloud Computing, 1*(3), 81–84.
7. Docker Inc. *Docker Swarm—Container-Orchestrierung mit Docker*. https://docs.docker.com/engine/swarm/. Accessed 17. Feb. 2022.
8. Cloud Native Computing Foundation (CNCF). *CNCF annual survey 2021 report*. https://www.cncf.io/reports/cncf-annual-survey-2021/. Accessed 17. Feb. 2022.

9. Open Container Initiative. Standardisierungsgremium für Container-Technologien. https://opencontainers.org/. Accessed 22. Mar. 2022.
10. Open Container Initiative. *Technical oversight board (TOB).* https://github.com/opencontainers/tob. Accessed 22. Mar. 2022.
11. Cloud Native Computing Foundation—Projektwebsite. https://www.cncf.io/. Accessed 22. Mar. 2022.
12. Internet Engineering Task Force (IETF). Offizielle Seite des Standardisierungsgremiums. https://www.ietf.org/. Accessed 22. Mar. 2022.
13. Granata, D., & Rak, M. (2021). Design and development of a technique for the automation of the risk analysis process in IT security. *CLOSER 2021,* 87–98.
14. Schoeneberg, K.-P. (ed.). (2014). *Komplexitätsmanagement in Unternehmen: Herausforderungen im Umgang mit Dynamik, Unsicherheit und Komplexität meistern* (1st edn.). Springer/Gabler.
15. Mehraj, S., & Banday, M. T. (2020). Establishing a zero trust strategy in cloud computing environment. In *2020 international conference on computer communication and informatics (ICCCI)* (S. 1–6). IEEE.
16. Barker, E., & Barker, W. C. NIST, National Institute of Standards and Technology: Recommendation for key management part 2—Best practices for key management organisations. NIST Special Public Publication 800-57 Part 2, Revision 1. https://nvlpubs.nist.gov/nistpubs/SpecialPublications/NIST.SP.800-57pt2r1.pdf. Accessed 15. Feb. 2022.
17. Barker, E. NIST, National Institute of Standards and Technology: "Recommendation for key management part 1—General"—NIST Special Public Publication 800-57 Part 1, Revision 5. https://nvlpubs.nist.gov/nistpubs/SpecialPublications/NIST.SP.800-57pt1r5.pdf. Accessed 14. Feb. 2022.
18. Bundesamt für Sicherheit in der Informationstechnologie (BSI). (2021). "BSI—Technische Richtlinie—Kryptographische Verfahren: Empfehlungen und Schlüssellängen", BSI TR-02102-1 vom 24. März 2021. https://www.bsi.bund.de/SharedDocs/Downloads/DE/BSI/Publikationen/TechnischeRichtlinien/TR02102/BSI-TR-02102.pdf. Accessed 15. Feb. 2022.
19. NIST, National Institute of Standards and Technology: *"Definitions of public key infrastructure."* https://csrc.nist.gov/glossary/term/public_key_infrastructure. Accessed 16.Feb. 2022.
20. Tuecke, S., Welch, V., Engert, D., Pearlman, L., & Thompson, M. *Internet X.509 public key infrastructure (PKI) proxy certificate profile.* Rfc 3820—veröffentlicht im Juni 2004. https://www.hjp.at/doc/rfc/rfc3820.html. Accessed 13. Jan. 2022.
21. Hassan, S., Ali, N., & Bahsoon, R. (2017). Microservice ambients: An architectural meta-modelling approach for microservice granularity. In *2017 IEEE International Conference on Software Architecture (ICSA)* (S. 1–10). IEEE.
22. Taibi, D., & Lenarduzzi, V. (2018). On the definition of microservice bad smells. *IEEE Software, 35*(3), 56–62.
23. Fielding, R. T. (2000). *Architectural styles and the design of network-based software architectures.* Dissertation, Information and Computer Science, University of California, Irvine. https://www.ics.uci.edu/~fielding/pubs/dissertation/top.htm. Accessed 17. Feb. 2022.
24. DIN EN ISO 9241-11. *Ergonomie der Mensch-System-Interaktion—Teil 11: Gebrauchstauglichkeit: Begriffe und Konzepte* (ISO 9241-11:2018); Deutsche Fassung EN ISO 9241-11:2018. https://www.din.de/de/mitwirken/normenausschuesse/naerg/veroeffentlichungen/wdc-beuth:din21:279590417. Accessed 17. Mar. 2022.
25. World Wide Web Consortium (W3C). *Resource Description Framework (RDF).* https://www.w3.org/RDF/. Accessed 17. Mar. 2022.

26. Berners-Lee, et al. *RFC2396—Uniform Resource Identifiers (URI): Generic syntax.* Internet Engineering Task Force—08/1998. https://www.ietf.org/rfc/rfc2396.txt. Accessed 17. Mar. 2022.

27. OWASP, Open Web Application Security Project. *Top 10 web application security risks 2021.* https://owasp.org/www-project-top-ten/. Accessed 13. Jan. 2022.

28. OWASP, Open Web Application Security Project. *OWASP mobile security testing guide.* https://owasp.org/www-project-mobile-security-testing-guide/. Accessed 13. Jan. 2022.

29. BITKOM. *Position paper regulation on digital resilience for the financial sector (DORA).* https://www.bitkom.org/sites/default/files/2020-10/bitkom_position-paper_on_dora_20201016.pdf. Accessed 18. Feb. 2022.

30. Heise online. *Die Bedrohungslage verschärft sich—Log4j-Angriffe nehmen zu.* https://www.heise.de/news/Dienstag-Die-Bedrohungslage-verschaerft-sich-Log4j-Angriffe-nehmen-zu-6301155.html. Accessed 17. Mar. 2022.

31. Bundesamt für Sicherheit in der Informationstechnik (BSI). *Kritische Schwachstelle in Java-Bibliothek Log4j.* https://www.bsi.bund.de/DE/Themen/Unternehmen-und-Organisationen/Informationen-und-Empfehlungen/Empfehlungen-nach-Angriffszielen/Webanwendungen/log4j/log4j_node.html. Accessed 17. Feb. 2022.

32. Bryant, B. D., & Saiedian, H. (2017). A novel kill-chain framework for remote security log analysis with SIEM software. *Computers & Security, 67,* 198–210.

33. Microsoft Corp. (2009). *The STRIDE threat model.* Artikel vom 11.12.2009. https://docs.microsoft.com/en-us/previous-versions/commerce-server/ee823878(v=cs.20). Accessed 17. Mar. 2022.

34. Bundesamt für Sicherheit in der Informationstechnik (BSI). *Sicherheitsprofil für eine SaaS Collaboration Plattform—Teil 2: Bedrohungs- und Risikoanalyse.* https://www.bsi.bund.de/SharedDocs/Downloads/DE/BSI/CloudComputing/SaaS/SPC_Teil_2.pdf. Accessed 17. Mar. 2022.

35. Olsson, H. H., Alahyari, H., & Bosch, J. (2012). Climbing the „stairway to heaven"—A mulitiple-case study exploring barriers in the transition from agile development towards continuous deployment of software. In *2012 38th euromicro conference on software engineering and advanced applications* (S. 392–399). IEEE.

36. Humble, J., & Farley, D. (2010). *Continuous delivery: Reliable software releases through build, test, and deployment automation.* Pearson Education.

37. truffleHog. *Analyse-Software für Secrets in Git-Repositories.* https://github.com/trufflesecurity/truffleHog. Accessed 17. Mar. 2022.

38. Preston, D. (2005). Pair programming as a model of collaborative learning: A review of the research. *Journal of Computing Sciences in colleges, 20*(4), 39–45.

39. Williams, L. A. (2010). Pair programming. *Encyclopedia of software engineering, 2.*

40. Bundesverband Digitale Wirtschaft (BVDW) e. V. *EU-US Privacy Shield.* https://www.bvdw.org/themen/recht/eu-us-privacy-shield/. Accessed 27. Mai. 2022.

41. BSI—Bundesamt für Sicherheit in der Informationstechnik—IT Grundschutz, Lerneinheit 4.1: Grundlegende Definitionen. https://www.bsi.bund.de/DE/Themen/ITGrundschutz/ITGrundschutzSchulung/OnlinekursITGrundschutz2018/Lektion_4_Schutzbedarfsfeststellung/Lektion_4_01/Lektion_4_01_node.html.

42. Kerzazi, N., & Adams, B. (2016). *Who needs release and devops engineers, and why?* Proceedings of the international workshop on continuous software evolution and delivery, pp. 77–83.

43. Gerstbach, I. (2016). *Design Thinking im Unternehmen: Ein Workbook für die Einführung von Design Thinking* (1st edn.). GABAL Verlag GmbH.

44. Ernst, H., Schmidt, J., & Beneken, G. (2016). *Grundkurs Informatik: Grundlagen und Konzepte für die erfolgreiche IT-Praxis.—Eine umfassende praxisorientierte Einführung* (6th edn.). Springer/Vieweg.
45. Obermaier, R. (2016). *Industrie 4.0 als unternehmerische Gestaltungsaufgabe: Betriebswirtschaftliche, technische und rechtliche Herausforderungen* (1st edn.). Springer Gabler.
46. Gaubinger, K., Rabl, M., Swan, S., & Werani, T. (edn.). (2015). *Innovation and product management—A holistic and practical approach to uncertainty reduction* (1st edn.). Springer.
47. Fischer, P., & Hofer, P. (2011). *Lexikon der Informatik* (15th edn.). Springer.
48. Maaley, W. (2017). *Vorlesungsunterlagen Modul Empirical Software Engineering*—Software Requirements—Requirement Elicitation Methods und Foliensatz zum Themenkomplex Prototyping—Stand 09/2017—Universität Hamburg.
49. Richter, M., & Flückiger, M. (2013). *Usability Engineering kompakt: Benutzbare Produkte gezielt entwickeln* (3rd edn.). Springer/Vieweg.
50. Zimmermann, K. (August 2013). *Referenzprozessmodell für das Business-IT-Management—Vorgehen, Erstellung und Einsatz auf Basis qualitativer Forschungsmethoden.* Dissertation zur Erlangung des Doktorgrades (Dr. rer. nat.) am Fachbereich Informatik, Fakultät für Mathematik, Informatik und Naturwissenschaften der Universität Hamburg.
51. Pomberger, G., & Pree, W. (2004). *Software Engineering: Architektur-Design und Prozessorientierung* (3rd edn.). Hanser.
52. Alpar, P., Alt, R., Bensberg, F., Grob, H. L., Weimann, P., & Winter, R. (2016). *Anwendungsorientierte Wirtschaftsinformatik—Strategische Planung, Entwicklung und Nutzung von Informationssystemen* (8th edn.). Springer/Vieweg.
53. Cooper, A., et al. (2014). *About face: The essentials of interaction design.* Wiley.
54. Buber, R., & Holzmüller, H. H. (2007). *Qualitative Marktforschung.* Gabler.
55. Richter, M., & Flückiger, M. D. (2013). *Usability Engineering kompakt: benutzbare Produkte gezielt entwickeln.* Springer.
56. Dumke, R. (2013). *Software Engineering: Eine Einführung für Informatiker und Ingenieure: Systeme, Erfahrungen, Methoden, Tools.* Springer.
57. Weinreich, U., et al. (2016). *Lean digitization.* Springer.
58. Saadatmand, M. (2017). *Assessment of minimum viable product techniques: A literature.* Assessment.
59. Olsen, D. (2015). *The lean product playbook: How to innovate with minimum viable products and rapid customer feedback.* Wiley.
60. Hoffmann, C., et al. (eds.). (2016). *Business Innovation: Das St. Galler Modell.* Springer Gabler.
61. DIN EN ISO 9241-392. *Ergonomie der Mensch-System-Interaktion—Teil 392: Ergonomische Anforderungen zur Reduktion visueller Ermüdung durch stereoskopische Bilder* (ISO 9241-392:2015); Deutsche Fassung EN ISO 9241-392:2017. https://www.din.de/de/mitwirken/normenausschuesse/naerg/veroeffentlichungen/wdc-beuth:din21:270021604. Accessed 21.03.2022.
62. Böhringer, J., et al. (2014). *Kompendium der Mediengestaltung: IV. Medienproduktion Digital.* Springer.

Agile Prioritization Model for Software Manufacturers

5

In this section, a specially developed agile organizational and prioritization model for software manufacturers in the context of a software product family is presented.

This model is fundamentally universally valid for software manufacturers and equally usable for all organizations in which the development of software-based solutions and digital services plays a central role.

It is obvious that this model will also deliver precise results in favor of your company's success in comparable constellations. Otherwise, you can intervene at any time and adapt the agile model to your organization and needs. The decisive factor here is the democratic inclusion of all stakeholders, as we have described in detail how you should proceed.

The aim of modeling the presented Large-Scale Agile Framework is to develop an agile organizational and prioritization model suitable for software manufacturers in the context of a software product family in order to improve the cross-product organization and prioritization. With a focus on the efficient design of software product lines, optimization, dimensions of technical framework conditions, professional documentation, and inter-process communication are at the center of such a model.

For software manufacturers, projects that represent individual software products are the actual value drivers. Thus, the success of a software manufacturer's company is directly dependent on software projects, so that a detailed structured multi-project management and controlling is of great importance. This applies equally to organizations whose value drivers are digital services. This includes platform operators who pursue an analogous strategy. In addition to the project level, all processes that reflect the life cycle of software products must be considered specifically for software manufacturers.

Pure multi-project management (MPM) does not offer suitable solutions for this. The desire for increasing flexibility also requires moving away from conventional, rigid structures. In contrast, pure MPM is a strictly hierarchical organizational model with typical

S. Block, *Large-Scale Agile Frameworks*, https://doi.org/10.1007/978-3-662-67782-7_5

top-down structures in its purest form and is therefore not a contemporary organizational model for a software manufacturer.

Requirement of key figure-based control and synchronization of a large number of projects
Crucial for companies in the role of a software manufacturer is rather that coordinated planning, control, and synchronization take place with regard to success-relevant key figures for a large number of projects, between which strong dependencies exist. For this purpose, the Balanced Scorecard model presented based on the life cycle of software products appears to be a sensible approach for such key figure-based control. The developed model is closely based on SAFe but also includes elements from the team concept of the Spotify Engineering Model, as well as the architecture and domain-related recommendations from Domain-Driven Design. The requirements for the efficient design of software product lines are also taken into account.

Embedding quality criteria for software in the software release cycle
Furthermore, the development of software products within a software product family must meet the qualitative requirements defined in ISO/IEC 25010, achieve corresponding economic efficiency with regard to the resources used, and at the same time meet the ever faster changing requirements in terms of agile software development.

Cross-functional prioritization of processes and activities in the agile software release cycle
Concrete questions are suitable for organizing an agile software release cycle in order to prioritize the internal processes and activities in the company that uses software for its business processes and digital services.

In the prioritization of processes and activities, the focus is on the different agile teams with their specialized tasks and roles.

5.1 To What Extent Does Your Organization Act in the Role of a Software Manufacturer?

Engaging with the question of to what extent your organization acts in the role of a software manufacturer is extremely rewarding. Even if the distribution of software—in contrast to traditional software manufacturers—is not a defined corporate goal for your organization, you will recognize many factors along the way to answering the question that also apply to your organization.

For organizations where digital services are the main value drivers, the focus is even more on digital marketing aspects, but the development of digital services should be understood analogously to the corresponding software releases of a software manufacturer.

Companies in the Role of Software Manufacturer

If a company designs its software for other companies, then it is in the role of a software manufacturer.

To find an answer to the question of to what extent your organization acts in the role of a software manufacturer, please consider that the transition to a software manufacturer in an increasingly digitalized world is fluid. While many companies such as retail groups and product manufacturers may not be software manufacturers, software products and digital services currently represent the central challenges for these companies.

To illustrate this, the following section presents examples of companies and their services that are suitable for highlighting important aspects. Use the examples listed to reflect on how dependent your organization is on software-based processes and agile transformation...

Outsourcing of IT Development

If your organization pursues an outsourcing strategy or has no sufficient internal capacities for the complete development of its software-side services and products, then the associated restrictions and limitations must be clear.

As soon as IT development is outsourced, the responsibility for requirement definition increases even more. The internal IT strategy of your organization remains the responsibility of your organization, even if external consulting is involved, as an IT strategy is inseparably linked to the positioning and overall strategy of your organization.

In addition, topics such as data structures, data management, and IT security must be optimally aligned with the service-oriented aspects of your organization's target groups. Long-term outsourcing based solely on cost savings or because internal know-how and employee-related resources are lacking is always strategically inferior in the long run.

Moreover, the more dependent your organization is on software, the greater the degree of customization and individualization of the software used. This already brings with it the need for differentiation from competitors, and this differentiation is increasingly shifting to the quality of digital services.

5.1.1   Example 1: Is LEGO a Software Manufacturer?

Consider, for example, the company that has become globally known and successful with the LEGO brand. Do software products play a central role for this company—in addition to the actual LEGO products? ...

Figure 5.1 "Screenshot of the LEGO online shop as part of the LEGO world" illustrates how the LEGO brand integrates the online shop as part of the LEGO website and demonstrates that the frontend development of a website is closely linked to backend

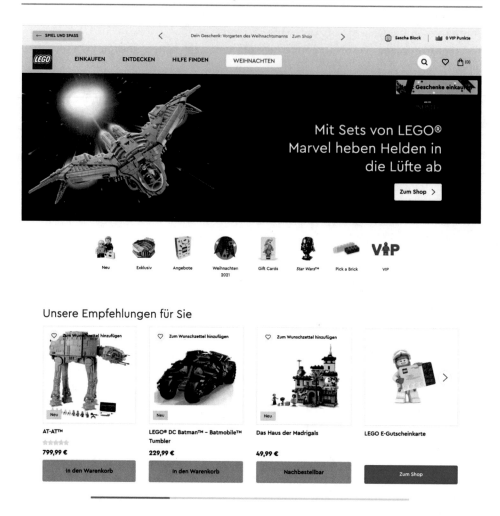

Fig. 5.1 Screenshot of the LEGO online shop as part of the LEGO website

systems and the underlying data models in order to offer customers service-oriented experience worlds with up-to-date data.

In this context, digital experience worlds and offer platforms play far more significant roles than merely promoting digital marketing. Digital service offerings and products in the form of apps and digital services on the international LEGO website have long complemented the globally popular colorful building blocks.

Figure 5.2 "LEGO Apps in the iOS Store" are evidence that numerous additional software artifacts—here in the form of iOS apps—are important experience and feedback channels. Each company, in turn, will be interested in integrating a single artifact as a functioning component within its entire digital experience world. With such an IT

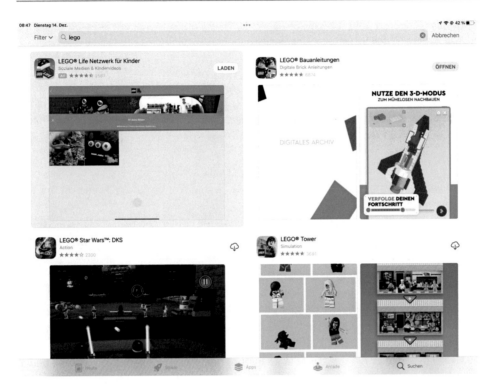

Fig. 5.2 LEGO Apps in the iOS Store

strategy, customer-oriented services always work across products and offer the best possible user experience.

The LEGO Group already initiated an agile transformation of its digital business departments in 2016, which also includes the introduction of a new digital operating model [1]. The decision-makers at the LEGO Group recognized that the transition to a digital company places special demands on adaptability. Over the years, the corporate group has been able to build a powerful enterprise platform.

> *"What is often overlooked is the massive system integration and the extent to which the LEGO Group is actually an IT and a brand-oriented company."—Jørgen Vig Knudstorp*

Jørgen Vig Knudstorp has been part of the LEGO Group since 1995 and was its CEO until January 1, 2017, and was significantly involved in its current corporate success. He recognized early on fundamental problems within the organization regarding agility and digital strategies [1]:

> *"We are not adept enough when it comes to developing software, such as smaller applications, disruptive business models, omnichannel landscapes, e-commerce, web-based services, cloud-based services, and so on. We are not agile enough there. And we could risk ending up with a legacy platform instead of an advantage platform."—Jørgen Vig*

*Knudstorp*One year after the transformation, the effects of the new model are evident in a significant reduction in response time to changes—from months to weeks—in the core functions of the company [2].

The example of the LEGO Group is, on the one hand, good evidence of how heavily companies in every industry now depend on software and digital services. On the other hand, the clearly defined role of software manufacturers recedes into the background insofar as the need for digitization and agile processes is of the utmost relevance in any case.

Even if it is to be ensured that published apps and software releases are always compatible with new devices and technologies, there is a direct proximity to the role of the software manufacturer.

It is also secondary whether a company commissions other companies to produce custom software for its own organization or whether this software is to be heavily adapted to the respective company processes by third parties, i.e., whether the software development is provided entirely internally or not. The LEGO Group, for example, not only uses software solutions such as those from SAP but also serves an ever-growing demand for digital toys and promotes the sale of LEGO bricks with video games, programmable LEGO robots, augmented reality offerings, and is strongly committed to intensifying customer relationships.

This is evident, on the one hand, in a rapidly growing LEGO online community and a rapidly growing library of digital content offerings. The official LEGO YouTube channel, which was registered in 2005, currently has almost 14 million subscribers and has over 17 billion video views [3].

From the service perspective of customers and consumers, it is entirely irrelevant who designed a digital service; the only decisive factors for them are service and product quality, combined with their experience.

In this context, it also fits into the overall picture that the influencer who became known as the "Hero of the Stones," who had already built up a considerable reach as a YouTuber with around 727,000 subscribers and over 233 million video views on YouTube [4], was perceived as a serious threat to the brand. The LEGO Group had taken legal action against the YouTube star and had sued him for trademark infringement, in which the generic term "LEGO" was at the center, which did not diminish the popularity of the "Hero-of-the-Stones format." On the contrary, the legal action taken by the corporation has been met with incomprehension by a broad section of LEGO fans [5]. Purely in terms of the share of video views on YouTube, this amounts to "only" 1.33% reach of an influencer in direct comparison.

The example of the trademark dispute à la David and Goliath, in the context of the above quote from the former LEGO CEO, illustrates all the more how important it is to establish agile processes within large organizations that are capable of responding not only quickly but also appropriately to any occurrences. Such events also fall into the category of emergency management, which requires close cooperation between various agile teams.

The example of the LEGO Group also shows that a transformation to agile processes and digital strategies is an ongoing, continuous process. It is obvious that transformations take longer the larger and more heterogeneous an organization is and the lower the agile maturity level of individual teams within the organization. Furthermore, the example illustrates how obvious it is to consider an organization as a software manufacturer.

5.1.2 Example 2: Flaschenpost.de—Innovative, App-driven Beverage Service

The digital beverage delivery service Flaschenpost is a good example of how traditional processes can be successfully digitized and a disruptive approach to established market participants. Started as a company from Münster, the innovative delivery service now exists in numerous cities and dominates not only with its innovative service concept in the industry.

Flaschenpost offers online ordering of beverages, groceries, and everyday products and delivers them to customers within 120 min. No delivery fee is charged, and deposit bottles can be returned to the supplier. As of 2022, Flaschenpost offers the delivery service, starting from over 30 warehouse locations, nationwide in 170 German cities and municipalities [6]. The option of online ordering via the website was quickly supplemented by a native iOS and Android app, thus intensifying the customer relationship in parallel to the email newsletter by adding another level of customer loyalty.

Functionally, the app also offers additional features, such as customer-specific tracking for tracking one's beverage order, push notifications for status changes, and information on current special offers, for example.

Figure 5.3 shows the "ordering process via the Flaschenpost app". The almost negligible delay of 3 minutes and the precise delivery in real-time can be tracked based on the time.

As a Flaschenpost customer, it is an invaluable advantage for me to know exactly when I will be supplied, as I am also informed in advance about the start of the delivery. And of course, the delivery almost always takes place within the desired 2-hour interval of my pre-order.

A win-win situation for both sides: For both the Flaschenpost company and me as a customer, the beverage delivery is predictable, reliable, and always a positive experience. Of course, I also receive the receipt of my order as a digital proof of purchase. And, naturally, the return of empties is handled and easily digitally accounted for.

In October 2020, the successful company changed ownership and is now part of the Oetker Group with an estimated purchase price of around 1 billion euros [7]. This is an impressive achievement, especially since the founder Dieter Büchl had founded the beverage delivery service in 2015 with substantial venture capital support amounting to 3 million EUR. By 2019, Flaschenpost had already achieved sales of around 90 million EUR. Due to the Corona crisis, beverage delivery services like Flaschenpost were

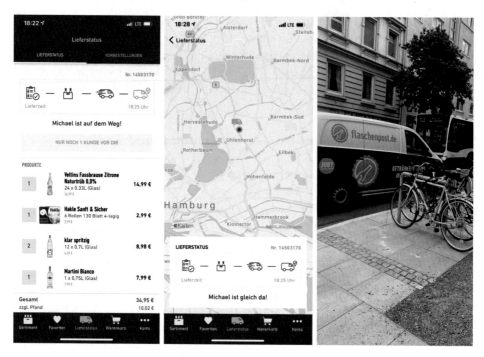

Fig. 5.3   Ordering process via the Flaschenpost app

rewarded with strong sales growth for their digital business model. The takeover by the Oetker Group impressively demonstrates how much manufacturers value direct touch-points with customers and how little corporations seem to trust themselves with such projects. In addition, Flaschenpost had succeeded in placing beer and water private labels alongside its digital service offering.

5.1.3   Example 3: Moia—Digital Shuttle Service

Moia is a service offering with which the Volkswagen Group has prototypically started an independent company with locations in Berlin and Hamburg and has since success-fully operated a popular ride-pooling service in Hamburg and Hanover.

MOIA serves as a current example of the close integration of hardware and software and at the same time for a clever, image-oriented service strategy with a green thumb-print.

Figure 5.4 shows the "iOS App of the digital shuttle service MOIA" and also illus-trates how pleasant and convenient a shuttle service can work in conjunction with a cus-tomer app. In addition to the number and type of passengers, a child seat and/or booster

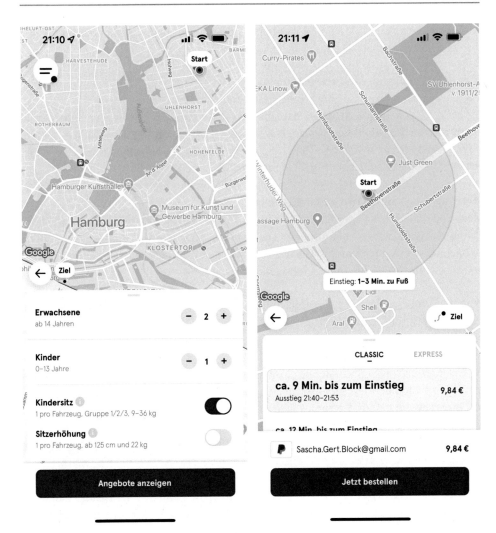

Fig. 5.4 iOS App of the digital shuttle service MOIA

seat can be easily booked. Different service offers can be selected, which may differ in waiting time or distance to the boarding point. Payment is, of course, cashless, and the tip can be chosen at the end of the ride or in advance. It's a pity that this service is only available in Hamburg and Hanover so far…

MOIA redefines mobility in urban spaces
The ride-sharing service Moia is VW's contribution to minimizing individual traffic in cities with electric shuttles. In Hamburg's cityscape, the extravagant electric cars stand out not only because of their striking gold color but also with their clear lines and

extravagant design. Moreover, a Moia offers its passengers luxury public transport at the push of a button and, above all, via an app.

With Moia, the group has been developing a system for shared electric shuttle rides in Hamburg since 2019. Hamburg residents have already ordered a Moia vehicle via the app four million times. At about half the taxi price, it takes passengers—often with minor detours for additional passengers—to their destination. So far, this has been a major subsidy business for VW: The group not only built the specially developed electric vehicles but also three depots with charging infrastructure [8].

MOIA develops tomorrow's mobility today
Meanwhile, the Volkswagen Group also wants to use its expertise to offer its own strategy in terms of autonomous driving. The company is currently testing the vision of autonomous driving with prototypes. By 2025, the autonomous technology of transportation should also be usable for the ridesharing service [9].

With this strategy, Volkswagen not only strengthens its technological know-how and launches as an official city partner in public transport (ÖPNV), but also improves its overall image with its emission-free mobility service and intensifies its customer relationships through the app service.

The three examples illustrate the close interlocking of digital services with a focus on maximum customer orientation. All three examples represent service scenarios from our real everyday life based on complex data and innovative technologies.

The result is always a service that customers are happy to use and, in doing so, naturally use and no longer want to do without the offered technologies—which are often a prerequisite for using the service scenario.

The necessary technologies and the associated know-how should ideally be best represented internally by companies offering such product or service scenarios, or at least be mastered so well that desired reaction times on the customer side can be realistically depicted. If call centers or third parties are involved as service partners, unwanted service efforts with usually long lead times inevitably arise. No one wants cascading service chains, telephone waiting loops, or email responses that take longer than expected…

Accordingly, the three practical examples also illustrate how important it is for companies and organizations to understand their role as software manufacturers. The sooner you can come to terms with this role, the better your service times will turn out, and the more pleasant the usability and benefits of your digital service will be for customers.

Why not give it a try and take on the role of a software manufacturer for your organization!

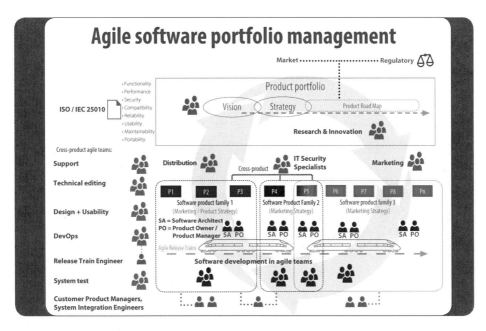

Fig. 5.5   Agile Software Portfolio Management. (*Source*: Sascha Block)

5.2   Agile Teams and Roles At Software Manufacturers

In order for organizations in the role of a software manufacturer to effectively design digital services and software products as the main value drivers in the course of digital transformation, the focus must be as closely aligned as possible with digital marketing options.

To achieve this, the development of digital services must be realized with Git repository-based software releases.

The central role is played by the Agile Release Train concept presented, which is at the center of the interaction of all agile teams and reflects all IT security aspects from the beginning with the Security-by-Design approach.

In Fig. 5.5 "Agile Software Portfolio Management", such an agile prioritization model for software manufacturers is shown.

The teams and roles recommended for the model are derived from practical requirements and a comparison with the current state of research. Table 5.1 "Overview Table Teams and Roles" lists the essential roles, teams, and their functions together with a compact task description, which are recommended for an agile prioritization model for software development.

Table 5.1 Overview Table Teams and Roles. (Source: Sascha Block, Own Representation)

Teams	Description and Tasks	Roles
Executive Board/ Management	The Executive Board/Management is responsible for the company strategy and positioning in the market. With active networking, they also shape and coordinate partnerships and alliances. They are responsible for the distribution of financial resources and, together with the Product Owners, shape the project budgets. In close coordination with the CDO and the agile software development teams, they coordinate the vision, strategy, and software product portfolio aligned with all software products. They maintain close contact with the Product Owners and agile teams and support them in achieving their goals. Active support is provided, for example, in removing existing obstacles or mediating in existing conflicts and bringing about objective decisions.	
Chief Digital Officer (CDO)	The CDO's goal is to develop a clear digitalization strategy and implement it continuously. To this end, he/she develops digital processes and services for customers, suppliers, partners, and internal processes in close cooperation with all agile teams. He/she ensures that the teams aligned with this can work optimally and achieve their goals. In doing so, he/she ensures that the defined goals harmonize with the legal framework conditions and that optimal IT security is guaranteed.	
Product Owner/ Software Product Manager	In addition to market observation and positioning of software products in relation to customer-specific business cases, Product Owners primarily are responsible for: • Software products within the software product portfolio • Software product roadmap and corresponding agile release plans • Agile prioritization of requirements	
Research & Innovation	Product-wide support function:	Technical Consultants
Marketing	Product-wide support function: • Development of brand strategy • Establishing a consistent brand communication • Marketing across all channels and media • …	Team leader, Marketing staff
Sales	Product-wide support function:	Team leader, Account Manager
Support	Product-wide support function: • Responding to support requests • Internal and customer-side license management for software products	Team leader, Support staff

(continued)

Table 5.1   (continued)

Teams	Description and Tasks	Roles
DevOps	Product-wide support function: Infrastructure services specialized in the area of hardware and tools for software development, as well as DevOps support for test environments.	Team leader, DevOps Engineers
IT-Security/ SecDevOps	Product-wide support function: • Requirement definitions for the IT security of software products • IT security-focused technology analysis • Organization and execution of penetration tests • Stakeholder briefing on the status of IT security, especially CDO, software architects, and product owners	IT security specialists, e.g. SecDevOps Engineer, IT Security Consultants
Technical Documentation	Product-wide support function: Multilingual, cross-media software product documentation for customers, e.g. in the form of online help, installation manuals, tutorials, etc. Partially overlapping area of activity in coordination with marketing (e.g. product flyers, proofreading function, graphics) and in close cooperation with development teams, marketing, sales, and product management.	Team leader, Technical Editors
Design/Usability	Cross-product support function: Standardization of interfaces in software products and development of technical frontend and usability solutions.	Team leader, project leader, usability experts, usability engineers
System test	Cross-product support function: Quality assurance using different testing methods at the level of individual products, as well as across products.	Team leader, software tester
Customer Product Manager	Representative of licensees and customers of custom software solutions. Represents customer interests, collects direct feedback from customers on site	Customer product manager
System integration	Cross-product support function: Integration of products into the heterogeneous IT landscape of license customers.	Team leader, integration engineers

(continued)

Table 5.1 (continued)

Teams	Description and Tasks	Roles
Agile Software Product Teams	Specialized development teams, assigned at the product level. Initial and ongoing further development of technical software solutions. Internal developer tests, which are automated as far as possible. The type of technical architecture and detailed process documentation is also in the hands of the product-specific development teams.	Product manager, project leader, team leader, software architects, software developers, maintenance officers
Release Train Engineer	Cross-functional role for organizing and coordinating cross-product release dates with regard to the product roadmap. Possibly attached to the DevOps team.	Release Train Engineer

5.3   Processes and Activities

The following section describes the essential processes and activities relevant to the model:

Agile Product Management
Executive board/management, CDO, and Product Owner are jointly responsible, in close cooperation with the agile development teams, for the vision and strategy aligned with all software products, as well as the product portfolio.

The cross-product vision and strategy are mutually dependent and primarily focused on the company's economic objectives. The product/service portfolio represents all individual software products and software services with their specific characteristics.

A software product family is a group of functionally complementary software products; as such, it addresses the specific needs of defined customer groups and is related for strategic marketing reasons. Laukkanen et al. confirm that complex constellations—including the environment of a software product family in a highly regulated market—require a correspondingly stringent release engineering [10, Sect. 5.3]. The same applies analogously to the bundling of software services.

Technically speaking, a single software product can be represented within a Git-based repository branch. By using so-called feature branches, it becomes possible to bundle various variants within a product branch, making customer-specific customizations easily manageable through such feature branches. The same approach can be applied to software-based services, for example, within the scope of a SaaS platform strategy.

Product Owners actively contribute to product strategy

The role of the software product manager is virtually identical to that of the Product Owner in agile framework models. Typically, the software product manager is responsible for defining the product strategy and defines it in relation to the product for a period of at least one to five years. This product strategy should be in line with the overarching portfolio strategy. In addition, there is a risk of bias and "tunnel vision"; a possible solution is the establishment of a committee that incorporates recommendations directly related to the product and between the product and portfolio. Product Owners will regularly have a higher level of detailed knowledge about their products/services than the more distant CDO, yet both actors align their strategies for the organization.

Increased IT security in the software lifecycle is essential

Moreover, the currently applicable requirements regarding IT security must be taken into account; these requirements are continuously introduced and monitored by the IT security team. IT security is a MUST criterion for software and thus also causes fixed cost components. These quality assurance efforts are relevant for both individual software products and the software portfolio, as well as within the entire DevOps cycle. Accordingly, the efforts for IT security must be made assignable and differentiated into cross-product/service and product/service-specific costs. In any case, IT security is indispensable and must be included in the pricing.

Agile change request process and cross-product product backlog in harmony

An agile change request process—in the context of a software product family and software product lines—is based on a cross-product product backlog and various product-specific product backlogs, with the cross-product product backlog synchronizing and prioritizing the requirements towards the individual software products.

The Product Owner manages the product backlog. At a central location, all features of the software product represented by him, which are coordinated with the software product portfolio, are transparently accessible. Software services are to be understood here as software products in the same way. The backlog organizes and prioritizes all requirements aligned with these features and submitted to the development team for implementation.

In doing so, all Product Owners collectively—supported by the software architects—ensure that no disadvantages arise in terms of software architecture from a specific product configuration in the future. The Product Owner of an individual software product is responsible for the product strategy and aligns it with the cross-product strategy for the product portfolio.

Agile management of efficient software product lines

The main task of strategic and technically coordinated software product portfolio management—in the context of software engineering focused on software product lines—is

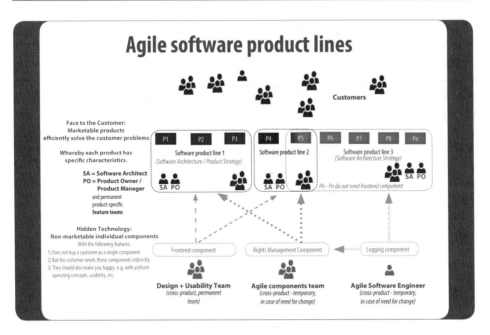

Fig. 5.6 Agile Software Product Lines—Sascha Block

the alignment of a product portfolio through the definition of distinguishable product features that characterize the essence of each individual line product.

Metzger/Pohl point out the importance of character features in software product lines: In defining such character features, there is a risk that the scope of a software product line becomes too large, so that domain artifacts become too general and the effort to realize them becomes too high. On the other hand, if the scope is defined too narrowly, potentially required features as well as functional and quality requirements of many customers may not be covered, and only very few applications can be derived from the product line. In both cases, the product line may not be economically viable [11, p. 189].

Figure 5.6 "Agile Software Product Lines" illustrates the interaction of agile teams, showing how non-marketable individual components represent technologically required basic functions, while the functions directly perceivable by the customer efficiently solve customer problems in the form of marketable software products.

Identifying Basic Components

Product Owners and Software Architects ensure that the software product lines represent valid variants of a base product, which have a common software architecture as far as possible and are based on identical basic components that are incorporated into each individual product of this line according to prescribed architectural specifications [12,

p. 23]. Agile component teams develop the necessary, cross-product base technologies for this purpose.

Cooperation of Feature Teams, Product Owners, Software Architects, and Security Specialists

The product teams develop the actual software products as permanent feature teams and are responsible—together with Product Owners, Software Architects, and Security Specialists—for the product architecture with the product-specific characteristics.

Analogous to the recommendations of Dingsøyr et al., the iterative development process of the feature teams is divided into four phases [13, p. 501]:

1. **Requirements Analysis:** This phase begins with the transfer of defined functionalities in the form of roughly abstracted User Stories. The Product Owner prioritizes the product backlog.
2. **Solution Description:** The User Stories are described in more detail and assigned to Epics, which also cover the design and architecture. Then, the individual User Stories are estimated in terms of effort and assigned to a feature team.
3. **Construction:** Development of the functionalities commissioned via the backlog in the form of tested, fully functional solutions.
4. **Release:** A formal functional and non-functional test to ensure that the entire release works according to expectations. This includes internal and external interfaces as well as the interaction between components and systems.

The Release Train Engineer (RTE) organizes the release processes and coordinates the release dates across all Product Owners and agile teams.

Whether the role of the RTE is functionally close to the agile software development teams or in the overarching DevOps team depends closely on the company processes and is crucial as long as such responsibility is not clearly regulated. Paasivaara comes to the same conclusion and classifies the explicit application of the RTE role as a key success factor [14, pp. 39/49].

Hidden Technology in the Form of Non-Marketable Individual Components

In order to create market-ready software product lines that efficiently solve customer problems and are modularly coordinated and optimally complement each other, non-marketable individual components must be identified in an analysis and transformation process, which typically have the following three characteristics: First, these functional individual components are not in demand by the customer; second, the customer still needs these components indirectly; and third, such components should "round off" the software product as a whole and make the customer as a software user "happy".

Typical examples of such non-independently usable and marketable software components are logging or frontend components and rights management.

The goal of an efficient software product line design is now to identify product-wide functions required by multiple software products and to outsource them in the form of "Hidden Technology". The implementation of these hidden technology components is always product-wide and can be carried out by a permanently or temporarily defined team, depending on the need for change and the intensity of the task. In any case, it is important to ensure that all software products are integrated into the software architecture concept in a compatible manner. Because strong dependencies exist, proactive involvement of agile development teams facilitates consensus building and ultimately ensures a design and architecture concept that is coordinated across all software product lines. In this way, software product lines enable a differentiated marketing strategy and medium- and long-term measurable scaling and synergy effects with a clearly demonstrable economic benefit. At the same time, it is ensured at all times that the individual software products within the product portfolio offer smooth interaction and the most variable combination possible. In addition, testing efforts are significantly reduced [as also 15].

The Special Role of the Customer Product Manager
Customer product managers intensify cooperation with the customer and ensure active feedback processes from license customers. This ensures that largely standardized software product lines offer the highest possible scaling effect [11, pp. 70/71] and that the diametrical interest is optimally reconciled. Software platforms serve as control instruments for innovations; in this context, the research and innovation team assumes a product-wide advisory and mediation function for and between the agile teams.

Solutions for Dealing with Individualized Software License Products
With regard to individualizable software license products, customer product managers, together with the product manager and product management, clarify to what extent customer requirements are still product-compliant and can be incorporated into the further development of software product lines. In contrast, the high degree of customization to meet specific customer needs provides a valid reason to consistently separate such adapted release versions from the development branch of a software line and to label them in this way as clearly defined customer-specific special products. This has an impact on the Git repository-based organization of software releases. As a consequence, separate release plans must be maintained for such individualized software products. It is also necessary to decide when the effort of further development becomes too high and ties up too many valuable resources, so that licensees must decide to switch releases within the software product line with repeated individualization.

Life Cycles and Technology Phases of Software Products
Product owners should be able to name the phase of a software product within its life cycle at any time and align the release planning accordingly. This includes ongoing stra-

tegic decisions and a cost-benefit analysis [16], e.g., to answer the question of whether the introduction of new software products is justified.

To evaluate individual software products, product management is required to reliably recognize, analyze, and assess relevant innovations. Ford and Ryan recommend a coherent strategy based on a technology portfolio and introduce classified technology phases (Phase 1: Pacing technologies, Phase 2: Key technologies, Phase 3: Basic technologies) [17].

Goodwin et al. [18, pp. 1082–1097] express reservations regarding the validity of existing analysis methods for predicting the importance of technologies, as the required basic data is usually already lacking in the non-availability of time series data—especially the heterogeneity of customers—and the necessary macroeconomic basic data. Therefore, the accompanying support of a research- and innovation-oriented team in an advisory function plays an even more significant role.

Portfolio analysis and the relevance of key technologies

Portfolio analysis is an indispensable tool for software manufacturers. They are continuously dependent on integrating relevant key technologies in the development of innovative and competitive software products. Therefore, it is essential to prioritize the identification, evaluation, and investment in pacing technologies relevant to the software product portfolio at the right time to develop market-ready software technologies. This ensures that market and regulatory requirements are fully taken into account.

This enables the company to assume a market-leading role in a market segment. Furthermore, a healthy technology mix should ensure that innovative customer groups refinance the investment-intensive key technologies and less demanding customer groups support the profitability of the software manufacturer through the licensing of basic technologies. In addition, key technologies in the early stage require the willingness to change, primarily from innovative customer groups.

Effectively removing obstacles in the transformation process

In the transformation process, the executive board/management and product owner work together to remove opposing obstacles, support the relevance of feedback, promote the agile mindset, and the agile corporate organization across all levels.

Balance of prioritization top-down and bottom-up

The balance of prioritization is not only top-down but also bottom-up and externally influenced [19]. The optimization of quality and time-to-market are accompanying effects [20].

The cross-product teams (support, DevOps, IT security/DevSecOps, technical documentation, design + usability, system testing, marketing, sales, research and innovation, and customer product managers) support the agile software product teams in the further development and maintenance of the software products.

Dual role of the product owner

The product owners assume a dual role: On the one hand, they act as advocates and representatives of the interests of an agile software product team; on the other hand, they take responsibility for the software product they are responsible for as product owners.

The software architects and IT security specialists provide professional support to the individual software product teams regarding software architecture and the implementation of IT security standards and regulatory requirements. The software architects and IT security specialists coordinate the product-specific and cross-product software architecture optimally with the product owner and among themselves. The teams negotiate compromises among themselves, and the research & innovation team has an advisory and process-accompanying support function. It makes sense for these teams to be closely linked and mutually complement their skills and expertise.

The Release Engineering typically covers—according to the recommendations of Laukkanen et al. [10, p. 3]—six areas:

1. **Version control** (Branching and Merging),
2. **Deployment Pipeline** (Code generation and largely automated testing),
3. **Build systems** (Compiling, linking, and bundling in packages),
4. **Code-based infrastructures** such as automatic configuration of servers, middleware, applications, firewalls, etc.,
5. **Deployment:** Rolling out a new software version as well as
6. **Release:** The publication of a new software version.

Agile Feedback Processes and Knowledge Management

All agile teams are continuously actively involved through ongoing feedback processes. Product Owners have the following methods available for planning, prioritizing, organizing, risk minimization, and implementation of feedback processes and agile knowledge management:

- **RACI—Responsibility Matrix/Role Model Canvas**
- **Guiding questions for moderated prioritization**
- **Timeboxing/Feature Boxing**
- **Multi-point/Single-point query**
- **Liquid Democracy/Liquid Feedback**
- **Liberating Structures**

The arc42 template [21] provides Product Owners and software architects and IT security specialists with a proven framework for joint agile knowledge management, especially for:

- **Questions for architectural decisions and IT security**
- **Constraints, context delimitation**

A well-structured knowledge management also effectively supports all stakeholders in identifying cross-sectional topics and forming horizontal and vertical agile teams. The following information is helpful in this regard:

- **Personas of stakeholders**
- **Map of contact persons/"System" responsible persons**

Collaboration Tools provide valuable organization-wide support

Modern collaboration tools provide valuable, project-accompanying support for all employees and teams in an organization. When selecting such technology tools, it is essential to ensure that each stakeholder has access to all relevant areas for them.

External exchange is also recommended: Expertise is not only gained through internal organizational exchange with colleagues, but also through subject-related topic groups and Meetup events, professional conferences, online learning, etc.

This is relevant in terms of modern collaboration tools because, in addition to personal exchange, they significantly simplify knowledge management with regard to such events in the form of shared calendars and the integration of content and links.

Agile Software Tools for Support

By now, various tools are available for this purpose, and there are also suggestions with the arc42 template [21] on how to efficiently record architectural decisions. Nevertheless, in the context of agile software development, there is still a lack of established methods for effectively managing software projects centrally across departments within the company and across company boundaries and providing support throughout all project phases.

- How can changes be effectively communicated?
- How are milestones documented in an easily understandable way across disciplines, and how can task allocation in interdisciplinary teams be effectively managed?

Artifacts for Knowledge Management

- Scalable software product lines offer advantages in economic and strategic terms through a differentiable orientation.
- Based on the factors of sales, liquidity, and profitability, product management should be able to identify the phase of a software product within its life cycle at any time and align release planning accordingly.

5.4   Conclusion

Based on the current state of research and taking into account various research-based approaches, it is possible to develop an effective agile organizational and prioritization model for software manufacturers in the context of a software product family for organizations. Such an Agile Framework then provides effective methods to effectively support software development and set the right priorities for digitalization.

Software product lines, as presented, offer medium and long-term measurable scaling and synergy effects and a demonstrable economic benefit in the interaction of individual software products within a product portfolio. Test efforts can be significantly reduced with such an approach model.

The presented concepts provide support in terms of easily understandable, transparent, and pragmatic documentation of software development.

It should also have become clear that agility must never be misused to justify uncoordinated prioritization. Nevertheless, this can be observed time and again in practice and can only be broken up through consistent action in the sense of an agile mindset and based on pragmatic software architecture documentation.

Agility here means the constantly present possibility not only to react quickly to changes but also to proactively shape the change. Continuous learning based on feedback processes creates an environment that is perceived as positive in terms of economy, quality, and simplicity—and leads to perfect cooperation.

5.5   Conclusions

License products, which are modified to a high degree based on a standard product due to customer-specific operating environments and customer-specific functions, represent individual solutions. The need for an integration team illustrates this deviation from standard software.

It follows that software manufacturers with software products that have a high proportion of individualization features require a different agile approach model than manufacturers of standard products. In addition, such a model requires clear rules to what extent such individualization takes place.

In a situation typical for the large-scale agile development environment, where a software product cannot be fully verified internally, it is advantageous and important to work towards effective communication between the various functional parts, development and deployment (Dev) and operations (Ops). The more an ideal-typical DevOps environment can be established towards the customer, the more knowledge gain is achieved within the feedback processes, and an improved time-to-market contributes to increased customer satisfaction and higher customer retention.

Software companies are challenged to maintain demand through constant product innovation. In view of the considerable costs and the additional organizational efforts required—which are associated with the introduction of a new software product—it should always be carefully considered whether innovations should be held back for the next major release or justify the introduction of a new software product. An alternative is to expand the portfolio within and beyond the product line. Based on the factors of sales, liquidity, and profitability, product management should be able to identify the phase of a software product within its life cycle at any time and align the release planning accordingly.

Market leaders in an industry often assume the role of innovators as early adopters of innovative software technologies and have a solid IT budget as such. Significant market changes or internal cost pressure also create a drive to use innovative information technologies. In both cases, software manufacturers have increased sales opportunities. The desire to intensify proximity to customers is also an important claim feature, which, closely related to the keywords Big Data and Smart Data, fuels demand through software services and can be justified with the increasing abundance and density of data and customer information.

Even though the practice-oriented case study provides an important and relevant research contribution, it is difficult to draw universally valid conclusions in the field of software engineering. This is due to the product context, which significantly influences development practices. In the context of a scientific work, it has been possible to mitigate these effects with the help of formative evaluation; the highly heterogeneous software products of different development teams play a significant role in this. Furthermore, the expert interviews conducted as part of a summative evaluation confirm the correctness of the results. The resulting artifact—in terms of a specifically adapted agile model for the organization and prioritization of software manufacturers—could also be confirmed.

A major challenge in studying very complex scenarios is the size of the case; the problem lies in understanding both the whole and the individual parts (principle of the hermeneutic circle). This problem was deliberately taken into account by reflecting a wide range of scientific viewpoints and, with the support of Action Design Research, iteratively questioning and adapting the selected concepts and scientific factual knowledge. In this way, a continuously developed understanding of the whole could be built up, and the three research questions embedded in the case study design could be ensured. In addition, there are a number of other subject areas that are relevant; these include, for example, dealing with software quality or the methodology of feedback from licensees.

The following checklist is intended to help software manufacturers consciously counteract disruptive factors and agility obstacles in order to eliminate them early on or, at best, proactively prevent them:

Checklist Agility Obstacles
Factors that prevent agility in software development:

- Change resistance
- Poorly defined or coordinated processes
- Homogeneous teams, lack of interdisciplinarity

- Poorly defined responsibilities
- Inappropriate role definition, leading to broad and complex process interfaces
- Rigid top-down dictated goals/dominant prioritization share
- Non-functioning feedback culture
- Disparaging appreciation within and between teams
- Lack of knowledge regarding agile methods and processes
- Factors that endanger the acceptance of direct user involvement:
- Keyword "Zombie Scrum"

All of these points—which oppose agility—apply not only to companies in the role of a software manufacturer but are fundamentally transferable to other organizations.

Organization-specific adaptations are important

The presented approach must be specifically adapted to the requirements of your organization and may only be transferable to any projects with adjustments or limitations.

The methodology of Design Thinking and Prototyping is particularly applicable to exploratory projects. Fully specified and fixed requirements from the beginning would require a less extensive anticipatory evaluation and collection of ideas and needs.

Depending on the finality of the product specification, a vertical prototype for clarifying technical questions should be implemented instead of a horizontal one.

Do not limit Design Thinking and Prototyping!

The approach using Design Thinking and Prototyping also has limited effectiveness if it is not possible to effectively involve the user and/or customer.

This should be taken into account as far as possible and any restrictions in this regard should be avoided!

Since software ultimately always has to support more decisions based on user feedback, this limitation has fortunately become rare, as feedback is desired on both sides.

Support method competence as best as possible

To apply the described approach, the project team also needs sufficient methodological competence in the areas of requirements elicitation, preparation of interviews/surveys, and independent requirements specification.

Large teams should supplement the procedural model with defined internal decision-making processes.

Also, real parallel work on prototypes can only be considered to a limited extent if features or components can only be developed cumbersomely across multiple teams.

For the efficient utilization of larger teams, concepts for task distribution and technical merging of designs must be added. Numerous project tools are suitable for this purpose, not least Confluence and Jira from Atlassian.

Agile methodology is also suitable for strongly hierarchical organizations
As is repeatedly demonstrated in IT projects, agile project methods can also be applied in strongly hierarchical organizations. Agile approaches are generally welcomed by large parts of the employees, regardless of the company culture, despite their novelty.

If there is no interest and openness towards the methods used, this can particularly hinder the involvement of third parties, such as customers or cooperation partners. Comprehensive project reporting obligations and requirements for a waterfall-like project planning in advance also tend to be contrary to the described approach.

For projects with a high budget, the risks must also be assessed differently. As a result, an extension of the shown approach would be necessary, including risk management processes and more precise project controlling.

5.6 Outlook

5.6.1 Implications for Practice

With reference to software product lines, the relevance of an excellent software architecture becomes particularly clear.

In case of conflicting interests of different stakeholders, quality requirements take precedence over the actual functions in the software requirements.

Product owners and software architects have three strategies available to manage this complexity:

Chunking—breaking down requirements into manageable components
First: *"Chunking"*—breaking down requirements into manageable components.

Prioritizing requirements in hierarchies
Second: *"Forming hierarchies—related to requirements"* and using them specifically for prioritization.

Using proven architecture patterns
Third: the targeted selection of proven architecture patterns—such as the Model-View-Controller concept, to design effective software solutions.

With this strategy, including the "Security-by-Design" concept, IT security can also be specifically increased, not only within software solutions but also in the processes taking place around them.

Establish ongoing access to the operating environment
If software manufacturers do not have ongoing access to the operating environment for the software products they develop and customize, a gap between Dev and Ops inevitably arises.

To a certain extent, the lack of an Ops environment can be compensated for by operating an internal staging area and systems on which software products complement each other in defined test scenarios. However, the system load and dynamically occurring difficulties in heterogeneous production environments can only be simulated to a very limited extent in this way.

Customer-specific operating environments pose a real challenge in terms of regulatory compliance and data protection, as well as operational components. However, it is already apparent that cloud solutions are suitable for dissolving this barrier as well.

Mature container technologies, the concept of a central secret vault, and role-based identity access management solutions contribute to this solution.

The strength of such system environments for software product lines, however, lies not only in the ability to demonstrate to licensees but also in the rapid response capability for reproducing deviating system scenarios.

With increasing technical virtualization possibilities and the corresponding DevOps maturity level, software manufacturers—based on a necessary agile organization and prioritization model—benefit from short release cycles and the fastest possible reaction times through the flexibility of such a model.

In the medium to long term, the increasing degree of dissemination of the underlying technologies will further expand agility towards licensees.

KPI-based Real-time Monitoring
The need for a unified, cross-product monitoring forms the technical bridge for a strategic expansion of software product lines. This also applies to website-based services, cloud-based platform solutions, and apps.

In the course of container-based virtualization, which is further driven by increasingly widespread private and public cloud environments, the striving for the greatest possible homogeneity also takes on a further very important and noteworthy role in the Ops area.

The Ops area benefits from this virtualization technology through highly efficient services, which are only made possible by machine-readable definition files, non-physical hardware configurations, or interactive configuration tools.

The spread of these virtual technologies based on the "Infrastructure-as-code concept" is thus continuously driven forward, with both Dev and Ops areas requiring highly agile methods to work together as effectively as possible.

Emergency concepts based on these principles prove to be particularly effective in order to intervene as quickly as possible in the event of a compromise. If permissions can be quickly and effectively revoked, damage can be limited, and data protection incidents can be avoided through established security concepts.

References

1. Andersen, P., & Ross, J. W. (2016). *Transforming the LEGO Group for the digital economy.* ICIS.
2. Sommer, A. F. (2019). Agile transformation at LEGO Group: Implementing agile methods in multiple departments changed not only processes but also employees' behavior and mindset. *Research-Technology Management, 62*(5), 20–29.
3. LEGO YouTube Kanal. https://www.youtube.com/c/LEGO/about. Accessed 22 Febr 2022.
4. Panke, T. alias HELD DER STEINE, YouTube Kanal. https://www.youtube.com/c/Heldder-Steine/about. Accessed 22 Febr 2022.
5. Richters, M., & Siethoff, P. *Held der Steine gegen Lego – Konzern nimmt Stellung.* Frankfurter Neue Presse vom 24.02.2021. https://www.fnp.de/frankfurt/held-der-steine-lego-frankfurt-youtube-streit-abmahnung-abo-fans-panke-zr-90193767.html. Accessed 22 Febr 2022.
6. Flaschenpost, Unternehmensangaben. https://www.wirsindflaschenpost.de/. Accessed 22 Febr 2022.
7. Ksienrzyk, L. Gründerszene. *Eigentlich wollte Flaschenpost nicht verkaufen, sondern 100 Millionen einnehmen* https://www.businessinsider.de/gruenderszene/food/flaschenpost-cherry-ventures-exit-r/. Accessed 22 Febr 2022.
8. Kapalschinski, C. (15. September 2021). *HANDELSBLATT.* https://www.handelsblatt.com/mobilitaet/elektromobilitaet/vw-shuttle-moia-vw-will-mit-moia-das-vollautomatische-fahren-zum-weltweiten-servicegeschaeft-machen-/27614874.html. Accessed 22 Febr 2022.
9. MOIA GmbH, Unternehmenswebsite. https://www.moia.io/de-DE/ueber-moia. Accessed 22 Febr 2022.
10. Laukkanen, E., et al. (2018). Comparison of release engineering practices in a large mature company and a startup. *Empirical Software Engineering, 2018, Jg.*(Nr. 6), 1–43.
11. Metzger, A., & Pohl, K. (2014). Software product line engineering and variability management: Achievements and challenges. In *Proceedings of the on future of software engineering* (S. 70–84). ACM.
12. Clements, P., & Northrop, L. (2012). *Software product lines: Practices and patterns* (8th edn.). Addison-Wesley.
13. Dingsøyr, T., et al. (2018). Exploring software development at the very largescale: A revelatory case study and research agenda for agile method adaptation. *Empirical Software Engineering, 23*(1), 490–520.
14. Paasivaara, M. (2017). Adopting SAFe to scale agile in a globally distributed organization. In *Global Software Engineering (ICGSE), 2017 IEEE 12th international conference on* (S. 36–40). IEEE.
15. Gustavsson, T. (2017). Assigned roles for Inter-team coordination in Large Scale agile development: A literature review. In *Proceedings of the XP2017 scientific workshops* (S. 15). ACM.
16. Baum, H.-G., et al. (2013). *Strategisches Controlling* (5th edn.). Schäffer-Poeschel.
17. Ford, D., & Ryan, C. (March–April 1981). Taking technology to market. *Harvard Business Review, 2.*

18. Goodwin, P., Meeran, S., & Dyussekeneva, K. (2014). The challenges of pre-launch forecasting of adoption time series for new durable products. *International Journal of Forecasting, 30*(4), 1082–1097.
19. Fitzgerald, B., & Stol, K.-J. (2017). Continuous software engineering: A roadmap and agenda. *Journal of Systems and Software, 123,* 176–189.
20. Perols, J., Zimmermann, C., & Kortmann, S. (2013). On the relationship between supplier integration and time-to-market. *Journal of Operations Management, 31*(3), 153–167.
21. Starke, G., & Hruschka, P. *Das arc42 Template für Architekturentscheidungen in Softwareprojekten.* www.arc42.de. Accessed 23 Febr 2022.

6

Challenges in Establishing a Large-Scale Agile Framework in the Enterprise

Regardless of the form of the Large-Scale Agile Framework that appears to be the most suitable model for your organizational form, almost the same questions and challenges arise that you and your agile teams must face.

These aspects are presented compactly in the following sections and can serve as a starting point for discussion and provide you with further suggestions for an optimal transformation process. If you recognize problems and challenges in the reading that already arise within your organization, then you should focus on the discussion and problem-solving here.

You will also find that you are not alone with a statement or perspective, but rather, alternatives in the sense of constructive problem-solving can often be found very quickly around you and in the most diverse teams.

6.1 Bringing Start-up Wind Into Established Organizations

For young companies like start-ups, digitization or the establishment of agile frameworks is often not necessary or even only to a limited extent as presented.

Reasons for this are:

- Digital natives find it easy to deal with the latest technology.
- Start-ups are usually small organizations with flat hierarchies, modern thinking, and few areas of competence/business.
- New strategies and changes are much easier to implement.
- Consistent digitization is already present at the time of company formation and is therefore a matter of course for every employee from the outset.

© The Author(s), under exclusive license to Springer-Verlag GmbH, DE, part of Springer Nature 2023
S. Block, *Large-Scale Agile Frameworks*, https://doi.org/10.1007/978-3-662-67782-7_6

- Start-ups consistently rely on DevOps strategies and new technologies from the very beginning.
- Start-ups act intuitively or through agile cultures shaped by the start-up initiators as digital leaders and are particularly agile in collaboration, or the start-up is already based on an agile organizational model similar to the Spotify model.

Open-mindedness & inventiveness are always a real enrichment!
Let yourself be inspired by the spirit, energy, and inventiveness—and also the open-mindedness—of start-ups …

Break away from entrenched processes and actively engage with your agile teams, your company, and its strengths and weaknesses! Put on the customer glasses, and actively involve your customers and partners in your company optimization.

Analyze processes, strengths, and weaknesses …
Which digitized processes give your customers and partners an advantage?

It is precisely these optimizations that advance your company because your customers generate your sales, and optimized processes with business partners give your company the competitive edge that moves you forward!

Do you and your teams already deal with these demands and goals 100% today, or does pure resignation prevail in large parts of your company or individual departments and specialist areas? It is your task to resolve this step by step.

Business model innovation
The aim of business model innovation is to combine the elements of the business model in such a way that they reinforce each other. This makes it possible to achieve growth and be difficult to imitate for competitors [1, Chap. 1, p. 5].

Prototypes, experiments, and a positive error culture put your company on the digital fast track!
Be courageous and start projects by continuously improving processes with prototypes. Initiate experiments; support creative thinking and new approaches that may not promise direct results at first glance.

Promote a new culture of learning in the company and, above all: Establish a positive error culture!

6.1.1   Agile Software Service Development

How much time elapses in your organization internally before a new release goes live in the production environment?

How agile is your release management?

Does it take months or even over half a year for desired changes to actually reach the user as results?

If you recognize yourself in such scenarios, your approaches to software development are accordingly extremely limited to probably not agile at all.

Even if the team-internal processes are already designed to reflect mockups according to the agile methodology, take the next step:

Test features not only within individual software teams, but always involve additional organizational units and especially even end customers in the testing phases.

6.1.2 Friendly User Tests (FUT)

A **Friendly User Test** is a test by the actual users of the software. Such tests are performed by people who are not part of the development team but are known to the organization conducting the test.

A **Friendly User** is a person who agrees to test an application or software in an unfinished version and before general introduction to discover errors.

The voluntary user of the new service agrees to collect valuable information from the developers. The resulting inconveniences are converted into active participation in fixing the errors that have occurred.

Steps to establish Friendly User Tests
- Planning and coordination of the deployment process for test versions;
- Definition of a main responsible person for test coordination;
- Ensuring that the test group uses a meaningful variety of test devices and devices, possibly providing these test devices as an incentive for testing an app for mobile devices;
- Briefing of frontend and backend teams;
- Support of overall project management, including stakeholder management and dissemination of agile working methods;
- Preparation of the execution of the Friendly User Test: Preparation of the test design, including customer journey, briefings, feedback options, etc.;
- Ensuring that test feedback can be easily given and provided in various ways and is comprehensively included in the evaluation.

Tests with real users are incredibly important for digital transformation and innovation. Even the best and most experienced developers can gain new insights through Friendly User Tests [2, p. 124 ff.] and further improve their software product or digital service.

6.1.3   Different Levels of Agility in Teams

To anticipate it: Different development levels of individual teams are not unusual, but rather the norm. It would be unusual and extremely unfavorable if an extreme manifestation were to accumulate within certain teams; in such a case, action would be needed.

While some software teams, for example, already use acceptance tests that are virtualized in Docker containers, other teams may not yet have this level of maturity by far.

- How far is your organization as a whole from a fully completed deployment process?
- What gaps do you still need to close and on which topics should the teams actively work to realize this target vision of agile software development for your organization?

DevOps is definitely a very relevant topic, which is closely related to the agility level of your organization [see also 3], and the technical development should therefore proceed in this direction.

Kubernetes and Docker are technically mature topics, i.e. these technologies have a low risk—not only large corporations like Google or Amazon have been using these technologies in productive operation for many years, but more and more medium-sized companies have also recognized the advantages of these container technologies.

6.1.4   Establishing Novel Development and Test Environments with Abstracted Hardware Layer

Agile software development and the products and services around it demand precisely such DevOps-based service solutions.

- Is the acceptance in your organization mature enough that everyone involved knows that DevOps technologies are an absolutely viable decision and a worthwhile investment, and that now is the right time to focus on such topics?

It is also relevant that the underlying technologies such as Kubernetes or API gateways are based on open-source solutions from disclosed sources. The primary goal is to create an abstracted layer to the hardware.

Gained Freedom for Development Processes & Test Scenarios
This creates a completely new space for the development process, allowing complex test scenarios in differentiated hardware environments to be possible, with the effort for provisioning, administration, and operation—in terms of time and cost—noticeably reduced.

The significantly noticeable reduced implementation time is particularly important for service-oriented scenarios. Shortest time-to-market cycles strengthen the positioning of your organization in important markets and customer segments for you.

With the standardization of the development strategy—e.g. through a uniform deploy-ment—a considerable savings potential also arises. There are hardly any significant dif-ficulties regarding the use of different technologies, e.g. within the build processes.

6.1.5   Transparent Decision-Making Processes and Agile Requirements Management

A transparent decision-making process regarding requirements management and archi-tectural decisions in the context of interconnected and interdependent software services is indispensable in an agile environment.

*"Conscious agile action should be understood as understanding the activities of others as well as understanding one's own activities in the context of other team members, teams, the organization, and their goals."—Sascha Block*In the context of transparent decision-making processes, various aspects are relevant:

- Openness of communication and information exchange;
- Visibility of and access to data, documents, and information;
- Visibility of decision-making processes and decisions;
- Visibility of processes;
- Transparency of collaboration;
- Transparency of tools;
- Awareness can be defined as openness, good observation skills, and proactive action

Transparent goals support collaboration and improve efficiency by reducing redundant work. Only when strategic goals are transparently and clearly communicated can such a strategy be effectively broken down and divided into work-sharing, agile packages. This results in small-scale, agile work packages with clearly defined and meaningful compo-nents, based on which each individual employee can act [4].

Strategies, visions, goals, and motives should be transparent and understandable at all levels of work and be understood at all levels of work, and the definition of portfolios and roadmaps based on corporate strategy and goals should be proposed [5].

Are all requirement descriptions clear and easy to understand?
- To what extent do the processes of requirement description in your organization require optimization?
- Are all affected organizational units involved in the calculation of releases to achieve a viable effort calculation?
- Are all relevant processes organized in regular cycles and designed transparently to provide more planning security and to be able to reliably and exclusively focus on software development outside of these cycles?

Only through solid requirements engineering can requirements be achieved with the desired effect and without unwanted side effects.

In this context, it is necessary, even if it may be more complex, to design the requirements in close relation between domain knowledge and the refinement of requirements.

For this purpose, minimum standards must be defined, which information must be presented in which level of detail and based on which specification [see also 6].

This requires agile methodology to effectively deal with requirements that develop quickly and may already be outdated before the project is completed [7].

Therefore, create control mechanisms and quality loops that regularly reassess the technologies used and ensure that you continue to "bet on the right horses."

Are time expenditures in projects measured in a usable way?

For organizational relief and optimization of project control, the recording of time expenditures and project planning should be carried out centrally in one tool. Collaboration tools like Jira offer excellent support for this, and of course, the commissioning should also be done centrally in the same tool—completely via Jira.

Do experience values flow into the effort calculation?

Effort calculation will always remain a real challenge. Experience from countless projects shows that the more minor the scope of a task, the closer the effort estimation and actual effort are to each other.

Therefore, break down tasks into packages as small as possible and necessary to achieve realistic estimates. Also, trust yourself to approach the results in estimation methods and deal openly with any mistakes made here.

Learn from your mistakes; you will hardly make them a second time in the same way!

The difficulty of unifying software and its architecture repeatedly proves to be particularly challenging. The life cycle of software products in relation to each other is far too different, and this will always be the case.

Product life cycle of components & basic technologies

The product life cycle of different software products is also closely interrelated and influences each other. It is difficult, if not impossible, for all software products to be based on the same framework.

The frameworks on which software solutions are based are also subject to a life cycle, so that these technology components automatically shape the character of the software products at different stages of age and maturity.

A uniform character of software services can only be realized with the simultaneous start of development for all software components. A uniform operating concept and usability, on the other hand, can be well implemented. These UX features are essential for successful software and are the key properties of good software.

6.2 Digital Leadership

Digital leadership means nothing less for a company than taking the lead in economically important competence fields with digital strategies. For digital leadership, it is not sufficient to merely understand digital changes. Rather, the challenge is to become an active shaper of change [8, Chap. 1, p. 3].

Agile Organization
In the sense of a digital version, being highly strategic and at the same time agile, i.e., flexible even with regard to contradictory interests, requires a new leadership style for digital transformation projects.

Interdisciplinary Teams
Successful digital companies use consistent collaboration in cross-functional teams. This influences the division of labor between regular corporate functions in terms of a strong emphasis on project-related collaboration across traditional organizational department boundaries and oriented towards a central success factor. Decision-making possibilities are shifted to the operational experts of the respective areas to optimally integrate their expertise into the digital development process [8, Chap. 2, p. 112].

Product Ownership
The role of the Product Owner is associated with the innovation and product development method "Scrum". Scrum is a popular agile approach model. The Product Owner takes responsibility for the (further) development of products and services. Unlike traditional development concepts, the advantage lies in the fact that regular feedback during the various development steps is directly incorporated into the design drafts and development concepts, both from the commissioning department and from the customer side through usability tests.

Communication
Digitizing companies also means using modern project tools, establishing new communication channels, and dissolving old thought patterns and structures. Arguments such as "We've always done it this way, it will still work tomorrow." must be actively refuted.

Pay attention to meaningful communication in meetings and in dialogue with each other. Table 6.1 "Communication examples and their meaning" lists some typical examples from everyday IT project life and at the same time provides an interpretation with possible recommendations for action on the communicative response to the respective statement. Feel free to use the following examples to illustrate how agility does not work, because each of these statements reflects how ideal communication, according to the understanding of the agile mindset, should not take place.

Table 6.1 Communication examples and their meaning

Statement	Interpretation and possible reaction
"We need to clarify this bilaterally"	I don't want to talk about it in this round/discuss the topic in detail. We can clarify this one-on-one. Often with fatal consequences! Relevant information remains opaque, and there is often little or no interest in an appropriate solution. You can actively counteract this by objecting that details can be clarified bilaterally, but you ask them to officially announce the results in the team.
"A colleague is working on it."	I don't know the current status. Often an indication of poor communication within or between teams. Unfavorable if only accurate information is not available at the moment, harmful if customer processes are affected or even security-relevant...
"I am not involved."	Another example of poor communication within or between teams. Why are you not involved? Are you aware of the connections? Do you know if and between whom/which teams agreements have been made on this? Has a deadline been agreed upon for the solution?
"I am not up to date."	Another example of poor communication within or between teams. Why are you not up to date? What needs to be changed so that you can make a statement on this? Are representation arrangements effectively made?
"We had no topics in the past few days."	Empty backlog? Okay if nothing important or even urgent was pending. Often this is also a good example of poor communication within or between teams. Is there regular information exchange? How is it organized and structured? Possibly also a sign of lack of motivation...

Flexible processes for action approval

Flexible processes for action approval, budgeting, and success control are essential to compete with start-ups and established players. Especially with regard to competitors, it is important to remain competitive with agile methods by ensuring that technological and strategic advantages are of the longest possible duration and maximum benefit.

6.2.1   Vision, Strategy, and Product/Service Roadmap

An organization-wide vision requires strategic decisions about products or services, such as setting priorities, determining the phasing out of product releases, or announcing the discontinuation of functionalities. This often requires the involvement of software architects and software development teams, as well as the executive board and other cross-product teams.

Many decisions are made in dialogue between specialists or managers and are not recorded. Agile collaboration tools like Confluence offer effective support in various ways to remedy this situation.

Use decision logs!

It is extremely important that decisions and information are transparent and easily accessible. This can be achieved with the help of decision logs, which also record the presence and absence of participants. Also important are communicated, clearly defined deadlines by which a decision is made jointly. An adequate preparation period should, of course, also be ensured.

Use graphical tools, decision trees, or the various functions of collaboration tools, such as appointment reminders or voting for decision-making. The only relevant thing is to make information as easily accessible as possible at all times and to make decisions transparently.

From "having a vision" to "living our vision!"

If the vision for a product/service and its associated business cases are shaped almost exclusively by the respective product owner, who closely coordinates with managers, the problem arises that there is not enough transparency regarding the vision and strategy. It is not sufficient to simply disseminate this information in a condensed form to the teams; instead, this information must be made permanently and easily accessible to all organization members via collaboration tools.

Product/Service Roadmap with defined features

This also requires a defined product/service roadmap, with definitions of usable features and service benefits. An active process for planning the lifecycle of products and services is also necessary.

Are your organization's customers actively involved in such decisions? After all, it is always the customers who contribute their value to your organization! Expand your organization's horizon and include all relevant stakeholders…

Two of the most important actors who **proactively support agile teams in digitalization projects** are the Chief Information Officer and the relatively new leadership role of the Chief Digital Officer:

6.2.2   Chief Information Officer

Role

The **Chief Information Officer** (CIO) is responsible for information technology and software systems in a company. The American-originated job title of Chief Information Officer is also widespread in German companies, and the position of CIO is common in most corporations and larger medium-sized companies. The position of Chief Information Officer is usually located directly in the upper management of a company.

Tasks

The tasks of the Chief Information Officer include **planning** and **strategic management** of the **information technology** used in the company. The range of tasks of a CIO includes **control, monitoring**, and **management** of activities, functions, and resources associated with digital information and IT systems, as well as the communication technologies used in the company.

The Chief Information Officer is the main person responsible for information technology within the company, responsible for the **management of IT planning,IT operations, and IT technology selection**. On the one hand, the CIO fulfills an **operational role**, focused on the **short-term corporate goals**. On the other hand, CIOs take on a **strategic role** within the company with the **long-term planning of IT strategies** [9].

Processes

The activities of the CIO can be primarily divided into three areas of responsibility:

1. **Operational tasks of the CIO**
   In day-to-day business, a CIO is fundamentally responsible for ensuring a **smooth flow of all IT-relevant processes** within the company. In addition to providing IT services, the CIO monitors the hardware and software used in the company through **monitoring and controlling**. In case of problems, the CIO must initiate the right measures for immediate error correction.
   - Implementation of legal requirements
   - Vendor management (control of external service providers)
   - Management of technical infrastructure and IT operations
   - Ensuring the successful execution of IT projects
2. **The strategic Chief Information Officer**
   The **strategic and continuous improvement of business processes through IT solutions** is the second area of responsibility for the CIO. By systematically ensuring **more efficient workflows,cost advantages within the company**, and **new solution approaches for business processes**, the CIO provides the company with a competitive advantage through IT.
   - Development of the IT strategy
   - Planning the technical advancement of IT and software solutions
   - IT coordination with departments and management
3. **The innovative CIO**
   The third area of responsibility for a CIO is focused on the **innovative aspects of corporate IT**. In this context, the Chief Information Officer identifies relevant technical innovations and their potential for the company and ensures that they are introduced at the right time within the company. Together with the IT architect, the CIO plans the structure of the IT architecture and the selection of optimally suitable technologies. The innovations of the CIO are primarily aimed at improving the **efficiency of**

internal processes, ensuring **effective IT communication**, and contributing to the **maximization of productivity within the company through optimal IT processes**.

History of the Chief Information Officer (CIO)
Until now, the Chief Information Officer was usually solely responsible for the **implementation and planning of** IT projects and thus **IT manager of the computer center**. Translated, the term Chief Information Officer most closely corresponds to a **Head of Information Technology**, **Computer Center Manager**, or **IT Executive**. The CIO is at the top of the management hierarchy and is primarily responsible for the IT infrastructure in a company. Equal to a manager, the Chief Information Officer is not involved in operational business areas. Rather, a CIO **operates at the strategic level** and makes fundamental decisions for the operational IT in the company.

Can a CIO program?
In practice, the CIO has no time for operational activities such as programming. However, most CIOs will be able to program themselves, as the majority of CIOs have a technical IT education, usually being computer scientists or having a comparable qualification.

Experienced CIOs are in high demand!
CIOs with a solid technological foundation for **project management** and several years of experience are highly sought after as executives. Those who can demonstrate a wide range and depth of skills and experiences for the position of Chief Information Officer are hot candidates for the CIO position in companies. Evidence of successfully completed projects, change management, and lean management with a focus on the efficient implementation of IT processes are advantageous.

What is the difference between a CIO and a CDO?
In many companies that have not yet adopted the role of the **Chief Digital Officer (CDO)**, the **Chief Information Officer (CIO)** continues to play the role of IT innovator to ensure that the company can keep pace with competitors both strategically and technologically. The CIO can also plan and implement the digital corporate strategy on an equal footing with the CDO.

6.2.3 Chief Digital Officer

Role
The Chief Digital Officer (CDO) is the central key figure of digital transformation in the company. A Chief Digital Officer aims to develop a clear strategy for the digitalization of the company and to implement it continuously.

Tasks

A Chief Digital Officer pursues several strategic goals for the digitalization of a company. Since most companies use IT solutions primarily to manage internal work processes, Chief Digital Officers assess the opportunities and risks of digitalization for companies. The task of the CDO is to develop digital processes and services for customers, suppliers, partners, and internal processes [10].

Processes

> *"CDOs design and optimize digital processes."*

In doing so, CDOs analyze and evaluate company processes entirely anew. For example, based on questions like the following:

- How can the company be made more efficient through the digitalization of internal processes and further increase business success?
- How can an effective digital strategy for marketing, customer communication, and sales be defined and individualized based on customer wishes?

"CDOs drive the use of digital channels."

- Which digital channels are used for internal and external communication?
- How can digital sales channels for products and services be used and intensified?
- What budget is required for optimal digitalization?
- How can customer acquisition, support, and sales be made more efficient through digital channels?
- How can sales through digital channels be further increased?
- Which digital social media channels should the company integrate into its marketing and corporate communication?

"CDOs modernize the digital infrastructure."

- What prerequisites in the form of changed or new structures need to be created for this?
- Which digital technologies are required to achieve the objectives?

"CDOs develop digital products and services."

- The Chief Digital Officer is challenged to identify the potentials through digitalization and to use them efficiently for the company. This includes the development of new digital products and services that, on the one hand, open up new sources of income for the company and, on the other hand, also increase customer satisfaction.

"The CDO enables the analysis of Big Data."

- What data is collected within the company and how is this information analyzed and used?
- Which relevant information is not yet digitally available and what strategies can be used to digitize such analog data?

"A Chief Digital Officer coordinates the digitalization of know-how & promotes the digital corporate culture."

- What knowledge must be present among the employees in the company in order to be able to implement the digital topics internally?
- Which new working methods and tools can be used to improve collaboration within the company and drive the **digital transformation** forward?

Skills of the Chief Digital Officer

1. **Business Skills**
   The Chief Digital Officer has a strong expertise in increasing a company's digital capital and integrating the best possible channels and tools. The CDO evaluates opportunities for diversification and strengthening the company strategy associated with digitalization.

2. **Marketing Skills**
   The CDO is familiar with all relevant marketing channels, recognizes crucial digital trends, and evaluates marketing opportunities of digitalization within the company. By analyzing and evaluating user behavior, the CDO increases the value of digital information within the company.

3. **Communication and Leadership Style**
   The Chief Digital Officer analyzes the habits of internal and external user groups and optimizes existing communication channels within and outside the company.

4. **IT and Digital Technologies**
   By using state-of-the-art digital communication and IT technology, the CDO expands the coverage of all relevant areas in which digital information processes make the company more efficient.

5. **Legal Expertise**
   The CDO is familiar with legal aspects of digitalization, even if they are not a legal expert in the strict sense. With a keen sense, the Chief Digital Officer finds the best possible solutions for the highest security and optimal data protection.

6. **Logistical Abilities**
   Experienced CDOs often have solid knowledge in the field of logistics or the efficient use of resources within the company and process optimization.

What is the difference between a CDO and a CIO?

In many companies where the role of the **Chief Digital Officer (CDO)** is still not adopted, the **Chief Information Officer (CIO)** continues to assume the role of IT innovator to ensure that the company can keep pace with competitors both strategically and technologically.

The CIO can also plan and implement the digital company strategy on an equal footing with the CDO.

6.3   Change Management—Digital Leadership in Management

Change management is particularly successful in digitalization projects as a proactive and thus prudent approach when it comes to achieving the greatest possible acceptance among affected executives and employees.

In particular, the support of top management is a critical success factor that ultimately shapes the efficiency of use and employee satisfaction [11].

Successful change management understands communication as a supporting element in change processes. Since inadequate communication is one of the main reasons for failed transformation projects, we align our strategy from the beginning to actively involve every employee in the company through communication.

Change management actively contributes to project success with two objectives:
1. Targeted coordination of processes, information technologies, and people
2. Control of change processes

6.3.1   Perspectives of Change Management

Successful change management focuses on the following three perspectives in your company:

1. **System-constructivist perspective:**
   Comprehensive consideration of all basic constants in the company (including barriers and boundary conditions) for organizing changes.
2. **Organizational development:**
   Inclusion of all affected people with their specific behavior and viewpoints.
3. **Learning organization:**
   Change processes should be designed as learning processes.

Invest in changes in this direction and use the tools and techniques presented in Part II to bring about and support positive changes in your company.

6.3.2   Change Request/Release Management

Focus on the following questions regarding change request and release management analytically. Experience shows that there is a lot of potential for optimization in the answers.

- Are the lived software development processes heavily change request-driven?
- How does fulfilling customer requests relate to your service/product vision?
- In what cycles and timeframes do requirements change?
- How dynamically do you react within requirement and implementation processes?
- How does your organization and individual teams deal with requirements, especially when customer interests are heterogeneous and not compatible with each other?
- How do you organize your software architecture and decide on the essential components, their essential quality properties, and at which points are you willing to compromise and where not?
- Has your organization recorded these central specifications and self-imposed goals for all team members in collaboration tools?

Each organization is challenged in its own decision-making and optimal use of limited resources—primarily time and development capacity. In doing so, the individual organizational areas must always be closely linked with software development.

A crucial aspect in implementation is to live processes agilely in all parts of the organization. Agility should not only be lived in the areas of software development but in all parts of your organization.

Even if projects and products and services are repeatedly worked towards hard-defined deadlines or executives expect fixed-price calculations in projects; to take customers along agilely, it is necessary to closely involve the participating organizational units in the agile software development process beforehand.

For this purpose, the tools used for change request requirement management, which records these rigid processes, must be replaced by agile alternatives (Jira, backlogs, dynamic prioritization—e.g., using story points and actual sprint planning—between the product owner and the project team).

6.3.3   Agile Academy

Take advantage of introductory events and coaching on relevant topics to prepare employees for your agile transformation journey and provide optimal support.

Under no circumstances should you introduce new tools that are not at least internally trained by colleagues who are well acquainted with their use.

A good option is regular training and active information events in which the employees of your organization are involved and can actively contribute.

The chosen event format should be recurring. How short the repetition intervals (monthly, quarterly, or even once a week) depend heavily on the agile maturity of the organization and employees.

It is important that emotions and thoughts are regularly reflected upon and appreciated.

An agile mindset should first be understood and internalized. For some, certain paradigms are at least unfamiliar, especially when breaking up leadership structures and dismantling hierarchies. Some also feel uncomfortable with the desire to take on more personal responsibility.

When employees can freely express their ideas, expectations, and desires and feel that they are being taken into account, participation and willingness to participate increase noticeably. This, in turn, has a very positive effect on the teams and the organization as a whole. Moreover, this effect is reinforced with an increasingly agile organizational culture. Suddenly, a pleasant feel-good atmosphere is realized, and productivity and diversity of ideas for problem-solving increase.

6.3.4   Establish Agile Values

Establish an agile mindset by clarifying for your organization and teams which values should shape their collaboration.

"Our Agile Manifesto"
For inspiration, here are some ideas of what such values might look like:

Values

- We are a team. And as such, we appear. Together.
- We have expertise. And if we want to know something, we learn.
- We respect and appreciate ourselves. And others.
- We give feedback. Constructive. Regularly.
- We see ourselves as service providers for *placeholder*. Customer-centric. Product-oriented. Service-oriented.
- We see digital transformation as an opportunity. And actively shape our change.
- We live a culture of error, are open-minded, and welcome diversity.
- We act sustainably, proactively, and avoid waste.
- We act in the interest of the company and the general society. Responsibly.
- We have open and transparent communication. Among ourselves. And towards others.
- We let go of our shame where it hinders us rather than helps.

With such an agile mindset, we can only win and achieve our goals together, thus unleashing the full potential of all our possibilities.

Symbolically, *"shame is the little sister of greatfear"* and illustrates what we can achieve when we reflect on what holds us back. In realizing goals or even just in open, mutual communication. And communication is an essential building block for success. On a small and large scale, as individuals and as a team. Then nothing and no one can stop us from achieving our goals. Everything suddenly becomes effortlessly possible when we can trust each other...

6.4   Emergency Management: Can Your Organization React Agilely in Emergency Situations?

A functioning emergency management system aims to ensure the continuity of business operations in emergencies. Carefully prepared emergency management enables organizations to respond appropriately and effectively to disruptions of critical business processes. Components of emergency management include emergency preparedness and emergency response.

With the rapidly increasing threat landscape regarding ransomware and cybercrime, the likelihood of any organization being affected by a cyber attack has increased significantly. However, regular IT failure scenarios should also be anticipated with foresight, so that employees of your organization can make informed decisions in emergency situations and initiate important steps to minimize the extent of damage.

Especially when reorienting towards an agile process organization, it is essential to deal with the components of emergency management.

Do you have planned IT Service Continuity Management?

IT Service Continuity Management does not necessarily assume dramatic emergency situations and therefore offers effective methods to defuse emergencies. The proactive management of unwanted effects that can affect your IT consists regularly of many interconnected processes, so it is of crucial advantage if you specifically think about the impacts and linked mechanisms in your organization.

> *Are you aware of the most important factors determining the quality level of the digital services you use?*One of the sub-goals, which should lead to the fulfillment of the main goals, is the improvement of service availability.

The goal of IT Service Continuity Management is to ensure the technical and programmatic tools, with the fulfillment of quality objectives primarily depending on the following critical success factors:

- the provision of information and
- the best possible support for all employees,
- a permanent updating of critical infrastructure artifacts,
- adequate response to corresponding changes in the organization ...

- … and its environment, including legal framework conditions or changes in the assessment of the threat situation and potential attack vectors,
- regular and serious check-ups of the effectiveness of protective measures and training,
- an effective configuration management process,
- the trained and routine use of effective tools.

The critical factors for the success of a specific quality objective can be designed expandable for your organization and may differ slightly in weighting, but the factors described above are generally valid for all organizations [12].

Benefits of proactive emergency planning
Every organization is now reducing the risks that can specifically impair performance and response time noticeably.

Directly achievable benefits of risk mitigation:

- lived adaptation of your organization to the constantly current situation—your customers and partners appreciate this too!,
- competitive advantages, e.g. through innovation and proactive communication,
- compliance with legal requirements,
- optimal understanding of business needs,
- increasing the credibility of your organization,
- reduction of insurance expenses.

6.4.1 How Can You Proactively Address Emergencies?

In critical security incidents, various steps must be executed very quickly to avert the acute threat. Time, communication, and optimal preparation for emergencies play a decisive role in this process.

Figure 6.1 "Schematic sequence of an emergency process" illustrates the typical sequence of an emergency process and can serve as an initial template for creating an emergency concept.

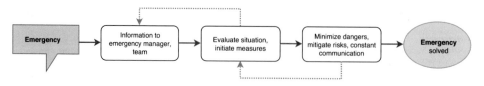

Fig. 6.1 Schematic sequence of an emergency process

Recommendations for implementing an emergency concept:

1. **Appropriate communication:** Be sure to clarify WHO should ideally be notified in WHAT order. Clear and unambiguous information about the occurred damage should, however, DEFINITELY be provided to all employees of your organization. External partners and/or customers should also be considered if they are affected by the extent of the damage.

2. **Initiation of individual measures:** For each previously identified emergency situation, individual steps and measures must be defined in preparation. You must not only discuss these action plans with your employees but actively practice them. With a prototypical approach, you will most likely identify further side effects and be able to take them into account as well. In an emergency, the training reflex kicks in and significantly increases the likelihood of correct action.

3. **Constant, up-to-date communication flow:** Especially in emergency situations, it is important to communicate with each other and ensure that important information reaches where it is urgently needed. Use the right communication channels for this purpose and have backup options in place in case of their failure?

4. **Troubleshooting:** The elimination of the damage is, of course, the focus of the respective emergency actions. In order for everyone to contribute effectively, it is not only important to know the individual steps for damage elimination but also necessary to assign the required roles to the involved actors.

5. **Documentation/Evaluation/Adjustment:** After one damage event is before the next damage event, or better before its prevention. It is important to learn from mistakes, effectively close gaps, and evaluate the corresponding findings within agile teams in a retrospective to learn from them and improve overall, both in the team and in the organization. Without analysis and evaluation of the events, this is simply not possible. Nevertheless, you should leave the non-implementation to others and put in the necessary diligence here…

Regardless of these factors, the resulting emergency concepts must be regularly reviewed and tested. Do not shy away from simulating the emergency as realistically as possible. These measures serve to protect your organization and to review the emergency concept, its effectiveness, and above all, the best possible training of the employees.

6.4.2   How Do We Approach an Emergency Concept Organizationally?

Ideally, each agile team independently assesses critical processes, and a higher-level team for emergency management acts as a coordinated control center and also supports the exchange of agile teams with each other.

Defining Technical & Organizational Measures (TOMs)

Technical and organizational measures define concrete actions to be implemented in the respective emergency situations. An example of such a TOM in a serious threat situation includes the appropriate measures to sever relevant network nodes and immediately disconnect hardware from the network in case of a serious threat. A corresponding TOM for this should read as follows:

Procedure in case of serious network compromise: 1) Disconnect server/component from external network (Internet); 2) Disconnect server/component from internal network; 3) Shut down server/component; 4) In case of hardware compromise or if hardware cannot be shut down: Do not disconnect from power supply, i.e., turn off BEFORE securing evidence such as log files.

Prioritize TOMs & Record All Services/Applications

Already in a first meeting, you can use a tool like Table 6.2 "Definition of technical organizational measures (TOMs)" to identify individual services and applications:

Table 6.3 "Priority labeling for TOMs according to the traffic light principle" is helpful as a legend to visually assign a corresponding priority rating to each defined TOM. When assigning priorities, the prioritizations according to the traffic light principle should be easily recognizable by color. Such a simplified presentation is invaluable in an emergency.

Table 6.2 Definition of technical organizational measures (TOMs)

Column	Description
Application/Service	Name of the application/service
Manufacturer	Name of the manufacturer/developer
Operator	Name of the operator/service provider
Prio	Classification of the application/service
Internal contact person	Contact information of the contact person within the organization
Internal contact person backup	Contact information of the substitute contact person as an internal backup
Operator contact person	Contact information of the contact person at the operator
Operator contact person backup	Contact information of the contact person backup at the operator
TOM	Stored TOM document (Technical & Organizational Measures)
TOM Date	Last review date of the TOM document regarding its currency

Table 6.3   Priority labeling for TOMs according to the traffic light principle

Colum	Description		
LOW		LOW	
MEDIUM		MEDIUM	
HIGH		HIGH	

Low damage (Affects a small amount of data records with non-critical significance/ application, etc.)

Medium damage

High damage (Affects many data records AND/OR critical data/application AND/OR significant impact on performance).

In total, the evaluation of all services/applications should result in a balanced picture, so that the different categories are represented approximately equally.

Framework conditions for emergency management

In each emergency concept, the required course of action is described. Guidelines, roles and tasks as well as delimitations and framework conditions should be listed.

This includes that the respective emergency concepts are tailored to the agile teams; it is very unlikely that these concepts can simply be transferred to other teams or organizational areas.

Also consider disasters caused by the influence of higher powers (flood, earthquake, war, building occupation), building damage (power outage, water damage, fire, evacuation, lightning strike) or severe disease events (epidemic, endemic, pandemic). Use In-Scope/Out-of-Scope to specifically exclude what is or has not been part of your consideration so far; this ensures that no threat situation is overlooked.

Level of detail & scaling effects

The focus of an individual emergency concept should always be traced back to the applications or services that are within the responsibility and maximum scope of action of a respective team. When considering the steps to be taken, a pragmatic balance between granularity and bundling must be observed so that the meaningfulness is not affected. The BSI standard 100-4 recommends between 5 and 15 processes per organizational unit [13]. The process should be tailored so that it is completely within an organizational unit and thus within a responsibility and accountability area.

According to the Single-Point-Of-Failure principle or the principle of broad impact, it is desirable to know components that have a large impact on other components when they fail.

It is also important to know which processes cause the greatest damage according to defined criteria when they fail, in order to prioritize them accordingly. Logical relationships and dependencies that require a specific sequence must also be identified. This is an important point insofar as this information is needed for the processes to restart.

References

1. Schallmo, D., et al. (2017). *Digitale Transformation von Geschäftsmodellen.* Grundlagen, Instrumente und Best Practices (1st edn.). Springer/Gabler.
2. Cooper, A. (2004). *The inmates are running the asylum: Why high tech products drive us crazy and how to restore the Sanity* (1. März 2004). Sams Publishing—2004 Que (2nd edn.).
3. Luz, W. P., Pinto, G., & Bonifácio, R. (2019). Adopting DevOps in the real world: A theory, a model, and a case study. *Journal of Systems and Software, 157,* 110–384.
4. Berggren, E., & Bernshteyn, R. (2007). *Organizational transparency drives company performance.* The *Journal of Management Development, 2007, 26. Jg., Nr. 5,* 411.
5. Kelanti, M., et al. (2013). A case study of requirements management: Toward transparency in requirements management tools. In *Proceedings of the eighth international conference on software engineering advances (ICSEA 2013)* (S. 597–604).
6. Zave, P., & Jackson, M. (1997). Four dark corners of requirements engineering. *ACM Transactions on Software Engineering and Methodology (TOSEM), 6*(1), 1–30.
7. Cao, L., & Ramesh, B. (2008). Agile requirements engineering practices: An empirical study. *IEEE Software, 25*(1), 60–67.
8. Kreutzer, R. T., et al. (2017). *Digital Business Leadership – Digitale Transformation – Geschäftsmodell-Innovation – agile Organisation – Change-Management* (1st edn.). Springer/Gabler.
9. Peppard, J. (2010). Unlocking the performance of the chief information officer (CIO). *California Management Review, 52*(4), 73–99.
10. Horlacher, A., & Hess, T. (2016). What does a chief digital officer do? Managerial tasks and roles of a new C-level position in the context of digital transformation. In *2016 49th Hawaii international conference on system sciences (HICSS)* (S. 5126–5135). IEEE.
11. Shao, Z., Feng, Y., & Hu, Q. (2016). Effectiveness of top management support in enterprise systems success: A contingency perspective of fit between leadership style and system lifecycle. *European Journal of Information Systems, 25*(2), 131–153.
12. Ministr, J., Stevko, M., & Fiala, J. (2009). The IT service continuity management principles implementation by method A2. In *IDIMT-2009 systems and humans–A complex relationship–17th interdisciplinary information management talks preceedings* (S. 131–139). Trauner Druck.
13. Bundesamt Für Sicherheit in Der Informationstechnik. BSI-Standard. 100-4: Notfallmanagement. 2008.

Part II
Agile Infrastructure

Agile Tools: Toolbox for Product Owners & Agile Teams

7

Numerous digital platforms are growing at a rate of three new members per second. With such rapid user growth, the infrastructure must be correspondingly agile and expandable.

This applies to internal IT systems as well as capacities in data centers or cloud infrastructure. And the collaboration tools you use should also be sized and licensed to ensure that every employee in your organization can work with these tools. This may seem obvious, but unfortunately, it is still very often reported from practice that it often fails due to these basic organizational hurdles.

There are missing Confluence licenses for new employees or entire teams, or Confluence areas or Slack channels have permissions only for specific teams or individuals but contain relevant, cross-functional knowledge.

If this sounds familiar to you, you know where to start. There are usually no good reasons to maintain such practices…

Moving to the cloud increases the need for agile infrastructure
Moving to the cloud provides you with such agile infrastructure, giving you access to thousands of servers and virtual nodes around the globe. This makes it easy to connect new systems and API interfaces. However, at no point should the aspect of IT security be lost sight of, even remotely.

An Amazon AWS Cloud account is generally well secured in its basic configuration, but even here, repeated reminders to activate two-factor authentication are often ignored…

To highlight just one more aspect that concerns many organizations: Agile infrastructure should also make it easy for you to connect new social media channels at any time and give you the ability to centrally control content. With these capabilities, you can significantly increase your potential reach, in line with your cloud infrastructure, and reach more influencers every day. However, the connection with data protection aspects must be taken into account. Make sure you know which data is flowing where. Especially the

S. Block, *Large-Scale Agile Frameworks*, https://doi.org/10.1007/978-3-662-67782-7_7

flow of data to third parties not only leads data into the unsuspecting control of third parties but also directly affects your terms of use. How do you organize the necessary consents within your consent management?

How is content management organized in your company? How do you ensure that content is optimized simultaneously for different social media channels, as almost every channel regularly has different requirements for the provided content, yet on the other hand, it should be ensured that you spread almost the same information content-wise on all channels at the same time. Your followers will thank you. Critical and attentive followers often notice more than what is known within an organization or, in the worst case, continues to be ignored... Often, negative feedback or constructive criticism from customers is not taken into account, not systematically evaluated at all or insufficiently, and thus no optimizations can be incorporated agilely.

Excellent if you and your organization already take all this feedback into account. Do you also communicate regularly and appreciatively that you consider such feedback and actively respond to customer requests?

Agile deployment of IT infrastructure

Effective mechanisms for agile deployment and management are essential to make your requirements for a highly scalable infrastructure practically usable.

You will quickly reach a point where the flexible connection of distributed applications becomes indispensable in an optimal way. For this, you need a highly responsive, distributed network infrastructure that is scalable and grows horizontally without changing the basic architecture or interrupting the data flow within your network with every change.

Requirement categories of an agile infrastructure

From this, the following categories of requirements for an agile infrastructure can be derived:

- **Security:** An important aspect of any global system and the strongest requirement for the defined API design.
- **Developer-friendly:** All developers working with your API should not suffer when working with your system.
- **Extensibility:** Our system should be able to handle the addition of new features without affecting your customers.
- **Up-to-date documentation:** Good documentation is key to getting your API adopted by new developers.
- **Proper error handling:** Because things will go wrong and we need to be well-prepared for that.
- **Offers a variety of SDK/API libraries:** The more work you simplify for developers, the more they will like your system.

- **Scalability:** The ability to scale is something every good API should have in order to properly deliver its services.

7.1   Agile Mindset & the 12 Principles of the Agile Manifesto

The increasing popularity of agile methodology and its importance for agile software development are a crucial reason why many organizations are adopting agile frameworks to accelerate and successfully shape the transition to agility.

A crucial factor for agility is an agile mindset, which is significantly influenced by the Agile Mindset and the Agile Manifesto.

Figure 7.1 "Agile Onion" illustrates how the Agile Mindset is related to values, principles, practices, processes, and tools. Intangible values have a strong impact on agility but are less visible. Processes and tools have high visibility but ultimately a weaker impact because they are ineffective without mindset and values, and cannot even unfold their full potential. The intangible values have a much longer-term validity, while processes and tools can be subject to a higher change interval depending on current needs.

The mindset of an organization is an essential part of the agile infrastructure. The employees of an organization—also referred to as *Human Resources* in a "classic" sense—are the capital of every organization. As banal as it sounds, it remains true: Without employees, no products and services. Without motivated and committed employees, no excellent products and services.

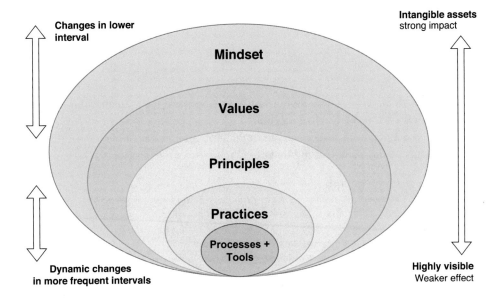

Fig. 7.1 Agile Onion

In terms of introducing an agile organizational structure, certain agile values and behaviors must also be known and lived.

The Agile Manifesto is an essential part of what defines the agile mindset. In many management levels, the content and its importance are still unknown. In the majority of agile software teams, the principles and their application have already become "second nature" to a large extent and are therefore passionately lived and defended in arguments.

Principles of the Agile Manifesto:
1. *Our highest priority is to satisfy the customer through early and continuous delivery of valuable software.*
2. *Welcome changing requirements, even late in development. Agile processes harness change for the customer's competitive advantage.*
3. *Deliver working software frequently, from a couple of weeks to a couple of months, with a preference to the shorter timescale.*
4. *Business people and developers must work together daily throughout the project.*
5. *Build projects around motivated individuals. Give them the environment and support they need, and trust them to get the job done.*
6. *The most efficient and effective method of conveying information to and within a development team is face-to-face conversation.*
7. *Working software is the primary measure of progress.*
8. Agile processes promote sustainable development. The sponsors, developers, and users should be able to maintain a constant pace indefinitely .
9. Continuous attention to technical excellence and good design enhances *agility.*
10. Simplicity—the art of maximizing the amount of work not done—is *essential.*
11. The best architectures, requirements, and designs emerge from self-organizing teams.
12. *At regular intervals, the team reflects on how to become more effective, then tunes and adjusts its behavior accordingly.*

Note: The 12 principles of the Agile Manifesto—Source: [1] , German translation by Sascha Block from the English original

Mordi and Schoop have made a significant contribution to developing a clear definition and understanding of the Agile Mindset with their scientific analysis [2, page 9]:

*"Agile Mindset is a way of thinking based on the values and principles of the Agile Manifesto and its main characteristics are trust, responsibility and self-responsibility, continuous improvement, willingness to learn, openness, and the readiness to constantly adapt and grow. It is underpinned by specific personal traits at the individual level and a supportive environment at the organizational level that enables the autonomy of people and teams, dealing with uncertainty, and a focus on customer benefit, with the aim of achieving a state of being agile rather than just acting agile."*Furthermore, Mordi and Schopp point out the direct connection to agile infrastructure: Having an agile mindset and being agile also means that the entire environment must be designed to take into account and support the attributes postulated in the definition.

It is not enough to merely acknowledge the importance and relevance of the Agile Mindset in theory; rather, it is essential to establish an organization-wide Agile Mindset that fulfills the following, partially overlapping characteristics:

Trust

Trust is an important characteristic, requiring explicit trust in the talents and abilities of those who do the work, which demands the ability to "let go" on the part of leaders, as without trust, true agility cannot exist. Trust also includes confidence in one's own expertise and encourages the courage to fight for one's ideas and not simply give in.

Responsibility and Self-Responsibility

Responsibility and self-responsibility are closely related to the value of trust and encompass both the collective responsibility of teams and the sole responsibility of an individual.

It is essential to promote the ability to make decisions instead of delegating decisions to others. To this end, everyone should be encouraged equally to maintain continuous attention in order to minimize errors and effectively respond to unexpected events. This fundamentally requires courage and genuine commitment. In extreme cases, this can result in triggering an emergency process—see emergency management—in a positive sense.

Continuous Improvement

Continuous improvement is based on the ability of independent or authorized **reflection** of personal behavior and individual skills, strengths, and weaknesses. It is desirable for each individual to **proactively** and tirelessly strive for improvements **in their work.**

Willingness to Learn

Continuous improvements are only possible if there is a willingness for constant learning and reflection. Analytical, science-oriented approaches and prototypical evaluation of hypotheses are part of this.

Curiosity and constructively questioning underlying assumptions and prerequisites, the willingness to experiment, error tolerance, and *"learning by doing"*, as well as feedback and short feedback cycles are the necessary prerequisites for this.

Openness and Readiness to Constantly Adapt and Grow

These characteristics are facilitated by a holistic view of life and an associated awareness of the environment and others, meaning they also involve being open and unbiased towards other perspectives.

Skills mature over time, just as technologies, in particular, develop rapidly. Recognizing similarities and patterns are not only technical skills but also of overarching importance.

Recognizing that we are on a journey together is preferable to the standpoint that a final state has been reached. This does not mean that defined goals are not achieved at a fixed point in time or are fundamentally questionable, but rather that they should always remain trustingly reflectable.

Specific personal characteristics

In order to develop and acquire an Agile Mindset, certain personality traits are significant; to personally support an Agile Mindset and enable it together with others, these include in particular: intention, integrity, honesty, transparency, courage, authenticity, empathy, proactivity, creativity, and problem orientation.

In combination with the other values, this leads to constructive, agile cooperation.

Creative environment

The creative environment is the infrastructure that supports the agility of individuals and teams through a pleasant, positive environment.

In addition to the physical aspects of a spatial environment with collaboration-friendly workspaces, this also includes open communication that does not follow hierarchical levels. In this context, managers take on the role of "enablers" and remove any obstacles, see also further explanations in the Change Management section.

Everyone contributes equally to goals, so that in the end we only win or lose together as a team. Constructive feedback following a "no-blame approach" should be promoted, meaning that mistakes are allowed and should be openly shared.

Autonomy of individuals and teams

The autonomy of individuals and teams means that agile work should be carried out in small, autonomous, cross-functional teams that in turn use a network of other agile teams. The respective individuals regulate and organize themselves as independently as the units of teams or team networks. Behind this is the conviction that people are intrinsically motivated and want to contribute if they understand the impact of their own work [3].

The result is mutual respect, trust, and self-organization. Technical tools and the physical environment provide the opportunity for interaction or (self-)information at any time.

Dealing with uncertainty

Uncertainties or extreme situations must not change the agile mindset. If it is accepted that simple solutions are rather rare than the rule—which is especially true for the increasingly complex technical infrastructure—it then also becomes the rule to validate knowledge and to allow the necessary time for this.

Creating facts and reflecting on them multiple times, i.e., from different perspectives and under different conditions, is useful and not a process that can be skipped.

Focus on customer benefit
An important driving force for agility is the creation of added value for the customer; this maxim is already contained in the agile manifesto. Every organization must therefore have goals and values that focus on added value and innovation for customers and deliver results that are meaningful to customers.

Prototypical approaches support this customer-oriented focus and include direct feedback from customers. It should be considered to what extent an internal idea and improvement management system transparently involves customers or to what extent unique selling points are worth protecting from competitors.

7.2   Agile Goals

Goal definitions are elementary guidelines according to which every organization aligns itself and its (economic) actions. Starting from a guiding vision and derived main goals, various goals result, which can be broken down into subgoals or project goals, or simply to be achieved by a defined date.

The concept of an agile goal does not currently seem to be defined in the literature but is indirectly derived from the previous explanations of the agile mindset:

After the goal is before the goal
On the one hand, every achieved or missed goal is followed by another, new goal definition. This ultimately follows from the definition of continuous improvement. By reaching the finish line, we are thus putting ourselves back in the starting position.

Do not cling to rigid goal definitions at all costs
On the other hand—and this is the more significant point—we should not follow rigidly defined goals without constantly checking their current validity.

Uncertainties should smartly influence goals
Uncertainties should also smartly influence our goal definitions, namely by clarifying and eliminating uncertainties and then checking and, if necessary, adjusting already established goal definitions.

In software development, however, it is very often a technological change that can call a defined goal into question. In the spirit of an agile mindset, it is then logical to question a situation even in the middle of a project and admit that a decision was made when selecting a basic technology that is evaluated differently from today's standpoint. If it follows from this insight and situational assessment that the consequences of maintaining the status quo are acceptable, everyone will feel better than if they simply continued undeterred according to tacit agreements.

The mere reevaluation with a transparently communicated insight—especially beyond a single team or decision-maker—will have a positive impact.

If we take into account that we cannot always make the right decisions—there are certainly analogies to probability theory—then it can only be advantageous to speak of agile goals with an agile mindset, right?

Our customers provide us with agile goals

When we focus on customers, we should not neglect the fact that their requirements can also change. The good news is that with a prototypical approach, we not only greatly minimize the risk of not registering customer wishes, but we are also much more responsive because our entire approach is designed for adaptability. We are a bit chameleon-like. And not opportunistically, but in a purely positive sense!

How do we ensure that (adjusted) goals are visible?

To make a company vision and company goals visible, dialogue images are an excellent option; these are presented in detail in the section on dialogue images and infographics under Content.

With the agile approach and the focus on the customer, goal definitions have been established and proven that pursue the common goal of aligning agile software development more closely with people.

7.2.1 Personas

Personas support the project team in gaining a common understanding of users and stakeholders, as well as their needs and behaviors, by being used as actors in user stories.

Persona Profile

Personas help to understand how and when, that is, in which context tasks are performed. One of the main advantages of using personas is that the resulting scenarios and visual designs are prescriptive. This brings us back very close to prototyping, because prescription is a scientific method for developing a hypothesis, which must then be secured by empirical observation or an experiment following the formation of the hypothesis. And a

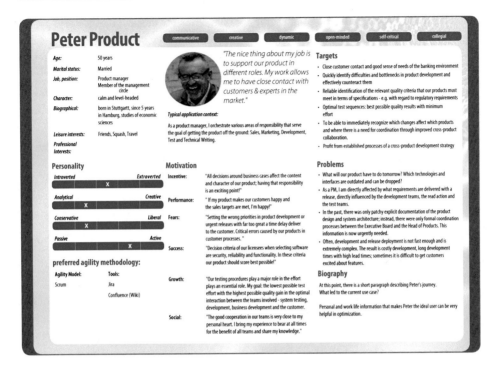

Fig. 7.2 Persona Profile

meaningful experiment requires as precise a description as possible of the test case and the test candidates.

If the test candidates do not have the right properties, the test results cannot provide correct statements either. Specifically: If the new gummy bear mix is tasted by test subjects who prefer chocolate, it misses its test target.

Figure 7.2 shows a "persona profile" in a graphically designed form. The visual representation with a concise, fictional name helps all teams optimally understand the motivation, goals, problems, and context of the persona.

7.2.2   User Story

User stories have their origin in eXtreme Programming [4] and are still referred to as "Customer Story" there.

A user story consists of three essential elements [5]:

- **the written part,**, which serves as a reminder of the requirement;
- **the conversation around the story,** which supports the development of a common understanding;

- and **the acceptance criteria,** which serve as boundaries for the scope of a story.

In recent years, this established schema of user stories has evolved. Cohn had already suggested in 2004 to supplement the story with personas.

Harbers introduces the concept of "value-based user stories" that are created in a "Value Story Workshop" attended by various interest groups and incorporating stakeholder values into the requirements [6].

Regardless of the individual weighting you choose, there are several sensible ways to incorporate the needs of users and stakeholders into the development of products, software, and services.

Personas always form the starting point for a User Story. In this way, the attributes of the personas are fully taken into account in the context of use. The following steps are taken to create User Stories:

- **Requirement analysis**: Identification of the content requirements in the context of the considered persona;
- **Identification of functional requirements,** e.g., regarding navigation, backend functions to be connected with the derivation of the minimally required permissions, etc.;
- within the Story Board, an overall view of the needs and business processes is thus created;
- the definition of interaction scenarios for different groups, for example, those of web users in comparison to app users.

With the transition to agile development, requirements are increasingly formulated in the form of textual User Stories. These User Stories capture only the essential elements of a requirement:

- for whom it is intended,
- what they expect from the system, and,
- optionally, why it is important.

What does a User Story look like?

The most well-known format, popularized by Mike Cohn [5], is:

> **"As a ⟨type of user⟩, I want ⟨goal⟩, [so that ⟨some reason⟩]".**
> "As a ⟨type of user⟩, I want ⟨goal⟩, [so that ⟨some reason⟩]"*Example of a correct User Story:* "As an administrator, I want to receive a notification when an untrustworthy event has occurred so that I can respond to it."

User Stories never contain the solution for technical implementation

As you may have already noticed, User Stories remain a clearly defined part of the requirement analysis and never contain specifications for a technical implementation.

This is a very common mistake made in the formulation of User Stories in practice.

Example of an incorrect User Story: "As an administrator, I want to receive an *email* when an untrustworthy event has occurred so that I can respond to it."

The modified User Story would already make a limited specification with email as the notification method, which may appear as a possible solution suggestion in connection with the User Story, but has no place in the User Story itself.

After all, it is quite possible that an SMS or push-up notification represents a better option or should also be included as a parallel notification option, so that three individual specifications result from this User Story.

A well-formulated User Story minimizes efforts

In practice, it is not uncommon for such trivial details to lead to functionalities never being questioned again. At the very least, the necessary efforts for subsequent implementation regularly turn out to be significantly higher.

Another mistake in the formulation of User Stories is the role designation, which often remains unchanged with the placeholder User and then does not provide any clarity regarding the actual role.

Example: Within the context—for example, in the registration process for an online service—complex, downstream authentication processes regularly occur, which are associated with completely different permissions.

Figure 7.3 "User Stories in Atlassian Jira" illustrates how user stories are represented in the collaboration tool Atlassian Jira.

How to improve the quality of a user story

For software engineering, there are eight quality characteristics that must apply to a requirement [7]:

1. **Correct**
2. **Unambiguous**
3. **Complete**
4. **Consistent**
5. **ordered by importance/stability**
6. **Verifiable**
7. **Modifiable** and
8. **Traceable**

Lucassen et al. recommend a methodical optimization of user stories, which is based on three complementary approaches and optimizes user stories from three different directions [8]:

Fig. 7.3 User Stories in Atlassian Jira

A. **Syntactic quality,** which refers to the textual structure of a user story without considering its meaning. The user story is therefore:
   - Atomic
   - Minimalistic
   - Well-defined

   If these requirements are taken into account, a user story expresses a requirement for exactly one feature, contains only one role, means, and purpose.
B. **Semantic quality,** which refers to the relationships and meaning of the text and their relation to the user story; The user story is therefore:
   - Conflict-free
   - Conceptually sound

- Problem-oriented
- Unambiguous

   Thus, a user story does not contradict another user story. The means of the user story expresses a function and its purpose a justification, not something else. In addition, a user story describes only the problem, not the solution for it. A user story avoids terms or abstractions that can lead to multiple interpretations.

C. **Pragmatic quality,** which refers to the selection of the most effective alternatives for communicating a specific set of requirements. The user story is therefore:

- Complete
- Without explicit dependencies
- Formulated as a complete sentence
- Independent
- Scalable
- Uniform
- Unique

If user stories are created according to these rules, you not only avoid associated problems, but also guarantee unambiguous and easily understandable user stories and at the same time use an agile task cut with separable and high-quality requirement definitions.

7.2.3 Epic

An Epic is a unit that encompasses a multitude of User Stories. The Epic construct, originating from Scrum—translated as epic—is a large User Story that summarizes several atomic User Stories to make them tangible and narratable, and is divided into smaller, implementable user stories.

Epics are thus units that aggregate User Stories and serve to organize agile work packages in this way. While User Stories reflect individual requirements in the form of needs from the customer's perspective, an Epic can be understood as an organizational unit.

An Epic is—viewed from a tree structure—the higher-level hierarchy for organization. Therefore, Epics regularly exist across multiple sprint cycles, while User Stories, Tasks, and Sub-Tasks can typically be completed, i.e., done, within a single sprint.

Figure 7.4 "Epic" illustrates—here in the detailed view—the relationship between Epics and individual User Stories.

Using Epics for KPIs and Management Reports

When an organization is just transitioning to agile methodology, it can be useful to define goals for Epics that are achievable quarterly or semi-annually.

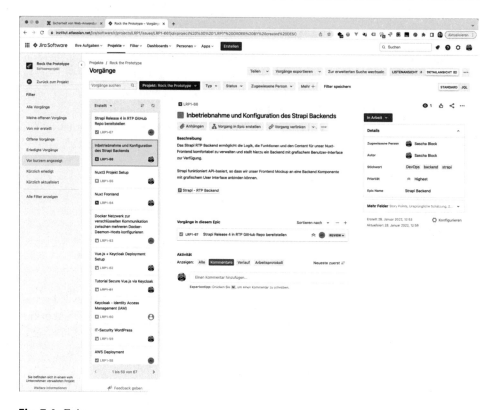

Fig. 7.4 Epic

Do not underestimate the initial planning effort associated with preparing the first rough plan. To complicate matters during this initial phase, you also need to familiarize yourself with the planning tools, which in most cases will be Jira from Atlassian.

Note that the following additional tasks are involved in the initial setup:

- **Reporting:** Reports for Product Owners, executives, or other stakeholders who want specific status information;
- **Representation of progress:** The textual description of all User Stories and their relationship, which converge in an Epic;
- **Check Time Estimate:** It should be taken into account that the tasks converging in an Epic are all based on initial time estimates from agile teams.
  The individual estimates are based on assumptions, at best on solid experience values. It is worth taking the time at this point to look at these effort estimates together with the teams and in the overarching and cross-team context of the Epic, in order to make any necessary adjustments in advance.

Tip Even though Epics represent a longer time unit, it is not recommended to define either too short or too long a time span for an Epic. It makes more sense to design the first Epics rather simpler and gradually approach the tools and methodology. Over time, you will develop a very keen sense of when an Epic is overloaded and time dimensions are either too generously sized or too ambitious. Keep in mind that it is always possible to transfer User Stories along with associated tasks to another Epic.

7.2.4   Task & Sub-Task

Tasks and sub-tasks dress a user story with the goal of organizational and technical implementation. Product owners and agile teams define the tasks required to implement a user story and organize these task packages into tasks and sub-tasks.

Planning tasks for sprints
For sprint planning, the product owners and teams decide which user stories and task packages to tackle. Sub-tasks often bundle preparatory measures, such as configuring a development, testing, and production environment. It has proven useful to adapt repeated steps in the process based on existing user stories—as a template. Furthermore, it is important that tasks and sub-tasks do not contain documentation-like detailed information but rather refer to corresponding wiki documentation or Confluence sections via direct links.

Clear recommendation: Separate tasks and documentation
The advantage is obvious: First, agile teams can focus on the current status information within the respective task artifacts and independently inform and exchange information about these agile artifacts at any time. Second, documentation takes place at a central, overarching location and forms a coherent artifact that grows over time and gradually complements a complete documentation that should also be easily understood by new team members.

Product owners, team members, and other stakeholders gain easily graspable priorities by breaking down task elements into granular sub-elements and estimates based on story points. Another positive side effect is that potentially hidden activities are uncovered and defined in the course of the estimate-based effort assessment. As a result, the product owner regularly reprioritizes the elements in the backlog after receiving estimates from the individual participants.

7.2.5   Backlog

A backlog, or product backlog, is a list of work items. Part of a backlog are, for example, user stories or software bugs that still need to be fixed, i.e., all the various tasks that agile teams need to coordinate to manage the upcoming work.

In agile software development, the product owner is responsible for setting priorities in the backlog. To do this, the respective tasks must be equipped with appropriate requirement definitions, brief descriptions of desired functions, or bug fixes for bug elimination for a software product.

For agile teams, the backlog is the most important project management tool and thus an indispensable tool for the agile working mode.

Close collaboration between product owners and teams
Product owners must work closely with the responsible agile teams to be able to use the most realistic effort estimates. Based on a good estimate and good, compact descriptions, product owners can evaluate the individual task elements and their priority in context and thus assess the relative priority of each element accurately.

Effort estimation clarifies questions and details
Regularly, questions about requirements and implementation arise within the agile teams when the estimation process begins. This effect is deliberately desired as a fixed component of the agile approach, as these questions help the entire team to understand the tasks in detail and to add any missing details or to further specify the respective task packages.

Sedano et al. have, through an extensive field study, made an important contribution to the basic principle of a backlog and provide the following results for this [9, page 210]:

1. Product Backlog **serve as an informal model** for the work to be done, and **do not contain requirement specifications.**
2. A backlog acts as a **boundary object**, and **bridges the gap between the creation of solution concepts and the development of software.**
3. The authors confirm the role and mode of operation of backlogs in **requirement specification** and their **functioning for team-oriented** evolution towards finding solutions specifically for software, as well as the **cross-team importance** of a backlog.
4. **Identification of design obstacles** that can arise within a backlog.Figure 7.5 illustrates the "basic principle of a Product Backlog" and thus provides a solid foundation for defining and implementing requirements in an agile manner.

Recommendation of specific backlog practices
Furthermore, the authors of the study define and recommend 13 specific backlog practices to minimize the emergence of requirement backlogs and to optimally use backlogs

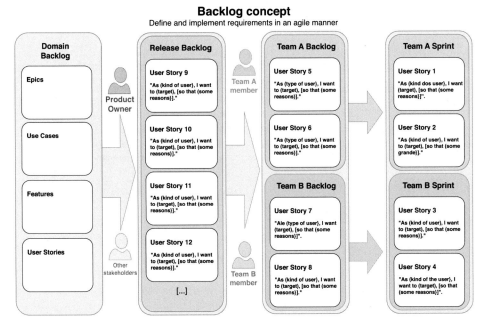

Fig. 7.5 Basic principle of a Product Backlog

[9, page 204 ff.], which was supplemented by their own practical experience as well as references to prototyping and Action Design Research.

Table 7.1 "Best Practices for Backlog Use" provides recommendations on which approach has a particularly positive effect on effective backlog use in practice.

Software teams can use the practice descriptions to improve the creation of their backlogs

7.3   Collaboration Tools

Collaboration tools are tools for effective collaboration with one or more other people to produce or create something.

The communication function is often an integral part of collaboration tools but far from the only benefit.

Many collaboration tools are based on traditional face-to-face interaction and use completely different functions and technologies. They all have the following characteristics in common [10]:

Table 7.1 Best Practices for Backlog Use

Best Practice for Backlog Use	Explanation
Balanced Teams	Well-balanced team composition with experts from the fields of business processes, product design, and software development.
Dual-Track Agility	It is recommended to organize work in parallel on two "tracks": • Track 1 usually includes research, negotiations with stakeholders, creating prototypes, and writing user stories. • Track 2 involves the creation, testing, software architecture, refactoring, as well as deployment and maintenance of the product.
Stakeholder Briefing	Identification and visualization of the individuals who are interested in the success of the product.
Interviews	Open interviews as well as (semi-)structured conversations with stakeholders such as users and product sponsors, i.e., stakeholders for e.g. (individual) functions
Persona	Creation of functional users with detailed character sketches to determine who will use the product features with which motivation and what specific needs.
Affinity-Based Task Assignment	Strengths and motivation-based, as well as voluntary assignment of tasks to promote the best possible intrinsic motivation of each individual as a contributor
Creative Idea Process & Action Design Research	Establishment of creative methods for problem-solving, organization of stakeholder interviews, and systematic processing of survey results.
Prototyping	Prototypical product conception through iteration between the phases of requirement definition, prototype creation, and discussion of prototype design.
Active Usability Testing and Validation of Functionality and Error-Free Operation	Technical and functional tests of prototypes and releases, including the implementation of (partially) automated test routes, i.e., definition of test cases and their verification using suitable test methodology.
User Stories	Building a common understanding within the team and together with connected teams for the implementation of upcoming user stories. Writing short, informal user stories with a connected reference to the overarching software architecture.
Story Showcase	Using story showcases and prototypes specifically to share goal definitions with other teams and to seek feedback and constructive solution/experience exchange.
Backlog Maintenance	Redefinition and re-sequencing of user stories and tasks within the backlog, checking for necessary updates—"Are all the information up-to-date?"
Acceptance Tests of User Stories,	Evaluation of the work performed by the stakeholders of the user stories. Establishing retrospectives for mutual reflection within the team.

- **Strong communication skills:** Whether through video, audio, or simple text, the most important characteristic of a tool for digital collaboration in agile teams is its ability to significantly support communication and interaction between participants.
- **Easy to understand and comfortable to use:** The user interface of the tool should be simple and intuitive to use. This is characterized by the simplest and most intuitive operation and easy navigation.
- **Excellent capabilities to support virtual collaboration:** Important are functions to support an optimal structure of information as well as well-functioning mechanisms for finding content, not solely through a very good search function. To encourage the numerous participants to contribute and also to structure their contributions, a collaboration tool should make it clear that contributions are expected and that they will elicit a response.

An online presentation is a good example of extended functionality, as it is clear to communication participants during use that they should actively respond to the presentation and interact with the presenter and other participants, rather than passively consuming a webcast.

The Periodic Table for DevOps Tools—see separate section—currently lists Slack, Microsoft Teams, Atlassian Confluence, Stack Overflow, and Mattermost as the most significant collaboration tools.

7.3.1 Confluence

Atlassian Confluence is a wiki software for collaboration within an organization. It is a commercial software that can be used as a platform-independent browser application as well as a native app in a mobile-optimized version. The name is programmatic, as all information from an organization converges in Confluence.

Confluence is primarily used for collaboration and knowledge management within an organization.

The most common use cases for Confluence:
- **Knowledge management**
- **Organization-wide wiki & glossary**
- **Collaborative platform**
- **Document management**
- **Requirement documentation**
- **Intranet**
- **Quality management system**
- **Project management**
- **Task management, if no Jira usage**
- **To support e-learning**

- **Content production and technical editing**
- **Troubleshooting articles**

Main features of Confluence:
- Teams can work together on documents simultaneously and track their changes in real-time;
- automatic versioning of content and files;
- comprehensive role and permission concept;
- templates for different content and reports;
- full-text search, which also includes attachments in the search;
- browser-based support for any language;
- extensive notification functions via email, popup, or push notification;
- integration of external user directories such as LDAP;
- export options for page content as PDF, Word, or HTML—the HTML function can be used, for example, to connect to a public website, e.g., for direct customer support;
- promotion of interaction through inline comments and notification options when mentioned;
- support for separation for specialized areas of teams or projects;
- very powerful WYSIWYG editor for creating appealing content, including an option for optimized color display of various programming languages;
- socializing features, e.g., comments and likes;
- tight integration with Atlassian Jira.

A page you should NOT actually see in Confluence is the error message *"You do not have permission to view this page"*. Confluence thrives as a collaboration tool on cooperation and transparency, and which information in your organization is so trustworthy that you entrust it to a cloud tool but want to hide it from your employees—regardless of their role and function?

7.3.2 Jira

Atlassian Jira is an essential tool for implementing agile projects and is also suitable for effectively structuring and organizing complex tasks. Jira allows agile teams to digitally map all essential artifacts and events according to Scrum or Kanban or even alternative agile methodologies.

Alternatives—mostly for smaller organizations are Trello and Asana—due to its wide distribution, importance, and functional superiority as well as the option to connect many other 3rd-party tools, Jira is presented here as an example.

The focus of Jira is on realizing the planning, all information on the current status, and the release process of software or products. To this end, the browser-based software—which has also been supplemented by native apps—offers real-time reporting and convenient features to keep an eye on progress and all relevant information.

Almost any conceivable customization towards individual team needs can be implemented, so that every agile team can find itself here. Jira works task or ticket-based. Transparency to individual information artifacts, just like in Confluence, forms the starting point for collaboration within and between agile teams. If desired, all information is available at any time.

Jira Backlog

Central elements here are the digital Scrum or Kanban boards, which can be freely chosen by the teams, on which the respective tasks with their status and the current processor are graphically visualized and thus plausibly and easily understandable represent the current project status.

Figure 7.6 illustrates a "Product Backlog in the form of a Kanban Board in Atlassian Jira". Here it is directly visible at a glance which requirements have already been fully implemented, which tasks are still in review or in progress, currently selected for development, or still in the backlog.

7.3.3 Git Repositories, GitHub, and GitLab

A **repository** is a software-managed directory for storing and describing objects. **Git**-repositories are such indispensable tools for software development in agile teams for versioned and centralized storage of source code. A Git-based repository database thus enables the systematic storage of program code, code fragments, technical documentation, and other components relevant to software development and at the same time allows their versioning.

While the Git environment on a local computer with one or more Git repositories represents a personal development environment, GitHub and GitLab are **online** platforms **for** remote repositories. Such a remote repository is a remote repository on another host to which development files are transferred. GitLab offers—unlike GitHub—the possibility to operate such remote repositories on your own servers, thus supporting the so-called **on-premise variant** for software operation.

Figure 7.7 shows a "Git Repository" in the form of a publicly accessible GitHub repository, here using the example of Keycloak, an open-source solution for identity and access management.

GitHub, on the other hand, is a purely cloud-based platform for versioning software based on Git versioning. GitHub online repositories are very popular and widely used in both open-source projects and commercial software.

Remote repositories and Git provide the particularly important functions and mechanisms for sharing code in a coordinated manner in a software project, for developing new software functionalities in parallel with other developers in agile teams, or for optimizing software.

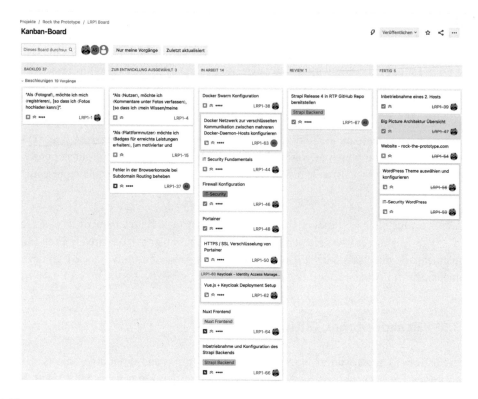

Fig. 7.6 Product Backlog in the form of a Kanban Board in Atlassian Jira

"For you as a software developer, it's only a small step to versioning with Git, but for every agile software project in a team, it's a big step—a milestone!"
  Sascha Block—IT Architect

Why is Git versioning of software so important?
The use of a Git versioning system (Git-CVS) not only solves many common problems when writing code but also significantly improves the entire software development process.

By allowing not only software developers and software architects to track code development via Git in near real-time as soon as code is hosted online, software development becomes transparent, reproducible, and open for collaboration in agile teams. Not only can other stakeholders and, in particular, penetration testers effectively assess the quality of software, but all automation processes are based on the basic technology of Git versioning.

It is secondary where code is hosted in Git repositories. The decisive factor is that online access is possible at any time. Closed-source projects can be hosted in a protected

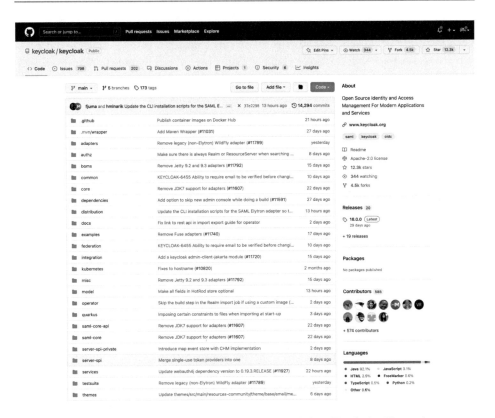

Fig. 7.7 GitHub Repository of the open-source IAM solution Keycloak. (Screenshot source: Sascha Block)

environment in the cloud or on private servers, the way and means are secondary. The primary goal is that code artifacts are available and versioned online in real-time.

The most important Git mechanisms explained compactly:

Commit

The commit is a snapshot of the changes made to source code via so-called staging files. A commit in a Git repository is like a backup of a developer's save state in the Git project with all the changes made to the stage files. All changes are saved with the commit command. The clever part—like with a backup—is that there is always the possibility to return to this state. Smart, right?

Stage

A stage—also referred to as the staging area—contains the files that should be included in the next Git transfer. With staging, the developer defines a file for the next transfer to the remote Git repository.

Track

When a Git file is tracked, an observer follows its changes and is informed about each such change. A tracked file is a Git element that is recognized by the Git repository as a single element. Tracking is not only relevant for software developers but also an invaluable mechanism for product owners, penetration testers, and various tasks within quality assurance and documentation of software.

Branch

A branch is a parallel version of the files in a repository.

Local

Newly defined source code artifacts regularly emerge as development files on the local development environment of individual software developers and thus contain the reference to their machine and their repository version.

Remote

The remote is the version of the repository that is stored on a remote host, such as a server. This remote repository can be hosted on GitHub, GitLab, or elsewhere. A URL or URI addresses this remote location.

Clone

A clone is a local copy of a remote project archive that has been created as a duplicate for a separate development environment.

Fork

A fork (fork) is a (modified) copy of a project archive and can be created at any time by any developer or Git user. It is a common strategy to fork a GitHub/GitLab project and create a 1:1 copy of this Git project as an archive. Likewise, a developer can transfer or merge a Git repo from another Git-Hub user's GitHub account to their own.

Merge

A merge is a versioning strategy to combine version files. With Git merge, a Git project is updated by incorporating all introduced changes via new commits into the remote repository through a merge.

Pull

With a pull or pull request, a developer retrieves modified files via commit from a remote repository and transfers them to their local repository. The release files are thus merged in the direction of a development environment.

Push

With a push or push request, developers send commits from a local repository to a remote repository.

Pull Request

The pull request is a request as a message sent by another GitHub user to incorporate the transfers in their remote repository into the remote repository of another user. Pull requests thus grant permissions for versioning into a remote repository.

Is Git versioning suitable only for code?

Git is not limited to code alone! There is no reason why this framework should be limited to code; a Versioning Control System (VCS) is well suited for tracking any plain text files:

- **Technical specifications**
- **Protocols**
- **Manuscripts**
- ...

Public and non-public Git versioning

Whether Git versioning is publicly visible (public) or private and thus not publicly visible is determined by the owner of a repository.

The permission control of repositories is diverse and offers a solution for every conceivable requirement.

Or to put it plainly and clearly differently:

There is no, absolutely no, good reason not to version software and source code with Git. Git is indispensable when programming.

In this sense: Happy Git versioning! ;-)

7.3.4 OpenAPI—Tools for API Design

Technically, APIs are often highly individual; mainly because new code in the form of definitions must be written for each interface. To keep time expenditures as efficient as possible and costs as low as possible, standardized **API protocols**, such as JSON-based REST APIs, ideally in RESTful API design, are often used.

For APIs for structured document formats like JSON, the use of the library must match the underlying specification for context-free documents.

Instances of context-free API protocols can, especially when misusing the APIs, lead to typical runtime exceptions or data leaks [11].

OpenAPI [12] is the leading specification and thus **tool for documenting APIs**.

OpenAPI, formerly known as Swagger, has now firmly established itself in software development. Swagger started as an open-source specification for the development and documentation of REST/RESTful APIs back in 2010.

In 2015, the Swagger project was acquired by SmartBear Software. The Swagger specification was donated to the Linux Foundation and renamed to OpenAPI.

The **OpenAPI Specification** is the cornerstone for a thoroughly proven open-source software, each with independent communities behind them, which further develop the respective open-source projects such as IAM-Keycloak with new IAM releases and a professional release plan.

With OpenAPI, countless OpenAPI tools are also available, which bring valuable functions to software projects, such as converters to alternative documentation formats, validators, editors, mock servers, test tools, etc.

From the OpenAPI specification, source code documentation can be generated for both client and server-side for over 50 languages. All of this is available as a free-to-use open-source contribution based on the OpenAPI specification.

OpenAPI Tools

In the freely accessible **OpenAPI GitHub** [13] you can find all known OpenAPI tools that implement the OpenAPI specification and are available for free use.

The number of tools is constantly growing, so it is worth checking regularly to benefit from further, new tools for API documentation via OpenAPI.

OpenAPI Schema

OpenAPI definitions should be used to make APIs transparent and easily understandable for all agile teams. In particular, the JSON schema for validating OpenAPI definitions of versions 3.1. [14] and the OpenAPI 3.1 YAML schema [15] are particularly popular.

OpenAPI Object

An OpenAPI object is, as illustrated in Fig. 7.8 "Component-based structure of an OpenAPI object," divided into components of an OpenApi object.

Fig. 7.8 "Component-based structure of an OpenAPI object" illustrates the component-based structure of an OpenApi object.

Analogous to representation 47, Table 7.2 explains the respective components of an OpenAPI object.

Advantages of OpenAPI Interface Documentation

The OpenAPI specification already forms the foundation of numerous field-tested open-source software, each backed by independent communities that further develop the respective open-source projects, such as IAM-Keycloak, with new IAM releases and a professional release plan.

Fig. 7.8 Component-based
structure of an OpenAPI object

- OpenAPI is the widely established standard for API specification.
- OpenAPI is an agnostic technology, meaning that all technology-independent technologies specified via OpenAPI, such as Java, .NET, PHP, etc., benefit.
- OpenAPI specifications are defined in YAML or JSON.
- The OpenAPI specifications are defined by a formal schema.
- Because OpenAPI specifications are organized in a structured document, all information is machine-readable.
- OpenAPI makes information objects and the relationships between them clear.
- Because all information is machine-readable, automatic API testing is possible.
- Tools like Swagger.io or Postman provide the appropriate working environment for any API testing.
- These tools are also a living API documentation.
- OpenApi CodeGen—Generate Server Code offers convenient templates for different programming languages.
- An OpenApi is a "single source of truth", meaning the API documentation is the only source and always up to date.

With OpenAPI, countless OpenAPI tools are also available, providing valuable functions in software projects, such as converters to alternative documentation formats, validators, editors, mock servers, test tools, SDK generators, etc.

From the OpenAPI specification, source code documentation can be generated for both client and server sides in over 50 languages. All of this is available as a free-to-use open-source contribution based on the OpenAPI specification.

How Agile Teams Benefit from OpenAPI Documentation
- Microservices define APIs, and these are defined through OpenAPI specifications.
- Through the OpenAPI Specs, the different code artifacts are defined, which can be comfortably versioned and organized via a Git-based repository. These code artifacts, in turn, are the different (information) objects in the API context, such as operation

Table 7.2 Field names and their meaning in the OpenAPI context

Field Name	Type	Explanation
openapi	string	REQUIRED. This string MUST be the version number of the OpenAPI specification used by the OpenAPI document. The openapi field SHOULD be used by tools to interpret the OpenAPI document. It is not related to the API info.version string.
info	Info Object	REQUIRED. Provides metadata about the API. The metadata MAY be used by tooling as needed.
jsonSchema-Dialect	string	The default value for the $schema keyword in the Schema Objects contained in this OAS document. This MUST be in the form of a URI.
servers	[Server Object]	An array of Server Objects, which provide connectivity information to a target server. If the servers property is not provided or is an empty array, the default value would be a Server Object with a url value of /.
paths	Paths Object	The available paths and operations for the API.
webhooks	Map[string, Path Item Object | Reference Object]]	The incoming webhooks that MAY be received as part of this API and that the API client MAY implement. This section is closely related to the "callbacks" feature and describes requests that are not initiated by an API call, e.g., by an out-of-band registration. The key name is a unique string to refer to each webhook, while the (optionally referenced) Path Item Object describes a request that can be initiated by the API provider, as well as the expected responses. An example is available.
components	Components Object	An element to hold various schemas for the document.
security	[Security Requirement Object]	A declaration of which security mechanisms can be used in the API. The list of values includes alternative Security Requirement Objects that can be used. Only one of the Security Requirement Objects needs to be satisfied to authorize a request. Individual operations can override this definition. To make security optional, an empty Security Requirement ({ }) can be included in the array.
tags	[Tag Object]	A list of tags used in the document with additional metadata. The order of the tags can be used to reflect on their order by the parsing tools. Not all tags that are used by the Operation Object have to be declared. The undeclared tags CAN be organized arbitrarily or based on the logic of the tooling. Each tag name in the list MUST be unique.
externalDocs	External Documenta-tion Object	Additional external documentation.

Note: Further details are explained in the root object of the OpenAPI document.

objects like user, documents, etc., and define with their properties and query parameters how an API works.

- Unit tests use OpenAPI to validate requests and responses.
- Tests can be cleanly separated for the respective test and deployment environments and realized and (partially) automated using continuous integration and continuous deployment.
- Consumer-driven APIs are defined through OpenAPI extensions.
- Authorization concepts are also API-based and are considered early on with an OpenAPI specification.
- The public API documentation is (automatically) generated from the OpenAPI specification, e.g., with Swagger tools, and made visible in the Swagger User Interface (see screenshot below).

Figure 7.9 shows how an "OpenAPI documentation" can be visualized clearly and easily comprehensible.

7.3.5 Messenger and Chat Systems

Messenger and chat systems support person-to-person or group-oriented communication. The messenger is an application for receiving and sending messages via a mostly native application, which is installed in addition to a browser. However, many messengers also support purely browser-based communication. Chat systems, on the other hand, are predominantly browser-based.

Almost all messenger and chat systems now offer a video conferencing function.

Even though Discord does not appear in the DevOps Periodic Table—see separate section—this application as a chat messenger has gained similar popularity as Slack in open source projects and is likely to be more widespread than Mattermost.

Fig. 7.10 illustrates how "Discord as a messenger-based collaboration tool" can be used for communication within and between teams. The Discord channel of Strapi shows the externally accessible communication channels in which the internal teams are directly integrated.

The mentioned representatives belong to the so-called messenger and chat clients, which serve for short-term communication and all support IP-based video telephony. Of course, video calls between several participants are supported. A standardized tool for this type of communication is absolutely essential for collaboration in agile teams.

In addition, your organization should—following the motto *"Bring your own device"*—also support alternative messengers and clients so that communication between participants of your organization and third parties is not unnecessarily complicated.

Certainly, IT security relevant aspects have to be considered, but basic support should definitely be ensured.

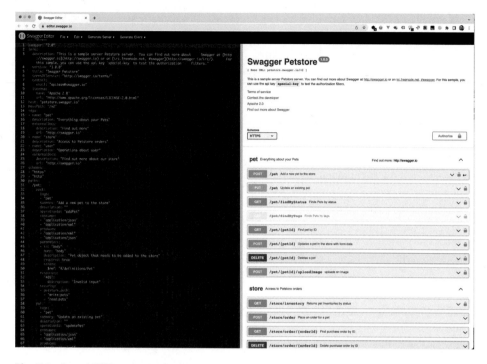

Fig. 7.9 OpenAPI Documentation

When introducing a messenger and chat system, you should consider how to plan the implementation of separate topic channels and team spaces within an agile framework. Separate retreat areas for coordinating individual teams with limited visibility are just as relevant as the correct bundling of different topics.

7.4 Agile Architectures—Foundation of Software-based Digitalization

Under rapid technological change, software architectures are changing at ever shorter intervals. What remains constant over a longer interval in these **agile architectures** are the underlying frameworks and patterns by which software does what you want it to do. That's why it's so important to continuously enrich this knowledge and incorporate this collection of values and practices into the development of digital solutions.

Even though cloud trends revolutionize many things, basic technologies that significantly ensure the security of cloud solutions are not new. The specification for the OAuth 2.0 Authorization Framework has existed since October 2012 [16], but is still current.

Technologies built on this, such as OpenID Connect, which have since extended the OAuth 2.0 protocol with additional functionalities, are continuously updated.

Fig. 7.10 Discord as a Messenger-based Collaboration Tool

For example, the OpenID Connect specification is currently being actively adapted with Draft 17 for OpenID Connect Federation 1.0 by the actors involved in standardization [17].

Software architecture is thus always to be understood as agile architecture and includes standardized software design. As such, it standardizes the technologies and components selected by your organization to be aligned with the most widely established standards. The underlying basic software architecture enables and shapes your organization-specific or company-internal processes.

How to become agile and shape your company innovatively:
Improve your agile software development and agile project management with agile processes, pragmatic tools, and methodological extensions within your company. Design the digital solutions for your company and your customers and users as effectively as possible!

Internalize how much you and your company are defined by agile processes! Take the initiative and shape your options according to your ideas. Which agile framework is ultimately the right one for your company can be found in the chapter on large-scale agile frameworks. Much more important than committing to a specific model or agile approach is understanding the agile mindset and the underlying idea and applying agile practices.

An agile software architecture enables customer-centric UX design
At the same time, an agile software architecture—in conjunction with prototyping—allows for the implementation of new system functions in close interaction with customer-centric goals in line with your organization's or company's strategy in the shortest possible time.

In the spirit of the lean-agile mindset, the verification of hypotheses regarding UX design and the targeted control of company-relevant KPIs in the form of accompanying usability tests are included.

7.4.1 Factors Influencing Agile IT Architectures

1. **High-speed architecture:** With the rapid growth of the internet, complex software systems, websites, online shops, and apps must be aligned for maximum speed. Infrastructure, code, and software-as-a-service are all concepts that further accelerate this trend of technological change.
2. **Mobile First, smart devices & IoT:** By the end of 2021, there will be two trillion smartphones worldwide and up to 12.3 trillion (equivalent to 12,300 billion) devices connected to the internet, ranging from Alexa to various IoT devices [18]. Regardless of whether digital identities generate revenue through websites and online shops, customers expect to be able to seamlessly switch between devices and media. The Mobile-First philosophy plays a crucial role in this, as does the ongoing consideration of applicable legal frameworks and IT security.
3. **Agile software and scalable services:**
   Loosely coupled systems are well-prepared for the future. Microservices enable agility for complex software systems by breaking down these software applications into individual components. This increases companies' agility, stability, and scalability.

Based on scalable software-as-a-service solutions, companies can provide transparent services and digital services to customers and bill them according to demand.

4. **The value of data is increasing:** Each year, the amount of data grows by up to 50%. The rapidly increasing amount of information requires not only powerful analysis tools and a solid, company-wide data concept but also the importance of new technologies such as artificial intelligence, neural networks, and smart data to analyze unstructured data from different sources in a targeted manner. At the same time, the responsibility of providers and operators to use data exclusively within the framework of applicable legal provisions is increasing. This also includes the right to delete personal data, which can be demanded by customers at any time.

5. **Cloud-based infrastructure:** In the digital age, the cloud is increasingly becoming an instrument for agile infrastructure. In most cases, several cloud solutions operate in parallel, complementing the market-leading cloud providers Amazon Web Services (AWS), Google Cloud, and Microsoft Azure. Solutions vary according to requirements and budget.

6. **Security and data protection:** With cloud-based systems and stricter data protection regulations—not just regarding GDPR—the requirements for security and data protection are growing. Every company is challenged to meet the necessary requirements of cybersecurity. Customers rightly expect transparent data protection and a fair, partnership-based customer relationship.

7. **DevOps and agile integration:** Companies, public organizations, and non-profit organizations inherently desire the transformation to agile customer service. In-house DevOps engineers, UX experts, and specialists in data management and analysis are just examples of central positions that enable the upcoming changes in companies. The introduction of agile methods requires company-wide support. In this context, the objective analysis and advice of external specialists, in close cooperation with company management, can prove successful. The crucial factor is that you approach and live the transformation towards agile architectures based on the agile mindset!

7.5 Pragmatic Software Architecture Documentation

A software architecture documentation is indispensable. For the creation of such a technical documentation, it is irrelevant whether a software system initially consists of a series of largely manageable functions or already a multitude of various components that are further divided into countless software services. In the worst case, a complex IT system exists for years without adequate architecture documentation.

Over the course of a project, software usually becomes more complex, rarely simplified. Especially with microservice architectures, the number of endpoints and functions increases, and the interaction between countless components and functional modules becomes more complex over time. Even if it is "only" an already functioning and complex software system—consisting of interacting individual applications in a corporate network—it is important to know architecture specifications; therefore, it is all the more important to record all relevant architectural decisions.

How to achieve pragmatic architecture documentation?
In pragmatic architecture documentation, the focus is primarily on fundamental decisions that are difficult to reverse in the future.

Interaction of collaboration tools and Git repositories
Pragmatic architecture documentation becomes manageable through the use of suitable collaboration tools and actively used tools for versioning software; primarily Git repositories.

With tools like OpenAPI tools and Postman, APIs can be flexibly documented. However, such predominantly technical documentation focused on data structures must always be supplemented with graphical and textual artifacts that can be displayed in a wiki like Confluence or directly with a web-based Git platform like GitHub or GitLab.

7.5.1   How to Create Visual Software Architecture Artifacts

Are all important software architecture artifacts in your projects well documented and visually represented? A well-designed and formally correct overview diagram and precise flowcharts often have more significance than countless words and numerous meetings.

Many projects lack meaningful, visualized architecture artifacts
Are your teams trained in the routine creation of these invaluable artifacts? Is the necessary time frame and importance given to architecture documentation, and is there a functioning interaction within prototyping and threat model-based penetration testing?

Clear recommendation: Start with simple representations and develop these representations further through refinement and detailing.

Draw.io as a simple visualization tool
For pragmatic architecture documentation, we briefly introduce the tool Draw.io as a best practice. The tool for graphical software architecture sketches, diagrams, and process representations is now available as a free desktop version, browser version, and as an add-on for Atlassian Confluence.

The operation is reminiscent of the alternative Microsoft Visio and is multilingual, the strength of the tool lies in its simplicity and equally in its easy availability for all. This is a crucial argument because the graphical design of architecture artifacts is not and should not be a science reserved for an elitist group of experts. Experts such as IT and software architects should rather support the optimization and refinement of such artifacts.

Moreover, with the attractive templates, even beginners can quickly create professional representations that can be saved and exported in various formats. The original file in Draw.io format, on the other hand, is not pixel-based and can therefore be scaled and, above all, modified as desired. With the easy availability and simple accessibility of the tool, everyone can contribute to the expansion of graphical architecture artifacts.

Figure 7.11 "Draw.io—Application for creating graphical artifacts for software architecture" shows the application interface of Draw.io and how this tool can effectively support you in creating graphical artifacts, e.g., for software architecture.

7.5.2   Standards, Criteria, and Norms for Software Architecture Artifacts

Ideally, these artifacts for documenting IT architecture comply with defined criteria and norms and are thus generally and easily understandable. To achieve this goal, the following criteria are defined, which should serve as a checklist for architecture artifacts.

Table 7.3 "Criteria and Checklist for Architecture Artifacts"

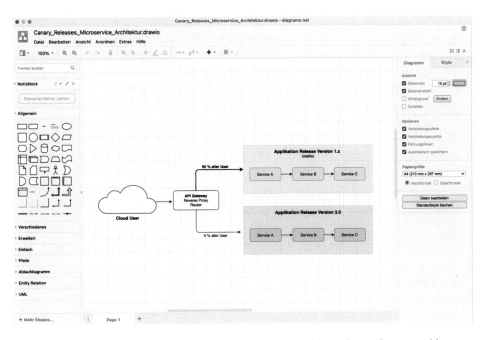

Fig. 7.11 Draw.io—Application for creating graphical artifacts for software architecture. (*Source:* Sascha Block)

Table 7.3 Criteria and Checklist for Architecture Artifacts

Criterion	Explanation
Comprehensibility	Representations should be intuitively comprehensible.
Legend	A legend explains the individual objects used and their meaning within the illustration. A centrally defined legend can be used, but ideally, the legend should always be provided with the respective representation.
Standards + Norms	Representations are easily understandable when they are created according to a specific convention or norm and the representation clearly refers to this specification in the form of a reference.
Readability	Texts, labels, and graphical objects must be of good readability in terms of display quality.

Designing easily understandable software architecture documentation

The documentation should be created as easily understandable as possible so that every potential recipient from the circle of stakeholders receives real assistance with the architecture documentation or is at least able to obtain a well-founded explanation with the help of other experts.

UML Diagrams

The Unified Modeling Language (UML) is a standard for describing software systems based on a uniform notation.

UML is the standard for analysis and design of IT architectures and object-oriented applications. Thus, UML provides a solid framework for representing complex software architectures uniformly and easily understandable.

  Goals of UML representations:

- Specification
- Visualization
- Documentation

Representation Forms and Diagram Types

UML essentially consists of nine diagram types, each serving a different purpose. These diagram types use different graphical elements, the semantics of which are precisely defined. Table 7.4 "Representation Forms and Diagram Types" lists the different UML representations in the context of their perspective in relation to requirements.

Auxiliary Cross Tables

As a pragmatic architectural artifact, easily readable cross tables prove to be useful. These cross tables contain both column and row headings, each representing a characteristic—e.g., different quality goals. Instead of a simple cross, an extension via weighting

Table 7.4 Representation Forms and Diagram Types of the Unified Modeling Language (UML)

Perspective	UML Representation	Representation of
Requirements (Requirements)	Use Case Diagram	• Actors • Scenarios
Static View	Class Diagram	• Classes • Relationships
	Package Diagram	• Structuring of used packages and/or libraries
	Collaboration Diagram	• Interaction of components
Dynamic View (Interactions, processes in the system)	Activity Diagram	• Sequence possibilities
	Sequence Diagram	• Objects • Interactions
	State Diagram	• internal behavior of objects
Implementation	Component Diagram	• inner structure of objects
	Deployment Diagram	• Embedding of objects in an environment

or values is also possible. Relationships can be color-coded in a simple cross table, or a UML tool such as the software *Enterprise Architect* can be chosen instead of, for example, Excel.

Table 7.5 "Cross tables as a pragmatic tool for software architectures" is recommended to illustrate the effects of technical decisions regarding architecture and corresponding software properties.

7.5.3 Addressing and Subject Areas of Software Architecture Documentation

According to Bass et al, software architecture addresses four different subject areas with heterogeneous interest groups in all cases [19]:

1. **The Technology** that provides measurable benefits to the company for problem-solving and ideally is based on established industry standards. The technical part of an architecture documentation includes all decisions relevant to system architecture, such as why a particular software architecture approach—like the Model-View-Controller concept—has been chosen for the design of a software system. In addition, it must be documented how the software system is structured as a whole, e.g., which individual systems make up the overall system and how they relate to each other.
2. **The Business Context** documents how the software system is suitable for mapping the company's objectives. Based solely on such a documentation component, the

Table 7.5 Cross tables as a pragmatic tool for software architectures

	Usability	Reliability	Maintainability
1. On which application environment is the server based?		X	X
2. Where is the state of an ongoing online session maintained?	X	X	
3. Which programming model/framework is used for the server?			X

management can verify whether all corporate goals are fully represented; deficits in software-based solution support can also be identified. Customers of the company typically also count as stakeholders of a software system, especially whenever products and services are prepared for customers as a target group via a software system—for example, in the form of an online shop. The description of the market situation allows changes to be perceived at any time and incorporated into the course of a software project.

3. **Software Projects** usually have a fixed project schedule from which corresponding milestones in the form of guaranteed functionalities at a specific point in time and scope, as well as within a defined cost framework, are agreed upon. Project management coordinates teams and tasks using appropriate planning tools such as Microsoft Visio or modern Software-as-a-Service tools like Atlassian Jira and Confluence.

4. **Professionals** are experts such as IT and software architects who accompany the involved teams and competently guide and coordinate specialist departments, ensuring that knowledge—in relation to deployed information technologies—is made available to all participants on an equal basis.Figure 7.12 illustrates "Subject Areas and Addressees of Software Architecture in accordance with Bass et al."

Determining Stakeholder Goals through Personas

Personas of Stakeholders: Appropriate personas of stakeholders precisely pinpoint their respective interests and clarify for all involved internal and external software developers who the respective user groups of the software solution are and what their main interests consist of.

7.5.4   Formulating Questions for Software Architecture Decisions

Zörner recommends using the following dimensions and questions to formulate architectural decisions [20, page 65]:

- **System context:** How do you involve the stakeholders?
- **Quality objectives:** Strategies and possible alternatives

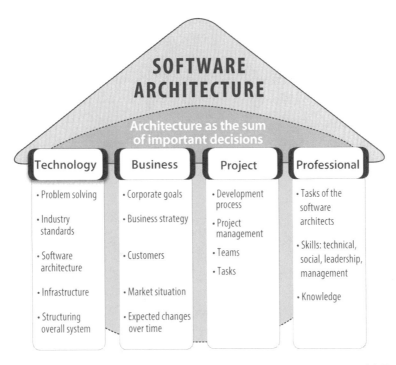

Fig. 7.12 Subject Areas and Addressees of Software Architecture in accordance with Bass et al. (*Source:* Sascha Block)

- **Project risks:** potential hurdles endangering the quality objectives
- **Identification of difficult-to-revise decisions**
- **Identification of framework conditions** with a large scope for decision-making
- **Technologies:** Which technology/product do we use for XY?

It is essential to evaluate possible alternatives. This also identifies corresponding questions, always with the evaluation of the subsequent solution strategies and alternatives. The respective conditions and relationships must be listed and evaluated accordingly.

Figure 7.13 illustrates the importance of the "context delimitation of software architecture".

Typical decisions for software architecture
Certain types of questions arise in every software project [20, page 64]:

- What interface will the users receive?
- How do we integrate external system XY?
- How do components of our system communicate with each other?

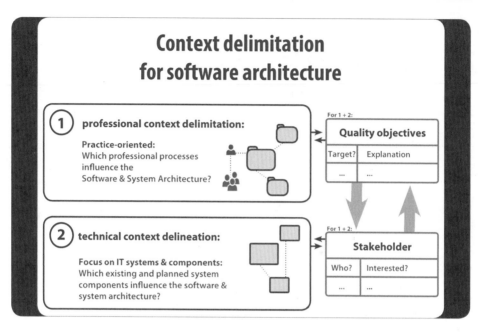

Fig. 7.13 Context delimitation for software architecture. (Source: Sascha Block)

- How do we address cross-cutting issues (e.g., persistence, distribution, ...)?
- Type of implementation for required functionalities: "Make or Buy Decision"
- Which product/technology do we use for XY?

Documentation tool "Software Architecture Decision"

In practice, a structured approach and the use of a template that documents the question, relevant influencing factors, assumptions, alternatives, and decisions made regarding software architecture have proven effective [20, page 62].

Zörner recommends incorporating lively questions (e.g., "Which framework do we choose for ...?") or the presentation of results (e.g., "ZEND as an object-oriented framework for implementing PHP-based web applications") specifically into the titles of the architecture documentation [20, page 66].

Figure 7.14 illustrates how the "building block view of a software architecture" can be depicted. Such visual artifacts are not only informative for new team members but also serve as fundamental information artifacts for software architects, IT security teams, and all other technically connected team members.

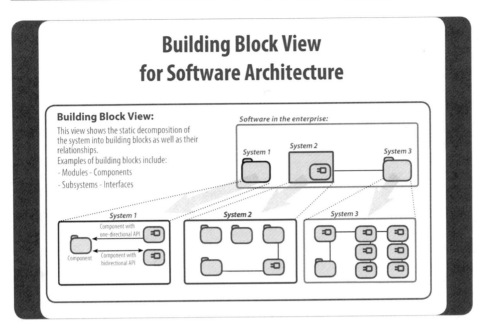

Fig. 7.14   Building block view of software architecture. (*Source:* Sascha Block)

7.5.5   Technical Debt

In a fast-paced digital world, technical debt is often overlooked. Cunningham defines technical debt as immature or faulty program code, thus providing a useful definition for software architecture artifacts that require urgent action in terms of correction and optimization [21].

Categorization of Technical Debt
The context and significance of technical debt have been continuously expanded and differentiated, ultimately allowing technical debt to be assigned to the following three categories [22]:

Requirement debts are caused by missing, insufficient, or subsequently added requirements (missing in the currently defined requirements) and inevitably result in inadequate software design or at least suboptimal software architecture. **Software design debts** reflect inadequate design in software architecture. It is obvious that poorly defined requirements can only lead to inadequate software architecture. However, even if requirements are complete, a deficient software architecture arises if proven software design patterns are unknown and/or ignored. It is irrelevant whether existing components do not fit together at all or at least not optimally due to different design patterns.

Typically, a historically grown software architecture prevents a robust, balanced software architecture, and the cloud trend makes these shortcomings even more apparent because suddenly applications are supposed to interact with each other that are completely incompatible. Only when these new requirements are defined in terms of technical debt and thus made visible and known to all stakeholders can these obstacles be overcome. **Test debts** reflect debts based on missing or insufficient tests. Inadequate tests affect the error-free, quality, and robustness at different levels, including a (partially/automated) error analysis at the code level.

Impact of Accumulated Technical Debt
Technical debt regularly refers to an accumulation of deficiencies that make it difficult to add new features to the system. The most common type of accumulation of technical debt is the rapid release of defined features without considering the future sustainability of the overall system or possible side effects.

That is precisely why it is essential for a large-scale agile framework to take this important aspect into account: Only if communicative mechanisms and overarching processes between the multitude of agile teams work can the implementation of desirable software architecture be achieved, which not only scores with a multitude of new features for the user but ultimately does not jeopardize the overall system with a balanced pace of new features, but supports all agile teams and the organization as a whole in their goals.

It is not always possible to completely avoid technical debt. Although it is regularly challenging to prevent technical debt, the efforts aimed at doing so are worthwhile. Not least, these efforts have a positive effect on the communication and satisfaction of all those involved...

7.5.6   Arc42 Template for Software Architecture Documentation

The arc42 template developed by Gernot Starke and Peter Hruschka is a proven proposal for pragmatically documenting software architectures [23]:

Structure of the arc42 Template
Figure 7.15 shows the "Structure of the arc42 Template" for organizing the subject areas of a software architecture.

Based on such a structure in a wiki like Confluence, the implementation of a complex software architecture can also be communicated across organizations.

The core of a software architecture documentation organized in this way consists of the **context boundary,** the three views on it are represented by the **building block view, runtime view,** and **deployment view,** and the **cross-cutting concepts** reflect the overarching, general principles and approaches that are used uniformly in many parts of

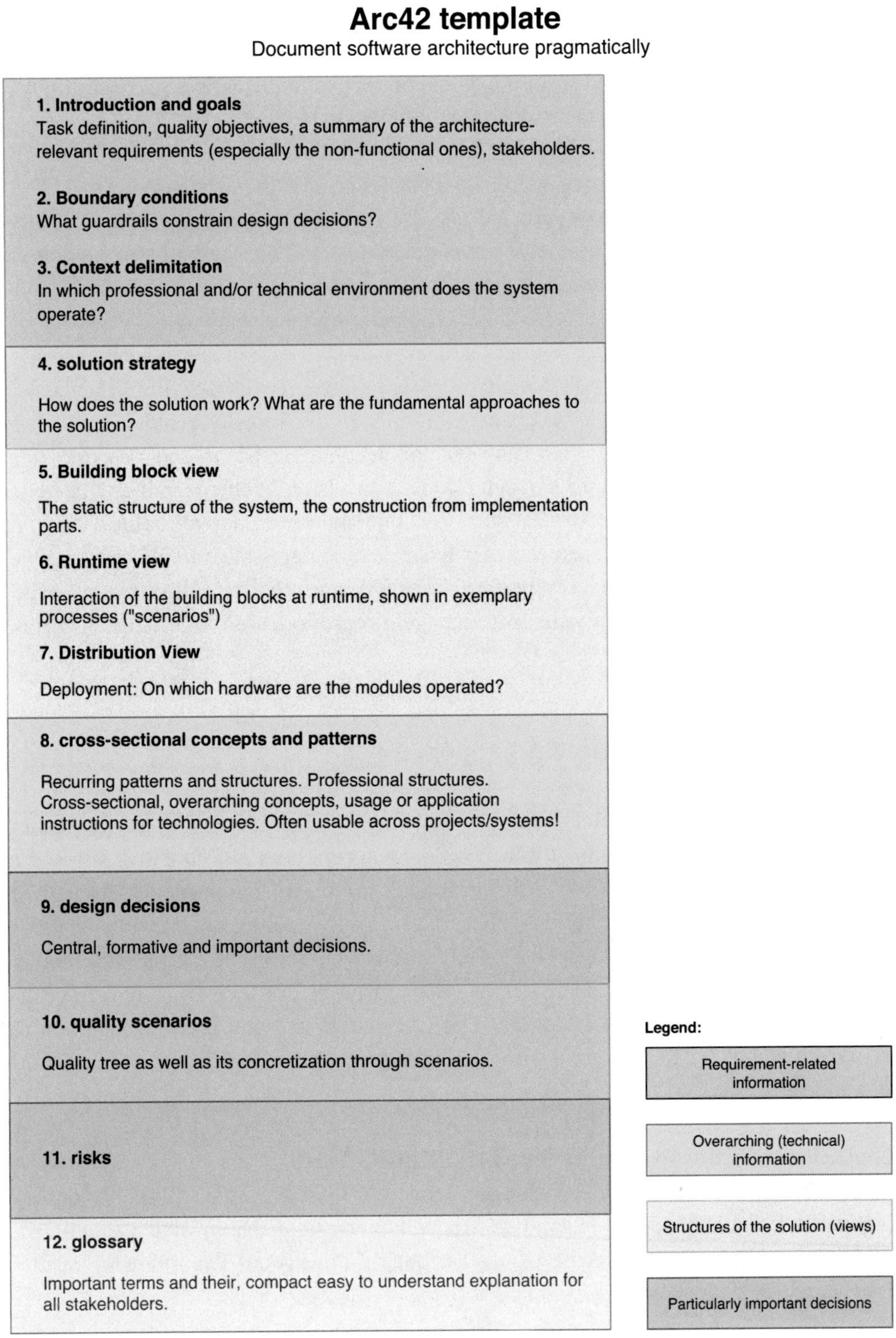

Arc42 template
Document software architecture pragmatically

1. Introduction and goals
Task definition, quality objectives, a summary of the architecture-relevant requirements (especially the non-functional ones), stakeholders.

2. Boundary conditions
What guardrails constrain design decisions?

3. Context delimitation
In which professional and/or technical environment does the system operate?

4. solution strategy

How does the solution work? What are the fundamental approaches to the solution?

5. Building block view

The static structure of the system, the construction from implementation parts.

6. Runtime view

Interaction of the building blocks at runtime, shown in exemplary processes ("scenarios")

7. Distribution View

Deployment: On which hardware are the modules operated?

8. cross-sectional concepts and patterns

Recurring patterns and structures. Professional structures. Cross-sectional, overarching concepts, usage or application instructions for technologies. Often usable across projects/systems!

9. design decisions

Central, formative and important decisions.

10. quality scenarios

Quality tree as well as its concretization through scenarios.

11. risks

12. glossary

Important terms and their, compact easy to understand explanation for all stakeholders.

Legend:

Requirement-related information

Overarching (technical) information

Structures of the solution (views)

Particularly important decisions

Fig. 7.15 Structure of the arc42 Template. (*Source:* Sascha Block in reference to Hruschka/Starke)

the architecture and follow the cross-cutting approach. This also includes concepts that relate equally to several components and can be centrally managed. For example, architectural patterns and styles, rules for cross-functional communication with regard to the agreement and use of specific technology stacks are included.

Particularly important decisions, including all **design decisions** and **risks and technical debt**, are documented separately and are thus permanently highly visible.

Introduction and objectives provide an easily understandable overview for every stakeholder with a brief description of the requirements and the three to a maximum of five most important quality goals for the software architecture. An overview with function and contact information for relevant stakeholders and their summarized expectations regarding the software architecture provides a good starting point for both newcomers and "old hands". **Constraints** capture what restricts design and implementation, including, for example, legal frameworks or defined IT security requirements. The **solution strategy** summarizes fundamental architectural decisions and describes the targeted solutions and is thus to be **understood** as a vision of the overall architecture. This includes the definition of partial steps for implementation and all defined IT strategic decisions. The **quality requirements** make requirements measurable and tangible through scenarios and defined key performance indicators (KPIs). **Glossary** and **Wiki** are central tools for technical and software architecture-oriented knowledge management.

7.5.7   ISO/IEC 25010—Quality of Software

Standards can also be understood as a tool for orientation; in particular, the guidelines for the quality of software and software development anchored in ISO 25010 should be taken into account within an agile organizational and prioritization model. As part of the adaptable framework conditions with a focus on software quality, the specifications of such quality guidelines correspond equally to the interests of the various stakeholder groups: organizations in the role of software manufacturers or for deriving defined qualitative specifications, possible operators (Ops), licensees, and end users. In addition to recommendations for the design of software, these guidelines also provide useful support for contract design.

Dimensions of Software Quality Based on ISO/IEC 25010

The qualitative dimensions of software are defined in ISO/IEC 25010 [24]. The quality dimensions complement each other and often lead to decisions that involve compromises in favor of one and at the expense of another quality dimension. The following quality dimensions are defined according to ISO 25010:

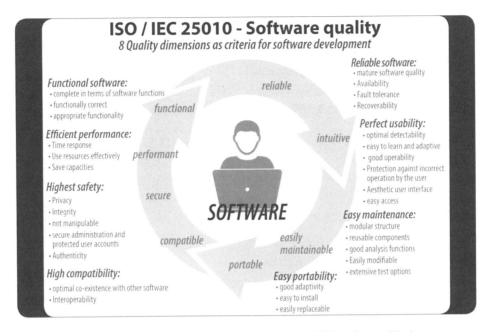

Fig. 7.16 Dimensions of Software Quality Based on ISO/IEC 25010—Sascha Block

• Functionality	• Compatibility	• Maintainability
• Performance	• Reliability	• Portability
• Security	• Usability	

Quality and effort are directly related: In general, software quality drives effort, i.e., increased quality increases effort. It makes sense for software manufacturers and clients to agree on contractually clearly defined specifications for technical parameters such as reaction times, system load, and other system-specific framework conditions that are fair to both sides.

Figure 7.16 illustrates the "Dimensions of Software Quality Based on ISO/IEC 25010".

7.6   DevOps Methods and DevOps Tools

DevOps combines development methodologies aimed at bridging the gap between development (Development, abbreviated: **Dev**) and operations (short: **Ops**).

DevOps as a Method Mix with Valuable Tools

The DevOps term is derived from the IT task areas Development and Operations. DevOps is a set of methods aimed at reducing the time required for changes to a software system or a digital IT solution from the initial change to the transfer to a defined target system—usually the test environment, the staging system, and the live environment (production environment) while ensuring the highest quality.

In contrast to alternative IT management practices such as ITIL, a proven DevOps strategy offers best practices and tools. ITIL, on the other hand, follows a strict approach and uses, for example, inventoried artifacts such as "Configuration Items (CI)", which can be useful but also involves considerable administrative effort and not to be underestimated complexity.

7.6.1   The DevOps Periodic Table

The Periodic Table of DevOps Tools provides a useful overview of tools that are relevant for actively supporting agility and DevOps practices while taking into account the entire lifecycle of software.

Figure 7.17 shows the infographic of the "Periodic Table of DevOps Tools" [25].

Over 18,000 votes for more than 400 products in 17 categories were evaluated in determining the listed DevOps tools [25]. No matter at which stage of implementing a DevOps strategy your organization is currently in, the tool provides a compact overview, brief explanations, and above all, a structured classification of the respective DevOps tools. Over time, it is also ideally suited to check to what extent new tools and technologies can improve your individual DevOps maturity level.

7.6.2   DevOps is More Than = Software Engineering + IT Management

A DevOps strategy deals with the question of how to optimally and efficiently design the software release process.

DevOps optimizes the software release process

DevOps as a paradigm in the form of a model, pattern, a set of methods with principles that support communication and collaboration in efficient teams from the areas of software development and software operations.

1. **Development** (software development) and **Operations**
2. **Communication, collaboration, and teamwork** between the software development and software operations departments

The Periodic Table of DevOps Tools (V4.2)

Legend / Categories:

- AIOps/Analytics
- Artifact/Package Management
- Cloud
- Collaboration
- Configuration Automation
- Containers
- Continuous Integration
- Database Management
- Deployment
- Enterprise Agile Planning
- Issue Tracking/ITSM
- Release Management
- Security
- Serverless/PaaS
- Source Control Management
- Testing
- Value Stream Management

Elements:

#	Symbol	Name	Tag
1	Aja	Atlassian Jira Align	En
2	Gi	Git	Os
3	Daa	Digital.ai Agility	En
4	Tp	Targetprocess	
5	Azp	Azure DevOps Pipelines	En
6	Ow	OWASP ZAP	Os
7	Dap	Digital.ai App Protect	En
8	Dar	Digital.ai Release	En
9	Acp	AWS CodePipeline	
10	Gh	GitHub	Fm
11	Pv	Planview	
12	Br	Broadcom Rally	
13	Dad	Digital.ai Deploy	En
14	Sni	Sonatype Nexus IQ	
15	Aq	Aqua Security	
16	Cfr	CloudBees Flow	
17	Brl	BMC RLM	
18	Gls	GitLab SCM	Os
19	In	Instana	Pd
20	Dd	Datadog	
21	Ja	JFrog Artifactory	En
22	Aws	AWS	En
23	Sl	Slack	En
24	Mt	Microsoft Teams	En
25	Rha	Red Hat Ansible	Os
26	Ht	HashiCorp Terraform	Os
27	Dk	Docker	Os
28	Rho	Red Hat OpenShift	
29	Lb	Liquibase	En
30	Dp	Delphix	
31	Ud	UrbanCode Deploy	
32	Ck	CyberArk Conjur	
33	Hv	HashiCorp Vault	Os
34	Ur	UrbanCode Release	
35	Al	AWS Lambda	En
36	Abb	Atlassian Bitbucket	En
37	Sp	Splunk	En
38	Ad	AppDynamics	En
39	Snx	Sonatype Nexus	Os
40	Az	Azure	En
41	Gc	Google Cloud	En
42	Ac	Atlassian Confluence	
43	Ch	Chef	Os
44	Acf	AWS Cloud Formation	
45	Ku	Kubernetes	Os
46	Ak	Amazon EKS	
47	De	Docker Enterprise	En
48	Id	IDERA	
49	Ha	Harness	En
50	Vc	Veracode	
51	Sr	SonarQube	En
52	Ff	Micro Focus Fortify SCA	
53	Azf	Azure Functions	En
54	Ci	Compuware ISPW	
55	Dt	Dynatrace	
56	Nr	New Relic	
57	Dh	Docker Hub	
58	Np	npm	
59	Ic	IBM Cloud	
60	So	Stack Overflow	Fm
61	Pu	Puppet	
62	Hc	HashiCorp Consul	Os
63	Ae	Amazon ECS	
64	Azk	Azure AKS	
65	Ra	Rancher	
66	Qt	Quest Toad	
67	Sk	Spinnaker	
68	Od	Octopus Deploy	
69	Sb	Synopsys Black Duck	
70	Cx	Checkmarx SAST	
71	He	Heroku	Fm
72	Sv	Subversion	
73	Gr	Grafana	Os
74	El	Elastic ELK Stack	Os
75	Yn	Yarn	
76	Nu	NuGet	Os
77	Os	OpenStack	Os
78	Mm	Mattermost	
79	Sa	Salt	
80	Hg	HashiCorp Vagrant	
81	Hp	HashiCorp Packer	
82	Gk	Google GKE	
83	Hm	Helm	
84	Db	DBmaestro	
85	Cfd	CloudBees Flow	
86	Acd	AWS CodeDeploy	
87	Sn	Snort	
88	Pbs	PortSwigger Burp Suite	Fm
89	Gf	Google Firebase	En
90	Cf	Cloud Foundry	Os

Pricing legend: Os Open Source | Fr Free | Fm Freemium | Pd Paid | En Enterprise

#	Symbol	Name	Tag
91	Jn	Jenkins	Os
92	Azc	Azure DevOps Code	En
93	Glc	GitLab CI	Os
94	Tr	Travis CI	Os
95	Cc	CircleCI	Fm
96	Mv	Maven	Os
97	Ab	Atlassian Bamboo	Pd
98	Gd	Gradle	Os
99	Acb	AWS CodeBuild	En
100	Aj	Atlassian Jira	Fm
101	Bi	BMC Helix ITSM	
102	At	Atlassian Trello	Fm
103	Sw	ServiceNow	En
104	Td	TOPdesk	Pd
105	Pd	PagerDuty	Os
106	Tt	Tricentis Tosca	Fr
107	Nn	Neotys NeoLoad	Pd
108	Se	Selenium	Fm
109	Ju	JUnit	Fr
110	Sl	Sauce Labs	Pd
111	Ct	Compuware Topaz	En
112	Ap	Appium	Os
113	Sq	Squash TM	Os
114	Cu	Cucumber	Os
115	Jm	JMeter	Fr
116	Pa	Parasoft	Pd
117	Dai	Digital.ai	En
118	Tp	Tasktop	En
119	Pr	Plutora	En
120	Gl	GitLab	Os

digital.ai

CollabNetVersionOne, XebiaLabs, Arxan, Numerify & Experitest
are now Digital.ai

Fig. 7.17 Periodic Table of DevOps

3. **"Bridge the gap"** between software development and operations, i.e., the operation of the software

4. **Software development methods**

5. **Deployment of software and code**—Continuous software deployment enables stakeholders to receive continuous feedback, quick responses regarding desired changes, and the implementation of automated "delivery pipelines" to significantly reduce the time and resources required for the overall software integration process.

6. **Automated Deployment**—A central task is the support and establishment of an automated deployment process in which the source code is transferred and integrated from the development environment to the production systems via versioning tools.

7. **Continuous Integration**—As a practical approach, the task of continuous integration defines seamless code integration into the live environment, thus ensuring the smooth software integration of digital solutions into the direct operating environment of users.

8. **Quality Assurance**—Defined as a DevOps method, it combines the demands for quality assurance with the operation and development of software and continuously optimizes them.

How to become agile with DevOps and shape your organization innovatively:
With the DevOps approach, you effectively complement your agile software development and agile project management with pragmatic tools and methodological extensions within your company.

In combination with the use of personas, user stories, and prototyping, you thus design digital solutions for your organization and all users as effectively as possible.

Aligning IT strategy with DevOps:
A successful DevOps anchoring is significantly influenced by the corporate strategy. To implement DevOps effectively and sustainably, the following questions help in this context:

• Which products, services, and processes depend on the DevOps area?
• To what extent does an employee devote themselves to activities defined for the DevOps engineer within internal DevOps topics, and to what percentage is the DevOps engineer available for external DevOps projects?
• How is DevOps anchored company-wide as an IT strategy and in the sense of a jointly agreed mindset?

Defining internal and external DevOps KPIs:
To optimally and sustainably anchor DevOps in the company, it is essential to define company-internal performance indicators in the form of DevOps-related KPIs.

Based on these KPIs, DevOps activities and the company-wide DevOps strategy can then be represented internally and externally.

In doing so, it is important—in the spirit of the DevOps idea—to ensure that the success assessment is transparent to all employees and customers. Only in this way can it be ensured that continuous improvement is achievable and accessible to all.

"DevOps and release engineering are software engineering disciplines that deal with the development, implementation, and process optimization to create high-quality software reliably and predictably."

7.6.3   BizDevOps as a Consequence for Agile Companies

Fitzgerald and Stol recognize the importance of DevOps for the close integration between software development and its operational deployment, which must be continuous, and call for a similar continuity between business strategy and its development, for which the authors have coined the term BizDevOps [26]. Fitzgerald and Stol consider a decoupling of IT and business strategies to be even more problematic, as the complex and data-intensive systems being developed today must be reliable and resilient.

BizDevOps thus places further demands on an agile organizational form and calls for an agile strategy with a strong focus on IT-strategic aspects, which is aligned with the entire company.

Figure 7.18 illustrates the "BizDevOps model based on Fitzgerald/Stol".

BizDevOps takes into account, as a consistently agile corporate strategy, all cross-functional agile teams that enable innovations and customer-oriented solutions for your company.

In this context, BizDevOps as an **agile business strategy** encompasses all areas and processes of a company: from the production and distribution of products and services, corporate strategy, resource planning and budgeting, to IT strategy and relationships with customers and partners.

How does BizDevOps differ from DevOps?
While **DevOps practices** currently contribute to merging software development and integration, the same continuity between business strategy and corporate development is required. The abbreviation BizDev is deliberately based on the DevOps concept.

Why BizDezOps?
The separation of individual business areas is currently even more problematic, as reliability and resilience play an increasingly important role in complex and data-intensive systems.

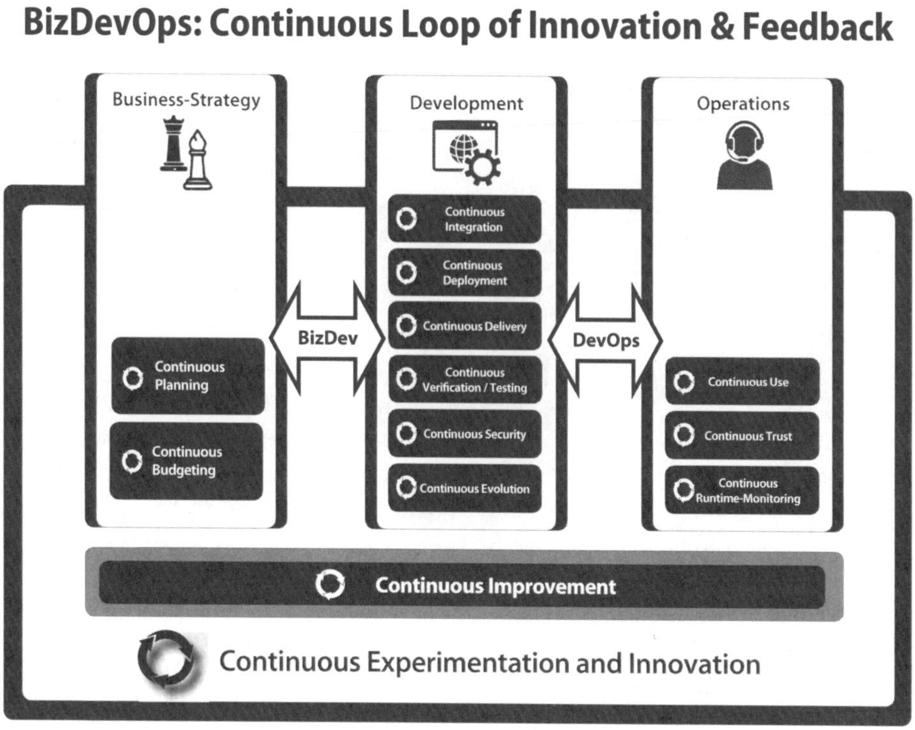
BizDevOps: Continuous Loop of Innovation & Feedback
Business-Strategy
Development
Operations
Continuous Integration
Continuous Deployment
Continuous Delivery
Continuous Verification / Testing
Continuous Security
Continuous Evolution
BizDev
DevOps
Continuous Planning
Continuous Budgeting
Continuous Use
Continuous Trust
Continuous Runtime-Monitoring
Continuous Improvement
Continuous Experimentation and Innovation

Fig. 7.18 BizDevOps model based on Fitzgerald/Stol. (*Source:* Sascha Block)

Above all, however, customer orientation plays a central role, and with it the desire on the part of companies to meet these requirements using the latest technologies. With the ongoing **digitalization,** new requirements arise in the form of new sales channels, customer communication, or customer tracking for success evaluation.

The functionally limited technologies of company-owned frameworks and internal IT solutions hardly meet these agile requirements anymore and require new tools and new organizational forms such as BizDevOps teams. Such a BizDevOps team is responsible for accompanying service processes, defining and monitoring relevant quality projects, and supporting development and operation; these teams have a high degree of autonomy [27].

There are therefore considerable risks if, as a result of non-agile structures and due to lengthy processes and sluggish reaction speeds, entire customer groups migrate to providers who have optimally adapted to technological change and are thus able to respond adequately to customer requests. Innovation through digital technologies is only possible and successful if the most suitable solution is always used and not the one that is merely optimally aligned with internal company operating aspects.

Higher motivation of employees through BizDevOps
Good employees and IT professionals want innovations and want to work with new technologies. This is because they know that this is also the best way to implement innovations and customer-oriented solutions.

However, if a company restricts its employees so much with its IT strategy that only a very small number of technologies are supported—which is usually due to a centrally organized IT operation—real innovations and customer-oriented solutions become simply impossible. As a result, not only does employee motivation drop rapidly, but customers also turn away from such traditional companies.

This situation will continue to intensify in the future. It has long been foreseeable that innovations will increasingly come from IT. With digital transformation, organizations in all industries are thus challenged to introduce agile business strategies that follow the orientation of a BizDevOps team.

Make cross-disciplinary decisions together
When cross-disciplinary teams are jointly responsible for project success, it ensures that the requirements of all business areas are taken into account and enables customer-oriented innovation across teams.

Risk assessment can be the responsibility of a specialized BizDevOps team, so that decisions are neither one-sided nor made lightly. It is important that agile teams jointly take responsibility for the development, operation, and optimization of applications.

Modernization of IT Strategy
To achieve this, modernization of the IT infrastructure is absolutely necessary: From **Continuous Deployment** to technologies such as Docker, virtual machines, and orchestration tools like Kubernetes, to automated system tests and standardized version control. Realize user satisfaction for user groups through design thinking and prototyping, resulting in comfortable usage. Guarantee quality and IT security based on continuous and detailed logging, and align key performance indicators to operate robust systems and effectively monitor them with connected processes and monitoring.

Cross-interface, multiple DevOps teams operate across applications, so technology decisions are never made and managed independently. The cycle of system development, system operation, and optimization is closed with regularly conducted experiments. The company-wide IT landscape evolves towards flexibly interacting IT systems and microservices.

Strategy and Vision as an Integral Part
In contrast to traditional projects, agile teams always take on functional responsibility for processes at the same time. This ensures that processes are ideally represented for both

the organization and customers, even when existing applications are modernized or completely replaced.

Strategy and vision of an organization are an integral part of an organization-wide, agile organizational model. To make strategy and vision visible and to clarify understanding in all relevant perspectives, infographics and organization-specific dialogue images are suitable content media, which will be presented in the following section.

7.7   Content

Content is any material published and provided for a specific target audience.

Successful content is based on a fundamental content strategy. A content concept defines clear goals and individual steps in the content creation process.

Within a large-scale agile framework, the content process is also a very important component. Content significantly determines how your organization is perceived by the public and customers. Nothing should be left to chance here.

Single Source Publishing for Countless Platforms and Media Formats

Your customers also expect that, even with a large number of content channels and countless content formats used by your organization, recognizability and consistent, unambiguous communication are guaranteed. Information is now expected around the clock.

The only solution to this is a single-source publishing strategy, which must be an integral part of your agile framework. This involves considering the content process from conception, production, to feedback evaluation. You also want to use content controlling to find out which content is well received and which is less well received or not at all by your personas.

Flawless, i.e., correct and error-free information and high quality should be the goal. From the perspective of your personas, every relevant medium and platform should be usable; this effectively serves the media channels that your personas also use.

Of course, you should choose the optimal format and platform for your organization. Nevertheless, you should also communicate this selection transparently and comprehensibly. In any case, take into account the relevance of your feedback channels and, of course, evaluate from the perspective of your customers which are the right content channels.

7.7.1 Goals of a Content Strategy

The goal of every content strategy is to attractively address the respective target group through clear and easily understandable messages.

From content aimed at potential interested parties, it must be immediately apparent what the benefit of an offer is. Each message must therefore be prepared specifically for the target group.

Concrete Content Goals
Each content goal is directly connected to the benefit for the company.

- **Optimal information flow within the company**
- **Always available basic information**, e.g., in the form of FAQs
- **Current information** (many pieces of information have an expiration date in the form of a validity period)
- **Efficiently reach target audience**
- **Increase expert knowledge and position as an expert**
- **Increase brand awareness and reach (Branding)**
- **Increase trust**
- **Improve user experience**

7.7.2 Requirements for Content

To achieve these content goals, the following requirements for corresponding content result:

- We understand content consumers as customers and create content to increase employee satisfaction.
  Speaking of customer satisfaction in the context of content creation helps us to have external addressees in focus right from the start. Such external content addressees include, for example, partners, suppliers, or applicants, whom we directly focus on at the start of our content strategy.
- Content is provided regularly, thus continuously serving the target group
- Lower barriers to participation
- Obtain feedback and set incentives for high-quality feedback
- Remain unique and memorable
- Continuously deliver quality and be a reliable source of information
- Challenge: identify concrete wishes and determine exact needs (the more precisely we know the demand, the better the content will be)

Conclusion: Good content is by no means cheap, but ultimately what counts is that good content is sustainably valuable for every company.

Questions in Implementing a Content Strategy
- Are you already involved in the creation of professional content with relevant benefits?
- Does your company have a solid content strategy?
- Do you practice success monitoring and thus maintain full control over which existing content really convinces?
- Do you use a topic plan for creating new content?

7.7.3   Content Controlling

How can you determine if the provided content is successful? The following key performance indicators have become established for this purpose:

Measurable KPIs for content:
- Conversion rate
- Contact initiation per channel
- Social media response
- Followers (also differentiated in new and lost followers)
- Visibility (internal/external)
- Bounce rate
- User feedback
- Average visit duration
- Number of user sessions
- Exit rates

7.7.4   Content Process and Coordination

Content must be cross-departmental, even according to old rules. All teams actively and regularly contribute to the content strategy. For this purpose, appropriate resources are available, which the content team can access as the product owner of the content strategy.

The content manager ensures qualitative and quantitative goal achievement through regular success and deviation controls.

Employees not involved in the project can contribute to the content at any time by submitting topic suggestions or concepts. The topic and action planning is guided by overarching corporate goals.

5. Content Resources
- Content strategy manager (person-hours)
- Resources of specialist departments (person-hours)
- Budget (e.g., for image materials, maintenance and development of content tools, advertising, and similar for creation and distribution)

7.7.5 Content Guidelines

A content guideline defines your content strategy. Such a guideline is particularly oriented towards the personas. And the personas, as well as the culture of your organization, define the optimal approach for this.

Do you want a casual connection with your customers and use informal language, or is a more distant and very serious approach the better choice? Such and similar decisions are made for the content guidelines.

7.7.6 Design System

A design system is usually a **combination** of (living) **style guides, component or pattern libraries,** and general guidelines, e.g., for the use of elements. Ideally, it serves as a "single source of truth" to centrally control the design of various platforms and channels (e.g., web, print, app). This ensures that all aspects of design guidelines, such as a corporate design, have the same consistency and quality.

Creating a design system pays off if the project is designed to grow and scale. It also facilitates collaboration and the onboarding of new team members.

Why Style Guides?
A style guide is a general **description of the design principles.** Style guides have existed longer than the web; they have been (and still are) used to define the appearance of print materials such as brochures, catalogs, stationery, logos, and packaging. In this context, one often reads about **Corporate Design (CD)** or the even broader **Corporate Image** (CI). The corporate image not only specifies visual aspects but also includes aspects of text and the overall big picture of how one presents oneself to the outside world—the image one wants to convey to the public.

A style guide describes, among other things:

- Typography (specifications for fonts, typefaces, and sizes)
- Colors (used palettes)
- (Design) grids (grid system)
- Imagery, icons

In general terms, this guideline defines what the **face of the company** or product looks like. This ensures consistent design and recognition. This is a core aspect of marketing efforts and also benefits users, as they can better navigate thanks to this consistency.

It is always important to adhere to the **common UI conventions** for buttons, checkboxes, etc. For example, on websites, the logo should always be in the top left corner, followed by the menu. Red should be used as a warning color, while green should be used as a signal color for OK. Buttons should look like buttons, and links should look like links (preferably blue and underlined).

What can such a pattern library look like?

A pattern library is a collection of patterns, i.e., templates or models. These patterns describe, for example, how **interactive elements** on the website work. For instance, what an expandable element (accordion) looks like that displays additional information when clicked/tapped. This includes describing…

- when such an element is used,
- what it looks like,
- how the icon is designed that triggers the interaction,
- how the interaction works exactly,
- how the animation proceeds.

In most cases, the (HTML or script) code is also included in the pattern library to implement this element. This **facilitates work**, ensures consistency, and prevents errors.

The design system of the Otto Group, for example, demonstrates such a modular system used to develop the frontends of digital products at OTTO. As the illustration shows, such a design system consists of numerous fragments, components, and modules [28].

Figure 7.19 shows the "Otto Group Design System with an extensive pattern library".

All patterns serve as templates and follow a uniform, semantic naming scheme. Semantic naming means that the name is not based on the appearance of the pattern, but on its meaning in use. Examples of semantic names are Primary Button, Slider, Copy, or Headline. Descriptive names like shiny button, large button, red headline should be avoided. Names that refer to the context of the pattern, such as Button Footer or Headline Navigation, are also unsuitable.

Why does a company like Otto expose its design system—accessible to everyone—publicly on the internet?

This is done so that service providers and third parties, but above all, every in-house employee has uncomplicated access to—not trustworthy—but relevant information for the corporate identity. In other words: Why shouldn't you also use such proven

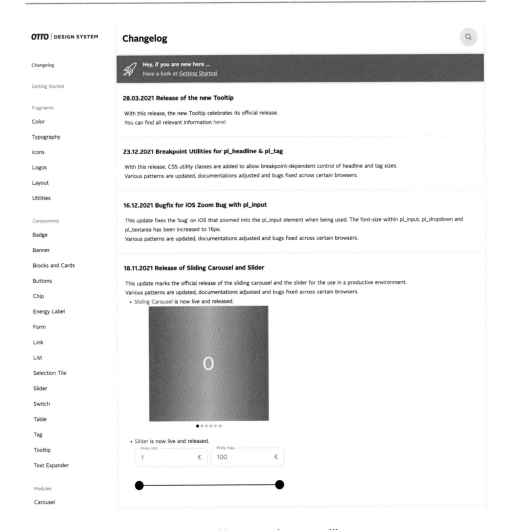

Fig. 7.19 Otto Group Design System with an extensive pattern library

approaches for your organization and benefit from simplified handling with clear transparency in the future?

7.7.7 Infographics

Infographics are visual representations of information and data. By combining text, images, diagrams, and in video-based channels also videos, infographics enable easy access to information.

Design complex information visually easy to understand

Infographics are suitable for presenting complex problems in an easily understandable and plausible way and encourage users to engage with more complex information through their entertaining and stimulating presentation.

With the content form of storytelling, a narrative method in which information is entertainingly processed, and which integrates graphics and images in digital media, infographics have gained in popularity. This is mainly due to the numerous social media platforms and website-based content platforms that intensively use these complex graphic media to generate attention among their target groups.

A good infographic conveys a central statement, which is reflected in a concise headline. In addition, a good infographic succeeds in presenting a complex issue or multiple pieces of information, i.e., data, in a visually appealing and concise manner.

Infographics should be part of every content strategy!

You should therefore include infographics directly in your content strategy and prepare the infographics in such a way that they precisely meet the information needs of your persona.

The actual purpose of an infographic is to convey information and a message to the viewer.

Four quality characteristics for infographics

Figure 7.20 illustrates quality characteristics as "dimensions of an infographic".

1. **Design**—The design should be convincing, with the chosen colors and fonts matching the theme and the graphic representation, and good readability is essential.
2. **Data**—The data contained must be relevant, current, and accurate.
3. **Story**—The story an infographic tells should be entertaining, exciting, or in some way particularly appealing, not for just anyone, but for your target audience. A problem, statement, message, or solution can be the focus.
4. **Shareability**—An infographic also achieves a further degree of dissemination through its metadata and, of course, the way in which and where you use and virally spread it.

A good example of an infographic, with direct context reference, is the DevOps Periodic Table presented in Sect. 7.6.2. Both as a pure graphic and as an interactive representation on the website, it meets all the requirements of a good infographic.

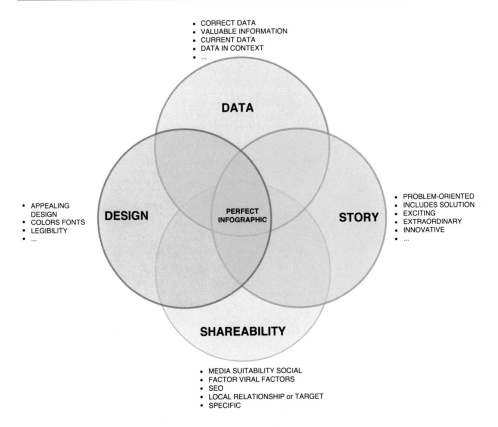

Fig. 7.20 Dimensions of an infographic

7.7.8 Dialogue Images

Dialogue images visualize complex topics in an illustrative way, similar to infographics. However, unlike infographics, dialogue images pursue a completely different goal: they aim to enable a dialogue between viewers based on their graphical representation.

Figure 7.21 illustrates the use of a "dialogue image for constructive exchange during a staff meeting".

The Design Process as Dialogue

When a dialogue image is developed during a joint workshop, it emerges step by step as a result of an intensive, topic-focused, and creative design process. In this process, one participant can take on the role of a moderator, while the participants are supported by an illustrator in working together with project managers, executives, and other stakeholders on the prototype sketch for the later dialogue image.

Fig. 7.21 Dialogue image for constructive exchange during a staff meeting. (Source: Dialogbild GmbH)

Such workshops demonstrate that discussions about what should be illustrated and to what extent contribute significantly to creating a common understanding of an organization's vision and strategy. Dialogue images not only support understanding of the prototypical approach but are also ideally suited to support agile transformation.

By the end of an eight-hour workshop, a complex prototype of a dialogue image in sketch form can be the creative result. Based on this specification, professionals for visual design then develop the actual dialogue image and, if desired, interactive versions of it.

In the interactive form of a dialogue image, content users can interact with the dialogue image via click points to playfully work out, for example, technical backgrounds and fact-based information on individual focus topics.

Fig. 7.22 Dialogue images for active customer communication. (*Source:* Dialogbild GmbH)

Conveying Vision & Goals of Your Organization Visually

They are an effective tool for conveying knowledge and illustrating relationships. They always provide orientation for the viewer.

Dialogue images are particularly well suited for graphically designing your organization to playfully and entertainingly convey the vision and goals of your organization.

Figure 7.22 illustrates the use of "dialogue images for active customer communication".

7.8 Monitoring & Controlling

As already clarified in the previous sections on Epics or within the framework of software architecture, controlling and monitoring based on defined metrics is necessary to measure and continuously monitor set goals.

Only based on identified quality indicators is it possible to determine the fundamental causes and facts of existing problems, and in the course of digital transformation, this information must be mapped in metrics in an organization's IT systems.

Discrete and Continuous Indicators

Quality indicators can be meaningfully classified into Discrete Indicators and Continuous Indicators.

Continuous indicators are used for factors that can be measured on an infinitely extendable scale or continuously. Typically, these are units such as weight, time, and money. Their measurement is determined and carried out repeatedly in advance.

Discrete indicators define characteristics that have a descriptive nature and can be well represented by personas in an agile context, for example.

Discrete indicators regularly have a certain frequency and can be in a relation (e.g., the number of orders of a defined persona classification). These can be assigned to artificially determined evaluation scales (satisfaction in relation to a specific service in quality levels such as excellent, satisfactory, unsatisfactory, etc.).

Such indicators can be repeatedly observed in predetermined periods and linked to conditions. Because discrete indicators sometimes pretend to be conjunctive with respect to observed properties and frequencies, percentage KPIs are recommended [29, page 970]. For simplification, conjunctive continuous indicators can also be converted into discrete indicators.

Example The delivery time is converted into the categories "on time" and "with delay," which makes the informative value clearer than if such a KPI were expressed in time units like days or minutes.

If customer satisfaction is to be investigated, an evaluation scale with a discrete character is always used. The direct advantage: observing and recording discrete data is generally easier. Disadvantages of discrete analysis are the requirement of a higher number of observations to obtain meaningful information. As a statistical guideline, a sample is considered reliably measured if at least 200 indicators can be reliably measured. For the precise definition of KPIs, further literature is referred to at this point; it is important to understand the indispensable necessity and significance of KPIs.

7.8.1 Key Performance Indicators (KPI)

Thus, it is also clear that continuous controlling and monitoring for the management and supervision of defined corporate goals are indispensable. Only on continuous data collection and measurement can you effectively assess whether strategic goals—also in view of competition—need to be adjusted.

Success indicators with the Business Motivation Model

The Business Motivation Model is suitable for defining corresponding success indicators. The Business Motivation Model is closely related to the motivation and business objectives of the Zachman Framework for Enterprise Architectures [29].

The vision of a corporate strategy is transformed into reality through quantifiable goals that are increased through controlling.

Defining KPI with the Balanced Scorecard method
Ganesan and Paturi suggest defining KPI based on Business Motivation Models and the Balanced Scorecard approach [31]. The defined KPIs must then be assigned to the decisive points within the process hierarchy at different organizational levels so that monitoring these KPIs becomes possible by multiple function carriers. The success factors are measured, analyzed, and evaluated at regular intervals through concrete projects within the corporate strategy, with specific KPIs. The excellent process knowledge of our as-is analysis mentioned at the beginning supports this (see Sect. "Excellent understanding of business processes").

7.8.2 Monitoring

Buschle, Johnson, and Shahzad recommend a specially designed analysis tool for monitoring enterprise architectures. While a large number of Enterprise Architecture Tools focus on documenting enterprise architectures, the authors present tool-based analysis functions for properties such as Business Fit, Security, and Interoperability. The article emphasizes that it is a real challenge to develop such a tool and adapt it to company-specific requirements [31].

Using proven methods such as Monte Carlo simulation, typical problems like server monitoring can be solved by observing certain object-oriented attributes. The introduced tool offers a Class Modeler and an Object Modeler as two separate tools for monitoring framework objects, their attributes, relations, and KPIs. In a second step, concrete analysis and monitoring scenarios can be implemented using the Object Modeler [32].

7.8.3 Strategies and Approaches to Digital Transformation

In addition to agile process models, other strategies and approaches are effective in successfully shaping digital transformation in companies. The following strategic approaches have proven particularly successful:

Forming cooperations and alliances
The economic dynamics on a rapidly changing digital playing field and the increasing competitive pressure in the market are pushing companies to cooperate to a much greater extent than before, even among strategic competitors. Often, a strategic goal can only be mastered due to its complexity if companies jointly lead projects to success in a cooperative network [33, Chapter 1, Page 6].

An example of such a partnership alliance is the cooperation between Audi, BMW, and Daimler, who jointly acquired Nokia's map and navigation service Here for 2.8 billion EUR [34]. The acquired digital assets in the form of highly precise digital road maps are a crucial technological component for autonomous driving. Building this data foundation alone would have required a high individual investment for each company without really being able to differentiate themselves in the competition. However, the acquisition of Here, which is considered one of the leading software companies for digital navigation maps and controls the world's largest map database, is also a strategic move against digital players like Google and Amazon and includes, above all, valuable access to new customers, as 80% of all cars driving in Europe and North America with integrated navigation systems use Here maps. This gives the automakers direct access to a petabyte-sized database that can store billions of events per week [35].

Mastering large amounts of data

Digital transformation is causing the amount of digital data to be processed to increase rapidly: Cloud computing, mobile internet, social media, digital sensors, machine networking, and Industry 4.0 are the drivers for data growth in companies according to a Bitkom study [36]. Google already exceeded a data volume of 24 petabytes during the 2009 fiscal year. The digital technology unit has 15 zeros. Today, the Californians process almost the same amount of data—daily [37]. For comparison: All books ever written together amount to hardly more than 50 petabytes.

Mastering large amounts of data is a real challenge for companies, both in terms of technology and the requirement to process and evaluate these vast amounts of data in a targeted manner.

Using strategic big data analyses

Big data analyses are undisputedly one of the core competencies for digital excellence. While digital players have long since firmly established the necessary expertise in their companies, managing even significantly smaller data volumes poses a serious threat to most medium-sized companies.

Strategic Goals of Big Data Analysis

In a study of 706 surveyed medium-sized companies with 100 employees or more in various industries, the goals of "optimizing the organization" and "better customer targeting" ranked equally at the top of the priority list for data analysis [38]. All relevant goals for big data analysis within a corporate strategy, with their percentage of mentions:

1. **Optimization of organization and processes—86%**
2. **Improvement of customer contact/customer targeting—86%**
3. **Better decision-making options—84%**
4. **Faster decision-making—78%**

5. **Development of innovative business models—73%**
6. **Better forecasts of future trends—69%**
7. **More targeted product design/product targeting—62%**
8. **More individual/targeted marketing—56%**
9. **Minimization of product launch time—56%**

7.8.4 The Optimal Architecture for the Digital Organization

Establishing the optimal software architecture for a company is not an easy task, but a constant challenge for all agile teams and decision-makers in the company. The use of tools can be helpful, but a clear and understandable architecture documentation is indispensable.

Enterprise Architecture Management (EAM) Tools for Planning Support
Both for the as-is analysis of the current IT landscape and for defining the target IT landscape as a target image of a digitization strategy, the use of EAM tools is an established method to methodically lead IT projects to success.

Software Cartography and IT Landscape Plans Provide an Overview
Software cartography and graphical representations and tools for organizing IT landscape plans, such as a functional, typical, or technical construction graphic, provide all participants with an easily understandable overview by hiding unimportant details and focusing on the relevant decision factors [39, page 176].

7.9 Methods & Tools for Agile Prioritization

In agile software development, prioritization is a crucial process in managing requirements, as poor prioritization of requirements can drastically increase development costs and even lead to production failures.

Agile prioritization is challenging, especially as more teams and stakeholders are involved, and requires at least a well-organized and possibly somewhat more formal process across the board, as changes in the priority list can lead to significant rework.

Furthermore, requirement prioritization in agile software development is a challenging task, as it is highly volatile. Neglecting critical requirements during prioritization leads to numerous problems such as poor product quality and dissatisfied stakeholders. In this section, we therefore present some techniques for agile prioritization of requirements.

7.9.1   Agile requirement prioritization with the Feature Graph

The Feature Graph offers a simple method for Product Owners to prioritize requirements in an agile manner.

Typically, stories with defined process descriptions are the starting point for an iteration. The essential selection criterion for which story the actual software development starts should be a benefit assessment of the respective features for the system and thus the user.

Requirement prioritization facilitates deciding whether the level of detail of the stories is already suitable for implementation and whether extensive stories need to be divided into smaller chapters. The first estimation round already provides concrete results for this: The developers estimate which artifacts can be implemented the fastest. This creates an order from the fastest realizable features to the most complex story.

In the second step, a dependency graph can be derived from this basic information: "Which features benefit in terms of effort from the existence of other defined features?"

Table 7.6 "Example table for a Feature Graph" illustrates the relationship of functions in mutual dependency on each other.

Visualization

Each outgoing arrow connection adds a score point in column B for a positive effect on another feature set. Each incoming arrow connection adds a score point in column C for an existing dependency on another feature set. Column D calculates the difference of the positive impacts of a feature set reduced by the number of existing dependencies on other feature sets. In a second step, the dependency graph can then be refined in a weighted variant by additional evaluation dimensions. Meaningful evaluation dimensions include, for example, the evaluation of easier implementation, improved usability, increased security, etc. Such a dependency graph visualizes the relationship in an easily understandable way for all participants [40, pages 47/48].

7.9.2   Agile Prioritization With the Single Point Query

In software product development, there is always a need to quickly and easily make an assessment of a group of people on a specific topic transparent. The question asked can relate to both the factual level and the relationship level. Single point queries can be represented on a scale, in a coordinate system, or through an evaluation table. Above all, a decision-making process with the single point query can also be quickly, easily, and conveniently carried out using modern collaboration tools or in a wiki. Table 7.7 "Application examples for single point queries" illustrates how effectively targeted questioning techniques can be used for current state analysis in teams.

Table 7.6 Example table for a Feature Graph. (Source: Sascha Block—Own illustration)

Step 1:		Step 2:	
A	B	C	D
Feature	Positive impact for feature set no.	Dependent on feature no.	Sum of positive feature impact minus feature dependencies
Set 1	$2,3,5,6,7 : \Sigma = 5$	none : $\Sigma = 0$	$5 - 0 = 5$ (Highest priority)
Set 2	$1,3,4,7 : \Sigma = 4$	$2 : \Sigma = 1$	$4 - 2 = 2$
Set 3	$2,4,6 : \Sigma = 3$	$5,6 : \Sigma = 2$	$3 - 2 = 1$
Set 4	$1,3,4 : \Sigma = 3$	$2,3,6 : \Sigma = 3$	$3 - 3 = 0$
Set 5	$3,4 : \Sigma = 2$	$1,3,4 : \Sigma = 3$	$2 - 3 = -1$
Set 6	$1,4 : \Sigma = 1$	$2,3,4,7 : \Sigma = 4$	$2 - 4 = -2$
Set 7	none : $\Sigma = 0$	$2,3,6 : \Sigma = 3$	$0 - 3 = -3$ (Lowest priority)

Table 7.7 Application examples for single point queries. (*Source:* Own representation based on Stach)

Application examples for single point queries:	
Factual level:	*How well informed do you feel about topic X?* Presentation option: Scale from "not at all" to "comprehensive"
Relationship level:	*How do you rate the mood in your team?* Presentation option: Scale with a smiling smiley to a sad smiley *How great is the understanding for each other in the team?* Presentation option: Evaluation table in five units from ++ to −−

The results of single point queries should be reflected upon together, and negative evaluations should be treated with appreciation and sovereignty. Then, the regular implementation of single point queries can be perceived as appreciative and is suitable for positively influencing a pleasant working atmosphere in the company.

7.9.3   Agile Prioritization with the Multi-point Query

Limited resources require prioritization with the decision of which projects to tackle and in what order. To find concrete results in such regularly recurring decisions, the multi-point query offers a methodology for moderating decision-making rounds [41, pages 144–147], which also ideally reflects the agile mindset.

The multi-point query is an approach to majority-capable decision-making and includes elements of estimation methods, as prioritization is based on experience and gut feeling rather than exclusively on hard facts.

What criteria should be used for prioritization?
In order to make well-founded decisions about prioritization, it makes sense to base them on a well-thought-out moderation concept that equally reflects all decision dimensions, so that no essential aspect of decision-making is lost.

Table 7.8 provides suggestions for important guiding questions for moderated prioritization.

With the help of a point allocation procedure, a majority-supported prioritization decision is now brought about—perfectly suited to an agility-oriented, democratic majority formation, reflecting and evaluating the alternatives in the community. Table 7.9 "Rules for Conducting the Multi-point Query" is a valuable guide on how to effectively apply this survey technique.

The multi-point query is suitable for decision-making as well as for agile prioritization of ideas, aspects, and solution approaches.

7.9.4   Agile Prioritization With Liquid Democracy

Liquid Democracy is a modern approach that optimally supports employee participation in companies or customer involvement in product development. Liquid Democracy reflects the wealth of experience of employees or customers by actively involving them in the decision-making process through received feedback.

What is Liquid Feedback?
Liquid Feedback is a freely available open source software that supports the Liquid Democracy principle for opinion formation and decision-making.

Table 7.8 Guiding questions for moderated prioritization. (*Source:* Own representation based on Stach)

Guiding questions for moderated prioritization:
Which topics are ...
... strategically important?
... the fastest to implement?
... the most cost-effective to realize?
... the most effective in terms of customers?
... the most innovative?
... suitable for clearly distinguishing oneself from competitors?

Table 7.9 Rules for conducting the multi-point query. (*Source:* Own representation based on Stach)

Rules for conducting the multi-point query:
• In a moderated process, all alternatives are collectively reflected upon.
• The formulated prioritization question must correspond to the goal of the moderation.
• The number of points to be awarded per participant is approximately half the number of alternatives, not the number of solutions to be implemented.
• The moderator takes over the evaluation and adjusts the result by cumulative rounding up or down.
• A maximum of two points may be awarded per option.
• The prioritization question is formulated and visualized according to the focus.

How does Liquid Feedback work?

The basic idea of Liquid Feedback is an openly designed grassroots democracy. To optimally involve all participants in important decision-making processes, the Liquid Feedback strategy provides for four stages [42]:

1. **New ideas and proposals:** In this liquid phase, a proposal must reach a certain quota in order to enter the voting process.
2. **Current discussion:** Discuss ideas, proposed changes, and improvements to the original quorum from Liquid Phase 1.
3. **Frozen Liquids:** If the necessary quota is reached through the discussion, there will be no further changes to the liquid proposal.
4. **Liquid Voting:** In the final liquid process, voting takes place. A minimum number of participating employees is required for valid liquid voting.

With the Liquid Democracy methodology, it is specifically avoided that decision-making processes are dominated by a few decision-makers or solitary decisions from a higher hierarchical level. This can increase the quality of decisions in companies, at least to the extent that liquid surveys at least contribute to sincerely appreciating the opinions of employees and customers.

In addition, Liquid Feedback sends a positive signal towards a modern-oriented societal or customer-oriented change in the company.

7.9.5   Timeboxing

The timeboxing approach, with fixed time intervals, enables the scheduling and project planning from an organizational perspective in the simplest way. The project team is free to choose their internal iteration cycle, for example, on a weekly basis, and for project management, the fixed cycles simplify project planning with regard to release dates.

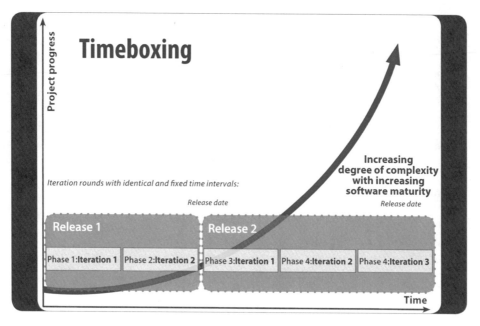

Fig. 7.23 Timeboxing for release planning with fixed time intervals

Figure 7.23 illustrates the method of "Timeboxing for release planning with fixed time intervals".

Table 7.10 "Timeboxing—Rules, Advantages, Disadvantages, and Risks" lists the respective rules, advantages, and disadvantages of the timeboxing method.

Table 7.10 Timeboxing—Rules, Advantages, Disadvantages, and Risks. (*Source:* Own representation—Sascha Block)

Rules:	• Fixed release dates • Free choice of iteration cycle • Variable scope of functions • If the complete scope of functions cannot be maintained, a functioning release will be delivered in any case
Advantages:	• Simplified release planning • A good prioritization allows for timely delivery with a meaningful scope of functions • Easier conclusions about team productivity possible • Over time, more confidence in performance and time estimation • Fixed cycle has a positive effect on the relationship with contractual partners
Disadvantages and Risks:	• Deadline adherence over quality?

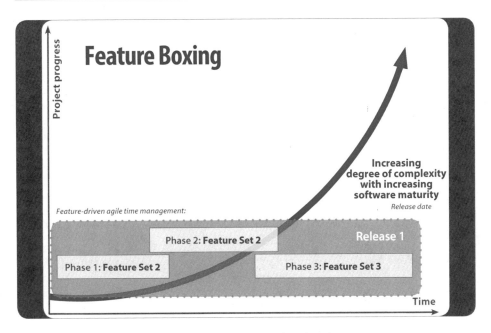

Fig. 7.24   Feature Boxing—Methodology of Feature-Driven Development

7.9.6   Feature-Driven Development

In the concept of Feature-Driven Development (FDD), no fixed time intervals for iterations are agreed upon, but the priority lies in the completion of defined work packages. The initial work package defines a rough, technical model of the software application.

Figure 7.24 "Feature Boxing" illustrates the functional principle of Feature-Driven Development. The release planning with variable time intervals of maximum duration focuses on software functionalities.

Table 7.11 "Feature Boxing—Rules, Advantages, Disadvantages, and Risks" lists the respective rules, advantages, and disadvantages of the Feature Boxing method.

Table 7.11 Feature Boxing—Rules, Advantages, Disadvantages, and Risks. (*Source:* Own representation, Sascha Block)

Rules:	• No fixed time intervals, only maximum time specifications • Planning for a maximum of 6 months • Initial planning never takes longer than 2 weeks • FDD-defined requirements are fine-grained and thus always evaluable in terms of the associated effort • Features are grouped into feature groups that contain technically meaningful units for delivery to users • The project manager only determines the calendar month of the completion of a feature group
Advantages:	• At the monthly level, it is always precisely recognizable whether an agile team is on schedule, over-fulfilled, or behind schedule • There are never any compromises at the expense of the functionality defined in advance for the delivery dates
Disadvantages and Risks:	• If functions are more time-consuming to implement than planned, the delivery date will be postponed

References

1. Beedle, et al. *Manifesto for Agile Software Development.* http://agilemanifesto.org/. Accessed 24 Febr 2022.
2. Mordi, A., & Schoop, M. (2020). *Making IT tangible-creating a definition of agile mindset.* ECIS.
3. Scheller, T. (2017). *Auf dem Weg zur agilen Organisation: Wie Sie Ihr Unternehmen dynamischer, flexibler und leistungsfähiger gestalten.* Vahlen.
4. Beck, K. (2000). *Extreme programming explained: Embrace change.* Addison-Wesley Professional.
5. Cohn, M. (2004). *User stories applied: For agile software development.* Addison-Wesley Professional.
6. Harbers, M., Detweiler, C., & Neerincx, M. A. (2015). Embedding stakeholder values in the requirements engineering process. In *International working conference on requirements engineering: Foundation for software quality* (pp. 318–332). Springer.
7. IEEE Standard Association, et al. (1998). *IEEE recommended practice for software requirements specifications.* IEEE Std-830.
8. Lucassen, G., et al. (2016). Improving agile requirements: The quality user story framework and tool. *Requirements Engineering, 21*(3), 383–403.
9. Sedano, T., Ralph, P., & Péraire, C. (2019). The product backlog. In *2019 IEEE/ACM 41st international conference on software engineering (ICSE)* (pp. 200–211). IEEE.
10. Lomas, C., Burke, M., & Page, C. L. (2008). Collaboration tools. *Educause Learning Initiative, 2*, 1–11).
11. Ferles, K., Stephens, J., & Dillig, I. (2020). *Verifying correct usage of context-free API protocols* (extended version). arXiv preprint arXiv:2010.09652.
12. Open API Initiative. *Linux foundation.* https://www.openapis.org/. Accessed 3 Mar 2022.

13. GitHub zur OpenAPI Spezifikation. *Werkzeuge zur Anwendung der OpenAPI-Spezifikation.* https://github.com/OAI/OpenAPI-Specification/blob/main/IMPLEMENTATIONS.md. Accessed 3 Mar 2022.

14. OpenApi 3.1 JSON Schema. https://github.com/OAI/OpenAPI-Specification/blob/main/schemas/v3.1/schema.json. Accessed 3 Mar 2022.

15. OpenApi 3.1 YAML Schema. https://github.com/OAI/OpenAPI-Specification/blob/main/schemas/v3.1/schema.yaml. Accessed 3 Mar 2022.

16. Hardt, D., et al. (Oktober 2012). *The OAuth 2.0 authorization framework.* Internet Engineering Task Force (IETF). https://datatracker.ietf.org/doc/html/rfc6749. Accessed 8 Mar 2022.

17. Hedberg, R., et al. (September Oktober 2021). *OpenID Connect Federation 1.0—draft 17.* Internet Engineering Task Force (IETF). https://openid.net/specs/openid-connect-federation-1_0.html#rfc.section.5.1. Accessed 8 Mar 2022.

18. Sinha, Satyajit—IOT Analytics. *State of IoT 2021: Number of connected IoT devices growing 9 % to 12.3 billion globally, cellular IoT now surpassing 2 billion.* https://iot-analytics.com/number-connected-iot-devices/. Accessed 8 Mar 2022.

19. Bass, L., Clements, P., & Kazman, R. (2012). *Software architecture in practice* (3rd edn.). Addison-Wesley Professional.

20. Zörner, S. (2012). *Softwarearchitekturen dokumentieren und kommunizieren* (1st edn.). Carl Hanser Verlag.

21. Cunningham, W. (1992). The WyCash portfolio management system. *ACM SIGPLAN OOPS Messenger, 4*(2), 29–30.

22. Abad, Z. S. H., & Ruhe, G. (2015). Using real options to manage technical debt in requirements engineering. In *2015 IEEE 23rd international requirements engineering conference (RE)* (pp. 230–235). IEEE.

23. Starke, G., & Hruschka, P. *Das arc42 Template für Architekturentscheidungen in Softwareprojekten.* https://www.arc42.de/overview/. Accessed 10 Mar 2022.

24. [URL:ISO/IEC 25010:2011]. *Leitfaden zur der ISO 25010 "Software product Quality Requirements and Evaluation (SQuaRE)".* https://www.iso.org/standard/35733.html. Accessed 3 Mar 2022.

25. Digital.ai Software Inc. *Periodic table of DevOps tools.* https://digital.ai/periodic-table-of-devops-tools/. Accessed 10 Mar 2022.

26. Fitzgerald, B., & Stol, K.-J. (2017). Continuous software engineering: A roadmap and agenda. *Journal of Systems and Software, 123*(Januar), 176–189.

27. Drews, P., et al. (2017). Bimodal enterprise architecture management: The emergence of a New EAM function for a BizDevOps-based fast IT. In *2017 IEEE 21st international enterprise distributed object computing workshop (EDOCW)* (pp. 57–64). IEEE.

28. Otto Group. *Design System der Otto Group.* https://www.otto.de/design-system. Accessed 14 Apr 2022.

29. Mikušová, M., & Janečková, V. (2010). Developing and implementing successful key performance indicators. *World Academy of Science, Engineering and Technology, 42*(6), 969–981.

30. Zachman, J. A. (2003). *The zachman framework for enterprise architecture. Primer for enterprise engineering and manufacturing.* Zachman International.

31. Ganesan, E., & Paturi, R. 2009. *Key performance indicators framework-a method to track business objectives, link business strategy to processes and detail importance of key performance indicators in enterprise business architecture. In: Americas Conference on Information Systems. 2009.*

32. Buschle, M., Johnson, P., & Shahzad, K. (2013). The enterprise architecture analysis tool–support for the predictive, probabilistic architecture modeling framework. In *19th Americas con-*

ference on information systems, AMCIS 2013; Chicago, IL; United States; 15 August 2013 through 17 August 2013 (pp. 3350–3364). Association for Information Systems.

33. Kreutzer, R. T., Neugebauer, T., & Pattloch, A. (2017). *Digital Business Leadership—Digitale Transformation —Geschäftsmodell-Innovation—agile Organisation—Change-Management* (1st edn.). Springer/Gabler.
34. FAZ vom 03.08.2015. http://www.faz.net/aktuell/wirtschaft/nokia-verkauft-kartendienst-here-an-deutsche-autokonzerne-13731935.html. Accessed 15 Apr 2022.
35. Becker, J. (14. Oktober 2016). Was Audi, BMW und Daimler mit dem Kartendienst Here vorhaben. *Süddeutsche Zeitung.*
36. Bitkom—KEMPF/FRESE. *Datability.* Accessed 9 Mar 2014.
37. Leetaru, K. (17. Januar 2017). Why are we so afraid of Petabytes? *Forbes Magazine.*
38. Bitkom Research/KPMG. *Mit Daten Werte schaffen.* Research Studie 2015.
39. Hanschke, Giesinger, & Goetze. (2016). *Business-Analyse—einfach und effektiv—Geschäftsanforderungen verstehen und in IT-Lösungen umsetzen* (2nd edn.). Carl Hanser.
40. Bleek, W.-G., & Wolf, H. (2011). *Agile Softwareentwicklung: Werte, Konzepte und Methoden.* dpunkt.
41. Stach, M. (2016). *Agil moderieren—Konkrete Ergebnisse statt endloser Diskussion* (1st edn.). Business Village.
42. Open-Source Software LiquidFeedback. https://liquidfeedback.org/ und https://www.public-software-group.org/liquid_feedback. Accessed 10 Mar 2022.

Data Quality—Lifeblood of Digitalization

8

The ubiquitous digitalization, with an increasingly purely digital data processing, Big Data and Smart Data, as well as complex and clever data analysis methods, form an inseparable unit that is becoming increasingly important for every organization—regardless of the industry.

"Garbage in, Garbage out"

The quantification and quality of data are—like two sides of a coin—equally important for good data management. The principle "Garbage in, Garbage out" applies to companies as well as any scenario in which digital data is processed. Only when working together and purposefully on the best possible data quality can powerful IT systems also deliver valid and meaningful data. Without valid data, there is no efficient system.

Digital transformation places high demands on data quality, and almost all employees in companies contribute to this. If incorrect product information ends up on websites or customer data is already recorded incorrectly during the ordering process in an online shop, this reduces data quality and has direct economic consequences.

Errors in the data cause errors in the generated reports; lack of trust in data leads to wrong decisions; opportunities are missed when data is outdated or incomprehensible.

What is Smart Data?

The term Smart Data extends basic data concepts and essentially describes intelligent concepts for the clever use of digital data, primarily in Big Data. Big Data stands for the rapidly increasing volume of digital data sets that arise in various ways within logging of IT processes, telecommunications, or in eCommerce. With the use and data protection-compliant evaluation of IoT devices, data volumes grow immensely.

S. Block, *Large-Scale Agile Frameworks*, https://doi.org/10.1007/978-3-662-67782-7_8

Fig. 8.1 Subject areas around "Smart Data". (*Source*: Sascha Block)

Smart Data pursues the goal and task of ensuring excellent data management to ensure that correct and error-free data remains meaningful.

In this sense, Smart Data strategies try to use digital data in different scenarios as effectively and purposefully as possible. Smart Data is therefore an imprecise term that combines novel data analytics practices with industry trends such as the Internet of Things (also known as IoT). The attribute smart refers not only to the data but also to applied knowledge of how this data is used in the application context and value-creating business scenarios [1, pp. 31/32].

Fig. 8.1 illustrates relevant subject areas around "Smart Data".

At the latest when Big Data is to be used, it becomes clear that IT managers must focus all efforts on intact data. Since data cleansing becomes more resource-intensive and sometimes impossible with increasing data volumes, it is logically indispensable to carry out data cleansing before the point of merging large amounts of data.

The enormous amounts of data require targeted and efficient methods for evaluating and web analysis of this data. As in Data Mining, knowledge evaluation within Smart Data is of central interest. The networking of different data sources—especially for companies—leads to new usage interests; however, existing data protection regulations must always be taken into account. Especially when using artificial intelligence, which consists largely of training neural networks, data quality is of high relevance.

8.1   Customer-Specific Products and Services Based on Smart Data

The benefits of smart data strategies in Industry 4.0 scenarios are only made possible by the Internet of Things: data on production performance and product quality can already be monitored in real-time [2, 457]. Customer data flows directly into the automatic production process, realizing exclusive custom-made products of the highest quality.

Customized sports shoes with Nike ID—while simultaneously analyzing the customer's running behavior via Apple iWatch or with Android Smart Watch—are just one real-life example from our consumer world.

In this economic scenario, two leading global corporations benefit from the cooperation in exchanging smart data of their mutual customers.

Data is the central raw material for economic value creation in the digital age. Data is available every day in ever-increasing quantities. With the worldwide rapidly increasing data volumes, the global data volume is expected to grow to a gigantic data volume of 163 zettabytes (ZB) [3].

Whether we believe the forecast of a leading international company for storage media or not is secondary. Even if the forecast only comes true at a later date, the increasingly vital importance of data in our modern society is a fact that we cannot escape—each and every one of us is directly affected!

The shift of our data to the cloud and the increase in devices that create data without human intervention is already happening. In this respect, the far more likely scenario is that the actual data volume is reached much earlier.

Challenges in Dealing with Immense Increase in Digital Data
When using smart data, many new questions arise, especially when the meaningful use of massive data streams is in the foreground. In addition to legal foundations that provide a legally secured space for companies to store and analyze data based on legal norms and regulations, societal acceptance must not be neglected.

It is precisely the emerging business models—particularly in sensitive areas such as finance, the insurance industry, and the clever handling of highly sensitive data in healthcare—that determine how consumers react to the intensive use of smart data. On the technical side, the primary question is the manageability of big data. With sensitive and highly protected data such as personal and health data, the complexity of data processing increases significantly. For example, by connecting effective solutions for pseudonymizing personal data and consent management.

From Theory to Practical Implementation
This section describes the mathematical foundations of computer science that apply to the successful validation of data. Plausibility checks and basic mechanisms of data collection, data analysis, and data correction are explained.

By the time you read this section, you will quickly realize why your company should definitely integrate this **building block for optimizing data quality** firmly into the selected Agile Framework and digitalization strategy…

8.2   Data Quality: Fundamentals and Preconditions

Five fundamental factors are crucial for high-quality data quality [4, Chap. 2, p. 1]:

- **Data consistency**
- **Deduplication**
- **Information completeness**
- **Data currency**
- **Data precision**

Scientific studies on data quality primarily focus on data consistency and deduplication of relational data. Nonetheless, all five factors for data quality are equally important, and each technical aspect poses fundamental challenges. The following sections provide a detailed explanation of these five fundamental factors.

Data consistency
The consistency of data is directly related to the plausibility and integrity of this data concerning its representation of existing values from the real world.

Using an easily understandable practical example, different methods for data optimization are explained. The connection to the real world is established by a manageable table with 5 data records containing personal data [4, Sect. 2.1, p. 2]:

Table 8.1 "Data record of personal data" represents the starting point of our dataset for data optimization and illustrates how quickly seemingly correct data can be contradictory.

Using plausible rules, it will be demonstrated step by step how many contradictions can already be contained in such a manageable amount of data, which are not recognizable at first glance. The term *"tuple"* used here is used in computer science for ordered collections of values (*one-dimensional arrays*) and—especially in relational algebra—as a synonym for data record. The values of a tuple are called attributes (data field) and can be seen in the example above in the table rows t_1 to t_5; a table row thus corresponds to a data record.

Consistent data are thus error-free within their data stock insofar as no contradictions arise from this data. To ensure this, it is necessary to continuously identify and eliminate errors within the data stocks using formal-logical plausibility checks.

Inconsistencies in data typically occur in the form of violations of data dependencies or violations of data integrity. The integrity of data is always directly related to the respective applicable conditions or relationships of data or data records to each other. Data integrity helps us repair data by correcting existing errors and inconsistencies in data records.

Table 8.1 D_0—Data record of personal data

T	First Name	Last Name	CC	AC	landline	Mobile	Street	City	ZIP	Status
t_1:	Marie	Schmidt	49	030	3855662	7966899	Unter den Linden 15	Berlin	10115	single
t_2:	Marie	Lutz	49	040	null	null	Jungfern-stieg 10	Hamburg	20095	married
t_3:	Marie	Lutz	49	040	6513877	7966899	Bee-thoven-str. 7	Hamburg	20095	married
t_4:	Tom	Walker	01	908	6512845	3393756	Post-fach 212	Trenton	08601	single
t_5:	Roberto	Blanco	01	908	6512845	null	6 N Broad St	Trenton	08601	single

Two central questions arise in direct relation to data consistency:

1. **Which data dependencies should we use to detect errors?**
2. **Which repair model should we apply for error correction?**

8.2.1 Data Dependencies

Dependencies of data exist in various forms. Such dependencies within data can be classified as follows:

1. A) **Functional Dependencies (FDs)** [5, Chap. 2.1.2, p. 24]:
   In a relation R, if an attribute set A defines an attribute set B such that for every tuple pair t_1, $t_2 \in R$, if $t_1^{A'} = t_2^{A'}$, then $t_1^{B'} = t_2^{B'}$.
   Functional dependencies typically arise directly from the application context. Accordingly, for our Table 8.1, each location is determined by a ZIP code.
   B) **Inclusion Dependencies (INDs)**:
   Inclusion dependencies are defined such that all values of an attribute a are contained in the values of another attribute b. In this case, a is the dependent attribute and b is the referenced attribute. It holds: $a \in A \subseteq b \in A$. Every foreign key automatically fulfills the requirement of inclusion dependency [6, p. 144].

Table 8.2 PatternTableaus PT_1, PT_2

PT_1	CC	ZIP	Street	PT_2	CC	AC	city
	44	*	*		*	*	*
					49	040	Hamburg
					01	908	Trenton

Note: Axiom φ_2 subsumes the conventional FD: $cc, ac \rightarrow city$ and thus marks the first data entry in PT_2 with its "* = Wildcard" entries.

2. **Conditional-functional dependencies (CFDs)**

   In the context of our example data, such a conditional-functional dependency can be created by combining the FD φ_1 and φ_2—supplemented with specific data patterns in the form of so-called Pattern Tableaus PT_1, PT_2 resulting from the logic of the respective data used. In the practical example of our dataset of personal data, such a CFD can be represented with the two axioms φ_1 and φ_2 as follows:

$$\varphi_1 : cc, zip \rightarrow street \quad \varphi_1 : cc, ac \rightarrow city$$

A CFD results from the integration of individual FDs into a combined quality rule:

$$CFDs : (\varphi_1, PT_1), (\varphi_1, PT_2), \text{thus } (\varphi_1, cc, zip \rightarrow street), (\varphi_1, cc, ac \rightarrow city),$$

PT_1 and PT_2 are each functional dependencies (FDs) as logical data fragments that we integrate into our formula in the form of a valid condition (Table 8.2).

CFD φ_1:$cc, zip \rightarrow street$ states that in Germany (i.e., where CC = "49"), the ZIP code uniquely determines the street. In other words, $cc, zip \rightarrow street$ is a functional dependency that is only valid for tuples with the country code CC = "49".

For our example data, FD φ_1 thus applies only to tuples t_1, t_2, and t_3, so that an inconsistency for tuples t_4, and t_5 becomes apparent due to these rules.

If we use φ as a data quality rule, we come to the conclusion that t_2 and t_3 violate the axiom φ_1:$cc, zip \rightarrow street$ and are therefore inconsistent: Both records have the same ZIP, but differ in the street. Such errors remain undetected when using regular FDs exclusively. Only by combining functional dependencies into a conditional functional dependency can inconsistencies in this form be detected.

CFD φ_2:$cc, ac \rightarrow city$ states that the Country Code (CC) and the Area Code (AC) uniquely determine the city. Moreover, for Germany (i.e., for the records in which CC = "49"), if the AC = "040", it must be the city of Hamburg. For the USA (i.e., for the records in which CC = "01"), if the AC = "908" (district of the State New Jersey), it must be the city of "Trenton". Thus, tuple t_1 is identified as the record that violates this rule.

3. **Denial Constraints (DCs)**

   Typically formulated by predicate logic statements of the form $\forall x : \neg (\phi(x) \wedge \beta(x))$, where $\phi(x)$ is a non-empty conjunction of relation atoms over x and $\beta(x)$ is a conjunction of the form $=; \neq, <, >, \leq, \geq$ for elements of x.

4. **Equality-Generated Dependencies (EGDs)**
   A special form of DCs, when $\beta(x)$ is of the form $x_i = x_j$.
5. **Tuple-Generated Dependencies (TGDs)**
   Predicate logic sentences of the form $\forall x(\phi(x) \rightarrow \exists y(\psi(x,y)))$, where $\phi(x)$ and $\psi(x,y)$ are conjunctions of relation atoms over x and $x \cup y$, so that each variable of x is related at least once with an atom of $\phi(x)$.
6. **Full TGDs**
   A special case of TGDs without existing quantifiers, for example in the form $\forall x(\phi(x) \rightarrow \psi(x))$.
7. **Local as View TGDs (LAV)**
   A special case of TGDs in which $\phi(x)$ is a single relation atom; LAV TGDs subsume INDs.

It is like a balancing act to decide which dependency class we should use as a data quality rule for repairing data. It is always necessary to ensure that the required computing power is sufficient. To assess the complexity of the chosen dependency class, computer scientists use the satisfiability problem of propositional logic and implication problems [7, Chap. 4: Relations and Mappings, p. 104].

Satisfiability
The satisfiability problem of propositional logic (engl.: Satisfiability) is a formal mathematical decision problem (predicate logic) that can be used to determine whether a propositional logic formula is satisfiable (true). Accordingly, unsatisfiable propositional logic formulas fundamentally yield the overall result false. A fundamental question that arises for the computer scientist is: *"Does the rapid identification of an NP-complex problem through correct solutions also mean that there is a fast way to find the solution path algorithmically?"* [8, pp. 279/280] Even if the available computing power increases year by year according to Moore's Law and thus the speed of solution calculation continuously improves, there remains a large number of non-trivial problems to solve, whose calculation is so complex that this solution is considered NP-complete. In terms of data quality, this means knowing whether the defined data quality rules are valid in relation to all defined dependencies.

Implications and Implication Analyses
Implication analysis can be used to remove redundant data quality rules and thus accelerate the process of error detection and data repair.

Complexity Levels of Implication Analysis
Table 8.3 "Complexity Levels of Implication Analysis" summarizes the complexity levels of the functions explained in the "Data Dependencies" section:

Table 8.3 Complexity Levels of Implication Analysis [4, Sect. 2.1, p. 3]

Dependencies	Implications (Runtime Estimation)
FDs	$O(n)$
INDs	PSpace-complete
FDs + INDs	Undecidable
CFDs	coNP-complete (Solutions can be falsified in polynomial time)
CINDs	EXPTIME (Solvable in exponential runtime)
CFDs + CINDs	Undecidable
DCs	coNP-complete (Solutions can be falsified in polynomial time)
TGDs	Undecidable

8.2.2 Data Repair

In practice, there are two approaches to cleaning an inconsistent database and optimizing data quality:

1. **Repairing data:** This approach is similar to creating a database copy that differs only minimally from the original database and contains only consistent information.
   and
2. **Consistent answering of queries:** This method performs repairs on data to be corrected directly in the original database and determines answers for correction based on predefined queries, with each individual repair operation corresponding to a database query.

Data Repair Models

Based on a distance function of graph theory, the change distance of a respective repair is evaluated, so that all dependencies to be fulfilled are preserved at the same time. In practice, there are various models with different repair semantics, each pursuing the goal of minimal cost:

1. **S-Repair:** The S-model assumes inconsistent but complete data. This model only allows the deletion of data tuples based on minimal set difference.
2. **C-Repair:** The C-model assumes both inconsistent and incomplete data. The C-model allows both the deletion and insertion of tuples. C-repairs are based on minimal cardinality and set difference [9, Sect. 5.7, p. 67].
3. **CC-Repair:** The CC-model extends the C-model so that the image of the database is smaller than the reference database in any case.
4. **U-Repair:** The U-model is a numerical aggregation method; this model supports the modification of attribute values. As a result, the costs for corrections are higher the further the values are from the actual starting attribute, as more processing cycles are required for correction.

Table 8.4 Complexity levels of repair checks [4, Sect. 2.1, p. 3]

Dependencies	Repair Model	Runtime Estimation of Repair Check
Complete TGDs	S-Repair	PTIME
1 FDs + 1 INDs	S-Repair	coNP-complete
DCs	S-Repair	LOGSPACE
WA LAV TGDs + EGDs	S-Repair	LOGSPACE
Complete TGDs + EGDs	S-Repair	PTIME-complete
WA TGDs + EGDs	S-Repair	coNP-complete
DCs	C-Repair	coNP-complete
Complete TGDs + EGDs	C-Repair	coNP-complete
WA TGDs + EGDs	C-Repair	coNP-complete
DCs	CC-Repair	coNP-complete
Complete TGDs + EGDs	CC-Repair	coNP-complete
WA TGDs + EGDs	CC-Repair	coNP-complete
Fixed FDs	U-Repair	coNP-complete
Fixed CINDs	U-Repair	coNP-complete

In practice, most data corrections are performed using the U-model. Unfortunately, applying the U-model is the most cost-intensive approach, especially when attribute values are also allowed to update continuously. The complexity level is already considered unsolvable when using the U-model as soon as only FDs or INDs are in use. Table 8.4 "Complexity levels of repair checks" illustrates how the classified dependencies are classified as a repair model and at the same time provides a runtime estimate of the respective repair checks.

8.2.3   Data Deduplication

The **data deduplication**—also known as **record-matching**—aims to eliminate redundant data and is therefore an indispensable step in optimizing data quality. The process of data deduplication can be divided into the identification and elimination of redundant data. Deduplication is based on complex mathematical operations; therefore, it is almost impossible to accurately predict the efficiency of deduplication algorithms.

Requirement for Redundancy Cleanup in Big Data
Cleaning up data to remove redundant records is essential, especially for large amounts of data.

In particular, when it comes to Big Data, the first step—before all other optimization steps—is to eliminate redundant data. This reduces the amount of data and automatically makes subsequent optimization methods more performant. Redundant data mainly occurs when data from a large number of different data sources with predominantly heterogeneous data sets are merged.

Deduplication Techniques

In practice, various deduplication techniques have proven successful, as there is no prevailing deduplication approach that is equally well applicable to all problem situations to handle all types of redundancies [10, Chap. 2 "Existing Deduplication Techniques", p. 23]. In terms of performance and implementation effort, the deduplication technique with its specific designs—depending on the particular characteristics of the prevailing data sets, the IT architecture of the involved systems, the available capacities, and the available deduplication time—offers special advantages. Thus, deduplication remains one of the most efficient methods in computer science to cleverly reduce data volumes. Four approaches to deduplication can be distinguished [4, Sect. 2.2, p. 3]:

1. **Probabilistic Deduplication**
2. **Learning-based Deduplication**
3. **Distance-based Deduplication**
4. **Rule-based Deduplication**

Collaborative Deduplication

Fan focuses in his introduction to data quality optimization on the approach of rule-based deduplication supplemented with directly connected repair processes (**collaborative deduplication**). Fan justifies this extension by stating that deduplication in its processes is always simultaneously aimed at data consistency analysis and data accuracy with data repair. Likewise, rule-based deduplication takes into account efficiency in terms of required resources (Data Currency). For this reason, it is understandable that the usually separate processes of data repair and deduplication are combined in the approach of collaborative deduplication to be used together for data precision.

In a previous study, Fan et al. demonstrate that record-matching and data repair complement each other and thus lay the foundation for data cleansing. While matching aims to identify tuples that refer to the same *"Real-World-Object"*, it is the accompanying task of data repair to make a database consistent by successively fixing errors within the data set [11, p. 16].

Deduplication and Bijectivity

To identify redundant data records, the mathematical function of bijectivity can be used. With the help of a bijection, it can be mathematically proven that a complete pairing between the elements of the domain and the target set takes place. Likewise, the inverse functions of a bijective mapping are always bijective [7, Chap. 11: Linear Mappings, p. 267]. This property of bijective relations can thus be used in the form of common

entity decompositions of relations to optimize data quality (deduplication). The field of entity resolution is receiving increasing attention to manage the growth of structured and semi-structured data from a variety of heterogeneous data sources. An exact resolution of existing relations is equally crucial for the cost-effectiveness of data cleansing algorithms, reducing data volumes, and precise data analysis for critical applications. It has been shown that, in particular for structured data, resolving entities from the relational perspective is effective. The collective resolution of relational entities is a powerful and promising approach that combines the attribute similarity method with relational evidence and enables improved performance compared to traditional approaches [12].

Matching Rules

Data Matching is the process of merging two or more data records into a single data record to eliminate duplicates [5, Chap. 7: Data Matching, p. 173]. With the help of rules defined closely to the respective data context, data records can be identified that, despite partially deviating content, have an identical meaning. This is usually done through recursive conclusions of identified data fragments with semantically equivalent content. With the help of **matching rules** with result inference, it is possible for deviating data fragments, despite different content in partial attributes, that both data records have the same meaning in the application context. Starting from the identical data fragments in the form of attribute tuples of both data records, the identical meaning of the partial fragments is inferred recursively. Of course, the applicable rules must be closely related to the context of the data sets to be optimized. In practice, matching rules are particularly helpful due to their practical benefits in transferring various data records into a single data record to limit data volumes and meaningfully improve data quality [5, Chap. 7: Data Matching, p. 177].

8.2.4   Information Completeness

The completeness of information is another important criterion for assessing data quality [7, Sect. 2.3 "Information Completeness", p. 4]. Only if the required basic data is available, database operations in the form of queries lead to the desired success by providing the desired answers to the database query.

Distinguishable are:

1. **Closed World Assumption (CWA):** In this case, the database is complete with all tuples in relation to the image of the real world, with only a few attribute values possibly being incomplete.
2. **Open World Assumption (OWA):** Here, in addition to missing attribute values, complete data records (tuples) are also missing, so that the image of the real value is incomplete.

The case of the CWA is practically always given, so that the attention is mainly focused on the case of the OWA, for which only a few queries are suitable to bring about a solution. It is precisely for these difficult problems that computer scientists strive to provide adequate solution strategies that can be demonstrably effectively applied.

Relative Completeness of Information

In order to ensure complete information as best as possible, computer science relies on the concept of **master data** (*Master Data* or *Reference Data*). To this end, companies establish a central repository of high-quality basic data that is used in various software applications in the corporate context. The concentration of data maintenance of such master data offers the advantage of consistent views and the supply of core processes in the company with pre-verified entities. Another advantage offered by master data is a stable framework in the form of a **master data validation framework**, which provides a secure foundation—based on precisely this completeness of master data—to derive applicable rules for data validation that facilitate further data processing or make it possible in the first place based on complexity barriers.

8.2.5 Data Currency

Data currency is aimed at evaluating the current value of data records in order to make well-founded decisions on data correction based on these evaluations. An existing approach to determining such data evaluations is timestamps in temporary databases. In practice, however, it has been found that these timestamps are often not available or imprecise [13, p. 251]. The crucial question, therefore, is how to make reliable data evaluations even without timestamps.

Modeling Data Currency

With the approach presented by Fan et al. for individual evaluation of tuples and attribute values, it also becomes possible to quantify the value of data [14, p. 44]. Using our example data set, it can be demonstrated analogously that a change from married status to single is impossible. Likewise, due to this rule definition, the conclusion is made that the last name and the status are directly related to each other, so that Marie's current last name is "Lutz". In combination with the unique mobile phone number, this leads to the conclusion that the data record t_3 is more current and thus more valuable than t_1.

8.2.6 Data Precision

Precision of data aims to ensure that values are as close to reality as possible, ideally representing it exactly. If precise data is not available, at least existing basic values (see explanations on the term master data) should be used to enable approximation or calculation. In this respect, there is still a wide field of activity for scientifically sound solutions, as only a few studies are dedicated to this subject area [4, Sect. 2.5 Data Accuray, p. 6].

8.3   Techniques for Data Cleansing

Data cleansing tools primarily offer enhancements for customer data or product data. For such auxiliary tools, there is an immense demand on the company side due to the rapidly increasing data volumes year after year. What functions must data cleansing tools provide? First and foremost, such data tools are expected to:

1. **Data profiling:** Identifying and creating rules for evaluating data quality
2. **Data cleansing:** Optimizing data so that it meets established quality guidelines, standards, business rules, and domain requirements.
3. **Data matching:** The identification, linking, and merging of existing data entries.

8.3.1   Discovering Data Quality Rules

While it is unrealistic to rely solely on business rules or experts from different application areas and domains to design valid data quality rules—especially since this is a manual and cost-intensive process—the question arises as to how it is possible to automatically derive such data quality rules. Since there is a possibility that the rule sets themselves are poorly defined or are based on invalid data, it is also useful to consider a mechanism that verifies the rules themselves [4, Sect. 3.1 Discovering Data Quality Rules, p. 6].

8.3.2   Error Detection for Data

Once the practically applicable data quality rules are qualified, the question arises as to how to efficiently capture errors in a database by applying these rules. For most users, it is sufficient if errors in data are automatically detected; data correction is often not even part of the requirement. Which methods for error detection are applicable depends on the prevailing dependencies. Which methods for error identification are effectively applicable depends in particular on which data quality rules are used and whether the data is stored in a local database or across multiple distributed databases. In practice, data is usually fragmented, scattered across various databases of different systems. In the first step, a consolidation of the data at a single location is necessary. Nevertheless, it remains an NP-complete problem to determine errors within vertically or horizontally fragmented data. While SQL-based approaches are still applicable for a single data source, this approach can no longer be used for fragmented data.

8.3.3   Data Repair

After errors in data sets have been detected, it is necessary to repair these faulty data. The only repair model of interest is the U-based repair model with a focus on correcting individual attribute values, as this is where the greatest need exists in practice.

Heuristic Data Corrections

Data repairs are often prohibitively expensive in terms of cost, but heuristic data corrections still offer acceptable solutions in such cases. A heuristic method refers to an analytical approach that achieves acceptable solutions despite limited knowledge and few available resources; heuristics use limited knowledge and make decisions through a clever system with the help of logical conclusions: "Initiating heuristic methods provide initial approximations, while optimizing methods gradually improve the solutions; above this are meta-methods that strategically control the discovery process even beyond local optima" [15, p. 388].

The complexity level is already coNP-complete for fixed FDs or INDs. For this reason, repair algorithms are usually heuristic and require 1:1 dependencies. With the separation of the decision which values are equal and the decision which values should be assigned to the respective equivalence class, there are guaranteed solutions for a data repair. The costs for this are determined based on the listed repair patterns from the table of the section Repair Models for Data.

Secured Repair Steps and Data Fixes

A main problem of heuristic repair methods is that they cannot guarantee corrections that are considered correct. To enable such a secured approach, correction assurance using master data is recommended. If this master data-enhanced framework is additionally secured by user interaction at the time of data entry using basic algorithms and optimization techniques, in any case, corrections that are considered correct and comprehensively secured are enabled [11, p. 237].

For our example data, the data structure can be extended in the master data by a postcode that secures all data applicable to the country code 49 = Germany as follows:

$$\sigma : (postal, zip) \rightarrow ((C, city), (A, AC))$$

This specifies for all input tuples that a uniquely assigned master data pair exists, which assigns a zip to a postal code. In this way, secured data corrections can be guaranteed, which in turn prevent correct values from being replaced by incorrect data corrections.

For critical application areas with highly sensitive data, heuristic methods are excluded from the outset because correct data may be replaced by faulty data. This results in the fact that for data-critical areas—such as for medical applications—only data correction methods that guarantee absolutely error-free data repairs are suitable.

8.4   Control Mechanisms for Optimizing Data Quality are Essential

The transition to a digital enterprise is inevitable. Competitive pressure under time constraints and the transformation of established companies with organically grown data structures over time require particularly careful handling of data for every IT project. The goal is not to accumulate every possible piece of data, but rather to interpret which data is correct, relevant, and of corresponding value and benefit to the company.

Careful handling of data requires diverse challenges in various areas. From the choice of the right data structures to the use of the right tools for digital data processing and data correction, to the creation and application of valid rules for data validation, it requires a wide range of expert knowledge. However, the effort to optimize the quality of one's own data is worthwhile, as data is of increasing value in a digital world. Only companies that continuously maintain their values in the form of existing data volumes and consistently focus all efforts on the continuous optimization of digital values will also increase their company value.

Precisely because their data volumes are constantly increasing and Big Data has long been prevalent in their company, but only correct and up-to-date data ultimately have value, their Large-Scale Agile Framework must include an effective mechanism for controlling data quality.

8.4.1   From Machine Learning to Smart Data

Large amounts of data can only be managed through machine-based methods. Artificial intelligence can be trained with algorithms and learns—guided by precise specifications from data specialists and algorithm experts—which patterns are present in the digital data streams. Especially with dynamic data streams—i.e., data that is constantly changing due to ongoing user interactions and machine behavior—humans rely on machine-assisted data analysis. Predictions and forecasts are often only possible through algorithm-based analysis methods that autonomously react to changes in data streams.

Stand-alone data mining programs can only analyze complex data volumes to a limited extent. The efficient integration of data and graph mining algorithms into relational database systems still poses a challenge in some cases. Some database systems, such as SAP HANA and Hyper, already integrate the various workloads OLAP and OLTP into a single system, so that the data basis only needs to be maintained once and ETL cycles are eliminated. SAP HANA's Predictive Analytics Library allows data mining algorithms to be executed individually, similar to SQL queries. The results of the algorithms are stored in tables to be specified and can thus be used in separate SQL queries [16, pp. 45/46].

8.4.2   Gaining Innovations from Data with Smart Data

Since various data is increasingly produced by diverse systems and stored in a distributed manner, it is important to evaluate whether merging the data streams creates relevant added value in the form of an information gain. If new information of relevant use is obtained through the aggregation of individual data fragments or if new business scenarios are only made possible through data bundling, innovations can be created based on data.

What is Smart Data Innovation?
Smart Data Innovation is therefore a process that aims to create new value based on data. Smart Data explores new structures in existing data. Just as untapped potentials are uncovered through the change of perspective in Design Thinking, Smart Data also detects innovations and unused values in data off the beaten path.

Agile Approach and Iterative Methodology Enrich Our Knowledge
The basis of Smart Data strategies is the concept of the continuous "Build Measure Learn Cycle". With this method, we quickly realize our idea in the form of a digital prototype, capture and collect digital data, and evaluate it based on previously established assumptions.

Figure 8.2 illustrates how the "Continuous Build Measure Learn Cycle" can be effectively used to optimize digital products and services using data.

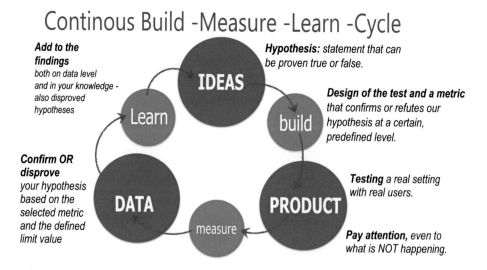

Fig. 8.2   Continuous Build Measure Learn Cycle. (*Source*: Sascha Block)

Our knowledge base is thus constantly expanding with relevant insights that continuously optimize our business model and our products. In this context, misjudgments in the form of invalid hypotheses are also relevant and valuable.

8.4.3   Semantic Data Analysis

Semantics usually refers to the meaning of data and is characterized by metadata structures. Supplementary sets of rules about the relationships between information objects and metadata complement a semantic data analysis. Semantic data analyses are complex and involve a high level of effort in creation. The evaluation and verification of rule systems are time-consuming, especially since each defined rule can generate new metadata and trigger new rules in turn. An important feature of semantic data analysis is that metadata description occurs decentrally: This enables the automatic integration of individual data silos. However, the inclusion of additional data from subsystems introduces new data rules. Although the computational effort increases and becomes more difficult to control as the system becomes more data-intensive, it is also possible that contradictions arise due to data integration. Nevertheless, semantic data analysis is an established methodology for enabling the integration of various data from different systems in the context of big data. Semantic context information is usually represented as so-called linked data in the form of interconnected graphs [1, p. 30].

Smart Data Optimization
Predictive Data Analytics, Cognitive Computing, Artificial Intelligence, and Machine Learning are central concepts that play an important role in the use of large amounts of data and smart data projects. As the processing of rapidly increasing data volumes becomes more and more complicated, the exploration of information and the search for exploitable patterns in big data are already impossible for individuals without technical aids.

Application example for artificial intelligence and machine learning: Image recognition on smartphones
A practical application example is the identification and logical sorting of people recognized in images. Over time, a large number of photographs accumulate on every smartphone; a large proportion of the images depict people.

Without our intervention or support, a smartphone is already capable of independently identifying people in images and sorting the images by the people depicted.

The manual and laborious process of tagging images is thus rendered obsolete and replaced by a true smart data innovation.

Figure 8.3 illustrates how artificial intelligence and machine learning can be used for image recognition on an Apple iPhone.

Fig. 8.3 Artificial intelligence
and machine learning using the
example of image recognition
on an Apple iPhone. (*Source*:
Sascha Block)

8.4.4 Framework for Data-Driven Design

Innovations and novel technologies require continuous improvement by optimally aligning the design and provided functions to the needs of users and consumers.

Design Thinking and agile development methods make a decisive contribution to success by using iterative procedures, starting with the minimal viable prototype (Minimal
Viable Product, or MVP) to verify or refute a hypothesis.

Such an MVP generates valuable data in a short time, which can be used directly for
the analysis and evaluation of new business models, business scenarios, and innovative
products and digital services.

Figure 8.4 Framework for Data-Driven Design—Using measurable Key Performance
Indicators (KPI), data-driven design is iteratively measured in 5 steps.

In a first step, we identify relevant KPIs and metrics that are important for achieving
our business goals. In the second step, we start generating digital data—directly with the
MVP or an existing business scenario—that appears valuable for the analysis and evaluation of our goals.

In step 3, we create assumptions and forecasts about the influences that the changes
we introduce or a newly provided digital service will have.

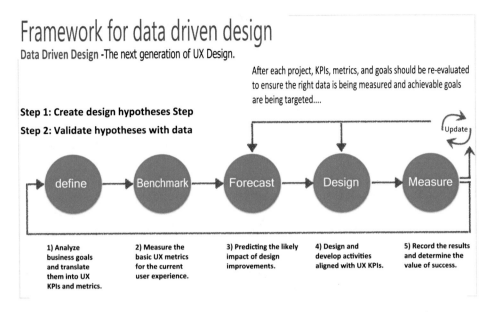

Framework for data driven design
Data Driven Design -The next generation of UX Design.

After each project, KPIs, metrics, and goals should be re-evaluated to ensure the right data is being measured and achievable goals are being targeted....

Step 1: Create design hypotheses Step

Step 2: Validate hypotheses with data

Update

define → Benchmark → Forecast → Design → Measure

| 1) Analyze business goals and translate them into UX KPIs and metrics. | 2) Measure the basic UX metrics for the current user experience. | 3) Predicting the likely impact of design improvements. | 4) Design and develop activities aligned with UX KPIs. | 5) Record the results and determine the value of success. |

Fig. 8.4   Framework for Data-Driven Design. (*Source*: Sascha Block)

In step 4, we implement the necessary prerequisites and go live with our MVP. In real operation, our digital prototype now generates digital data that we use in step 5 for analysis and success evaluation.

8.4.5   Conclusion

The transition to a digital enterprise is inevitable. Competitive pressure under time constraints and the transformation of established companies with organically grown data structures over time require particularly careful handling of data for every IT project. The goal is not to accumulate every possible piece of data, but rather to interpret which data is correct, relevant, and of corresponding value and benefit to the company.

Careful handling of data requires diverse challenges in various areas. From choosing the right data structures to using the right tools for digital data processing and data correction, to creating and applying valid rules for data validation, it requires a wide range of expert knowledge. However, the effort to optimize and evaluate the quality of one's own data is worthwhile, as data is of increasing value in a digital world. Only companies that continuously maintain their values in the form of existing data volumes and consistently focus all efforts on the ongoing optimization of digital values will simultaneously increase their company value.

Smart data is the regenerative energy source of the 21st century, and the value of data continues to grow unabated. Short-term and meaningful reports are as essential a part of entrepreneurial action as the consolidation of competitive positions based on one's own innovations. Technological progress, a significant advantage over competitors, and genuine innovations with economic benefits have always been a guarantee of entrepreneurial success and a solid foundation for successful business strategies.

Because smart data projects aim to promote innovations and because smart data analyses always have an exploratory character, it must be understood that insights and innovations in the basic process of their research are subject to a certain degree of uncertainty. Nevertheless, smart data technologies remain the only sensible option for handling constantly growing digital data streams. More than ever, a knowledge advantage is an indispensable competitive advantage, and smart data is ideally suited for creating novel digital products and innovative digital services. In addition, investing in expert knowledge around smart data is extremely lucrative, so not only companies like Google, Facebook, or Amazon are among the winners, but also medium-sized companies in every industry that specifically focus on these new digital technologies.

References

1. Wierse, A., & Riedel, T. (2017). *Smart Data Analytics – Zusammenhänge erkennen, Potentiale nutzen, Big Data verstehen* (1st edn.). De Gruyter.
2. Vogel-Heuser, B., Bauernhansel, T., & ten Hompel, M. (2017). *Handbuch Industrie 4.0 Bd. 2 – Automatisierung* (2nd edn.). Springer.
3. Unternehmenswesite Seagate Inc. *IDC-Whitepaper*. https://www.seagate.com/files/www-content/our-story/trends/files/idc-seagate-dataage-whitepaper.pdf. Accessed 10 March 2022.
4. Fan, W. (2015). Data quality: From theory to practice. *ACM SIGMOD Record, 44*(3), 7–18.
5. Doan, A. H., Halevy, A., & Ives, Z. (2012). *Principles of data integration*. Elsevier.
6. Bohannon, P., et al. (2005). A cost-based model and effective heuristic for repairing constraints by value modification. In *Proceedings of the 2005 ACM SIGMOD international conference on Management of data* (S. 143–154). ACM.
7. Brill, M. (2001). *Mathematik für Informatiker*. Hanser.
8. Hansen, P., & Jaumard, B. (1990). Algorithms for the maximum satisfiability problem. *Computing, 44*(4), 279–303.
9. Bertossi, L. (2011). Database repairing and consistent query answering. *Synthesis Lectures on Data Management, 3*(5), 1–121.
10. Choi, B.-Y., Kim, D., & Song, S. (2017). *Data deduplication for data optimization for storage and network systems*. Springer International Publishing.
11. Fan, W., et al. (2010). Towards certain fixes with editing rules and master data. *Proceedings of the VLDB Endowment, 3*(1–2), 173–184.
12. Bhattacharya, I., & Getoor, L. (2007). Collective entity resolution in relational data. *ACM Transactions on Knowledge Discovery from Data (TKDD), 1*(1), 5.
13. Zhang, H., Diao, Y., & Immerman, N. (2010). Recognizing patterns in streams with imprecise timestamps. *Proceedings of the VLDB Endowment, 3*(1–2), 244–255.
14. Fan, W., Geerts, F., & Wijsen, J. (2012). Determining the currency of data. *ACM Transactions on Database Systems (TODS), 37*(4), 25.

15. Fischer, P., & Hofer, P. (2011). *Lexikon der Informatik* (15. Aufl.). Springer.
16. Then, M., Passing, L., Hubig, N., Günnemann, S., Kemper, A., & Neumann, T. (2015). Effiziente Integration von Data- und GraphMining-Algorithmen in relationale Datenbanksysteme. *TU München – Proceedings of the LWA.*

Printed in the United States
by Baker & Taylor Publisher Services